DESIGN
DESTINATIONS
WORLDWIDE

© 2008 Tandem Verlag GmbH
h.f.ullmann is an imprint of Tandem Verlag GmbH

Editor:
Joachim Fischer
Editorial coordination:
Sabine Marinescu
Layout:
Arne Alexander Klett
Imaging:
Stefan Eisele

Produced by
Klett Fischer architecture & design
www.klett-fischer.com

**Project coordination
for h.f.ullmann:**
Dania D'Eramo

Coordination of the translations:
Textcase, Hilversum
Translation into English:
Trahern Gemmell for Textcase
Translation into French:
Aurélie Blain for Textcase
Translation into Dutch:
Céline Jongert for Textcase

Printed in China

ISBN 978-3-8331-4746-3

10 9 8 7 6 5 4 3 2 1
X IX VIII VII VI V IV III II I

www.ullmann-publishing.com

JOACHIM FISCHER

DESIGN DESTINATIONS WORLDWIDE

h.f.ullmann

Hotels, shops, museums and public squares are simultaneously meeting points, stages, theaters, venues for seeing and being seen, oases of relaxation, they are parts of a landscape in which people's lives unfold. These are often places far ahead of their time, forging their own style and setting new examples. They are cultural phenomena which are continually evolving, locales which offer the most diverse outlets for society's age-old urge to express itself. All over the world, shops, bars, restaurants and hotels are opening their doors – or being reinterpreted with a boundless wealth of imagination and the financial investment this requires. Of all public spaces, these are without a doubt the ones subject to the greatest changes. The creation of these places incorporates not only the work of the finest architects, but also designers, artists and fashion leaders, ever striving to satisfy the growing demands of a self-aware clientele with the use of innovative materials and ideas so original they truly break the mould. These are the eternal buds of creative trends – never finished, always exciting.

This contemporary, experimental character is what distinguishes these places from other buildings and large-scale city planning projects: on the one hand, their designs go far beyond the construction of mere architectural structures; on the other hand, these creations are increasingly seen as canvases where new ideas can be tried out before being applied to other constructions of different scope and function. Through thick and thin, these locations manage to keep their own unique character, though ever dependent on the functions and capabilities of a given project and the goals which have been set for it. They are places which are defined by the people passing through, people who have contributed to their success in one way or another. In this manner, interstices of public life are created, defining new atmospheres and offering a show of hospitality and inter-personal contact.

The credo of life, lifestyle and superior modes of living is the over-arching motif of "DESIGN DESTINATIONS WORLDWIDE". Such superlatives are always subjective, thus a mere matter of taste. What is indisputable, however, is that this selection of special places is unique in its design and presentation.

550 SHOPPING | STELLA McCARTNEY | LONDON | GREAT BRITAIN

Hotels, Shops, Museen und Plätze sind Treffpunkt, Bühne, Theater, Schauplatz, Ruhepunkt, Aussichtspunkt, sind Teile einer Landschaft, in denen die Menschen ihr Leben verbringen. Oft sind diese Orte ihrer Zeit voraus, prägen einen Stil und übernehmen Vorbildfunktion. Sie sind kulturelle Phänomene, die sich beständig weiterentwickeln und dem Drang der Gesellschaft, sich selbst darzustellen auf vielfältige Weise Ausdruck verleihen. Rund um den Globus eröffnen neue Shops, Bars, Restaurants und Hotels oder werden mit viel Einfallsreichtum und finanziellem Aufwand neu interpretiert. Sie sind von allen öffentlichen Räumen sicherlich diejenigen, die den stärksten Veränderungen unterworfen sind. Mit der Realisierung dieser Orte sind daher nicht nur Architekten befasst, sondern auch Designer, Künstler und Modeschöpfer, die mit neuartigen Materialien und originellen Ideen die wachsenden Ansprüche einer selbstbewussten Klientel zu erfüllen suchen. Sie sind Keimzelle kreativer Trends – nie fertig und immer aufregend.

Dieser bisweilen experimentelle Charakter ist es, der diese Orte von anderen Gebäuden und städteplanerischen Großprojekten unterscheidet: Einerseits gehen deren Entwürfe weit über die Planung rein baulicher Maßnahmen hinaus, andererseits werden an diesen Orten immer häufiger Möglichkeiten erprobt, die später auch in Bauten anderer Größenordnung und Funktion verwirklicht werden. Dennoch bewahren sich die verschiedenen Orte ihre spezifische Eigenständigkeit, allerdings in Abhängigkeit von den Möglichkeiten und Funktionen eines Projektes und den Absichten, die damit verfolgt werden. Sie sind Orte, geprägt durch die Menschen, die dort ein- und ausgehen, die auf die eine oder andere Weise zu deren Erfolg beigetragen haben. So entstehen Zwischen-Räume des öffentlichen Lebens, sie schaffen Atmosphäre und bieten somit einen Akt der Gastlichkeit und der Kontaktaufnahme mit anderen.

Das Credo von Lebensart, Lebensstil und gehobener Lebensführung zieht sich wie ein roter Faden durch den Band „DESIGN DESTINATIONS WORLDWIDE". Derartige Superlative sind immer subjektiv, also Geschmackssache. Unbestreitbar ist aber, dass diese Auswahl besonderer Orte in ihrer Art und Aufmachung einmalig ist.

Hôtels, boutiques, musées et lieux publics sont à la fois points de rencontre, scènes, théâtres, lieux pour voir et être vu ou havres de paix ; ils sont partie intégrante du paysage dans lequel nos vies évoluent. Ces endroits sont souvent en avance sur leur temps, par leur style unique et leur fonction exemplaire. Ce sont des phénomènes culturels en constante évolution, des lieux comblant des plus diverses manières ce besoin urgent et intemporel de s'exprimer, cher à toute société. De par le monde, boutiques, bars, restaurants et hôtels ouvrent leurs portes – ou sont réinterprétés par une imagination d'une richesse sans limites en bénéficiant de l'investissement financier que celle-ci requiert. Parmi tous les espaces publics, ceux-ci sont sans doute sujets aux changements les plus fascinants. La création de ces lieux n'implique pas uniquement le travail des meilleurs architectes, mais également de maîtres du design, de l'art ou de la mode, s'efforçant sans relâche de satisfaire les demandes croissantes d'une clientèle avertie, par l'usage de matériaux innovants et des idées si originales qu'elles rompent toute continuité avec le passé. Ce sont les bourgeons éternels de la tendance, toujours en mouvement, toujours excitante.

Ce caractère contemporain, expérimental, distingue ces lieux des autres édifices, des projets urbains à grande échelle : d'une part, leur design se place bien au-delà de l'édification de simples structures architecturales ; d'autre part, on considère de plus en plus ces créations comme des toiles d'expérimentation, avant d'appliquer les idées nouvelles à d'autres constructions, aux intentions et aux fonctions diverses. Contre vents et marées, ces endroits réussissent à garder une âme unique tout en dépendant des fonctions et des demandes du projet qui les a fait naître, ainsi que des résultats attendus qui lui sont liés. Ces endroits sont définis par les âmes qui les traversent, celles qui d'une manière ou d'une autre ont contribué à leur succès. De ce fait, des interstices de vie publique sont créés, définissant de nouvelles atmosphères et offrant une démonstration d'hospitalité et de contact interpersonnel.

Cette philosophie de vie, d'art de vivre et de modes de vie supérieurs est le fil rouge de « DESIGN DESTINATIONS WORLDWIDE ». Ces descriptions sont toujours subjectives et relèvent de ce fait d'une simple question de goût. Ce qui reste cependant indiscutable, c'est que la présente sélection de lieux hors du commun est unique tant dans sa forme que sa présentation.

52 HOTELS | FAENA HOTEL | BUENOS AIRES | ARGENTINA

Hotels, winkels, musea en pleinen zijn ontmoetingspunt, platform, theater, schouwplaats, rustpunt en uitzichtpunt. Ze vormen een onderdeel van het landschap waar mensen hun leven doorbrengen. Vaak zijn deze plekken hun tijd vooruit, drukken een stijl hun stempel op en hebben een voorbeeldfunctie. Het zijn culturele fenomenen die zich voortdurend verder ontwikkelen en de maatschappelijke druk om op te vallen op velerlei wijze tot uitdrukking brengen. Over de hele wereld ontstaan nieuwe winkels, bars, restaurants en hotels of ze worden met veel creativiteit en hoge kosten nieuw leven ingeblazen. Deze plekken zijn van alle openbare ruimten ongetwijfeld het meest aan veranderingen onderhevig. Bij de totstandkoming van deze plekken zijn dan ook niet alleen architecten betrokken maar ook designers, kunstenaars en mode-ontwerpers die met de nieuwste materialen en originele ideeën aan de groeiende wensen van een zelfbewust clientèle pogen tegemoet te komen. Het zijn bronnen van creatieve trends – nooit klaar en altijd opwindend.

Dit soms experimentele karakter zorgt er ook voor dat deze plekken zich onderscheiden van andere gebouwen en stedenbouwkundige projecten. Enerzijds gaan de ontwerpen veel verder dan alleen bouwkundige maatregelen en anderzijds worden op deze plekken steeds vaker mogelijkheden uitgeprobeerd die later ook in gebouwen van een andere omvang of functie worden omgezet. Toch behouden de verschillende plekken hun specifieke zelfstandigheid maar wel in afhankelijk-heid van de mogelijkheden en functies van een project en de doelen die worden nagestreefd. Het zijn plekken die worden gevormd door de mensen die hier in- en uitgaan en die op de een of de andere manier hebben bijgedragen aan het succes. Op deze manier ontstaan tussenruimten van het openbare leven, ze bieden atmosfeer en maken hiermee een gebaar van gastvrijheid en de mogelijkheid om contacten met andere mensen aan te knopen.

Het credo van levenswijze, levensstijl en hoogwaardige leefwijze loopt als een rode draad door het boek 'DESIGN DESTINATIONS WORLDWIDE'. Zulke superlatieven zijn altijd persoonlijk ofwel een kwestie van smaak. Maar onbetwistbaar is wel dat deze selectie van bijzondere plekken in zijn wijze en presentatie uniek is.

576 HEALTH & BEAUTY | BATHHOUSE | LAS VEGAS | USA

LUXURY LODGINGS AND RESORTS

HOTELS

This hotel has earned its slogan "the sexiest hotel in the world" – the hotel's pure white design offers the perfect, neutral canvas for diverse and surprising light effects. Every room in the hotel has its own spa as well as mirrored walls which reflect the Mediterranean Sea throughout the entire room. Guests can enjoy the use of a pool twice the length of an Olympic swimming pool.

Das Hotel wird seinem Werbeslogan „The sexiest Hotel in the World" gerecht – die pure weiße Einrichtung bietet die perfekte, neutrale Basisform für diverse und überraschende Lichteffekte. Hier verfügt jedes Zimmer über ein eigenes Spa sowie über Spiegelwände, die das Mittelmeer im ganzen Raum reflektieren. Die Gäste können in einem Pool schwimmen, der doppelt so lang wie ein olympisches Schwimmbecken ist.

Cet hôtel mérite son enseigne d' « hôtel le plus sexy du monde » ; le design d'un blanc immaculé de cette adresse offre une toile neutre et parfaite aux effets de lumière les plus surprenants. Chaque chambre possède son propre spa ainsi que des miroirs aux murs, reflétant la Méditerranée dans toute la chambre. La clientèle peut jouir d'une piscine deux fois plus longue qu'un bassin olympique.

Het hotel doet zijn reclameleus 'the sexiest hotel in the world' eer aan – de smetteloos witte inrichting biedt een perfecte en neutrale achtergrond voor de diverse, verrassende lichteffecten. Elke kamer beschikt over een eigen spa en over spiegelwanden die de Middellandse Zee door de hele ruimte weerkaatsen. De gasten kunnen gebruikmaken van een zwembad dat twee keer zo lang is als een olympisch bad.

These lavish and luxurious villas are inconspicuously integrated into the tropical world of this small island. From their sun decks, these water villas offer breathtaking views over sea and sky. All the villas are constructed from natural materials: wood, stone, palm roofs and fabrics in warm hues and traditional patterns. The guest here will be greeted by a typical "island style", accentuated by ethnic elements in a clear-cut and appealing design.

Die großzügigen und luxuriösen Villen fügen sich unauffällig in die tropische Welt der kleinen Insel ein. Von ihren Sonnen-decks aus gestatten die Wasser-Villen atemberaubende Ausblicke auf Himmel und Meer. Sämtliche Villen sind mit natür-lichen Materialien ausgestattet: Holz, Stein, Palmendächer und Stoffe in warmen Farbtönen mit traditionellen Mustern. Den Gast erwartet ein typischer „Island Style" mit ethnischen Akzenten in klarem und ansprechendem Design.

Ces villas somptueuses et empreintes de luxe sont discrètement intégrées dans l'univers tropical de cet îlot. Depuis leurs pontons, ces villas aquatiques offrent une vue imprenable sur la mer et le ciel. Toutes les villas sont faites de matériaux naturels : bois, pierre, toits de palmes et tissus aux tons chauds et motifs traditionnels. Les clients sont accueillis dans un parfait « style des îles », souligné par les accents ethniques d'un design précis et plaisant.

De ruime en luxueuze villa's gaan harmonisch op in de tropische omgeving van het kleine eiland. Vanaf de zonneterrassen bieden de watervilla's adembenemende uitzichten op de hemel en de zee. Alle villa's zijn opgetrokken uit natuurlijke ma-terialen: hout, steen, daken van palmenbladeren en stoffen in warme kleuren met traditionele patronen. De gasten staat typische 'island style' te wachten, geaccentueerd met etnische elementen met een sprekend en innemend design.

The Blue Palace Resort & Spa is the latest luxury hotel on the Greek Mediterranean isle of Crete. A resort of exceptional quality and style, constructed in the mythical atmosphere of the island of Spinalonga with its 16th-century Venetian fortress, it is the ideal place for rest and relaxation, offering unique and breathtaking views from all its luxury bungalows, suites and villas.

Das Blue Palace Resort & Spa ist das neueste Luxushotel auf der griechischen Mittelmeerinsel Kreta. Ein Resort von außergewöhnlicher Qualität und Stil, errichtet in mythischer Umgebung der vorgelagerten Insel Spinalonga mit seiner venezianischen Festung aus dem 16. Jahrhundert. Ein idealer Ort zum Erholen und Entspannen, mit einer einmaligen, atemberaubenden Aussicht von allen luxuriösen Bungalows, Suiten und Villen aus.

Le Blue Palace Resort & Spa est le dernier hôtel de luxe ouvert en Crête, cette célèbre île de Méditerranée. Ce complexe d'un style et d'une qualité exceptionnels, est construit au cœur de l'atmosphère mythique de l'île Spinalonga, où se dresse une forteresse vénitienne du XVIe siècle ; il est idéal au repos et à la relaxation, chacun de ses luxueux bungalows, suites et villas offrant une vue unique, à couper le souffle.

Het Blue Palace Resort & Spa is het nieuwste luxehotel op het Griekse eiland Kreta. Het is een resort van buitengewone kwaliteit en stijl en kijkt uit op de mythische omgeving van het eiland Spinalonga met zijn Venetiaanse zestiende-eeuwse vesting. Een ideale plek om tot rust te komen, met een uniek en adembenemend uitzicht vanuit alle luxeueze bungalows, suites en villa's.

The Bulgari Hotel combines contemporary design with comfort. The building consists of three parts, the oldest of the three facades going back to the 18th century. The hotel was redesigned by architect Antonio Citterio and stands in harmony with Bulgari's elegant style. Precious natural materials were integrated into the design, such as the black Zimbabwe marble in the lobby, the stone from Vicenza and the aphyon from Turkey in the spa area, the teak and precious oak in the guestrooms and suites.

Das Bulgari Hotel verbindet zeitgenössisches Design und Komfort. Das Gebäude besteht aus drei Teilen, die älteste der drei Fassaden geht auf das 18. Jahrhundert zurück. Neu gestaltet wurde das Hotel vom Architekten Antonio Citterio und steht im Einklang mit dem eleganten Stil Bulgaris. Verarbeitet wurden kostbare Materialien wie schwarzer Zimbabwe-Marmor in der Lobby, Stein aus Vicenza und Aphyon aus der Türkei im Spa-Bereich, hartes Teakholz und edles Eichenholz in den Gästezimmern und Suiten.

L'hôtel Bulgari allie design contemporain et confort. L'édifice est constitué de trois parties, la plus ancienne des trois façades datant du XVIIIᵉ siècle. L'hôtel a été redessiné par l'architecte Antonio Citterio et entre en parfaite harmonie avec l'élégance du style Bulgari. Les matériaux naturels précieux ont été privilégiés, comme le marbre noir du Zimbabwe présent dans le hall d'entrée, la pierre de Vicenza et l'Afyon de Turquie dans l'espace spa, le teck et le chêne précieux dans les chambres et les suites.

Het Bulgari Hotel verbindt eigentijds design met comfort. Het gebouw bestaat uit drie delen, de oudste van de drie gevels stamt uit de achttiende eeuw. De architect Antonio Citterio reconstrueerde het hotel in overeenstemming met de elegante stijl van Bulgari. Hij verwerkte waardevolle materialen zoals zwart marmer uit Zimbabwe in de lobby, steen uit Vicenza en aphyon uit Turkije in de spa en hard teakhout en kostbaar eikenhout in de gastenkamers en suites.

Casa Colombo is a retro-chic hotel for well-traveled architecture and design lovers. It will enchant you with its painstaking and detailed renovation of a 200-year-old colonial palace, while stimulating with the combination of a refreshing and unconventional type of European design with Asiatic products.

Die Casa Colombo ist ein retroschickes Hotel für weit gereiste Architektur- und Designfreunde. Es besticht einerseits durch seine aufwendige und detailgetreue Restaurierung eines 200 Jahre alten Kolonial-Palazzos, anderseits begeistert es durch eine erfrischend unkonventionelle Art europäisches Design mit asiatischen Produkten zu kombinieren.

Le Casa Colombo est un hôtel rétro-chic destiné aux amoureux du design et de l'architecture bien pensée. Il vous enchantera par sa rénovation soignée et détaillée d'un ancien palais colonial vieux de 200 ans, tout en vous stimulant par la combinaison d'un design européen rafraîchissant et inhabituel et de l'artisanat asiatique.

Het Casa Colombo is een chic retrohotel voor architectuur- en designvrienden van wijd en zijd. Het bekoort enerzijds door de grondige en minutieuze restauratie van het tweehonderd jaar oude koloniale palazzo en anderzijds door de verfrissende onconventionele wijze om Europees design met Aziatische producten te verenigen.

The hotel and resort Costa Lanta offers its own interpretation of originality through sleek and contemporary architecture. Set back from the beach, the twenty freestanding bungalows are nestled into the sprawling property between tropical trees and natural water courses. This exposed concrete cube with bedroom and bathroom opens out onto a wraparound terrace. Reduced to its essentials, the architecture here is the subdued background for views onto the Indian Ocean.

Das Hotel Resort Costa Lanta interpretiert das Thema Ursprünglichkeit mit zeitgemäßer, schlichter Architektur. Vom Strand zurückversetzt, sind die zwanzig freistehenden Bungalows zwischen tropischen Bäumen und natürlichen Wasserläufen in das weitläufige Grundstück eingebettet. Dem Sichtbetonkubus mit Schlafraum und Badezimmer ist eine membranüberspannte Terrasse vorgelagert. Auf das Wesentliche reduziert, bildet die Architektur den dezenten Hintergrund für den Ausblick auf den Indischen Ozean.

Le complexe hôtelier Costa Lanta offre sa propre interprétation de l'originalité par une architecture soignée et contemporaine. En retrait de la plage, les vingt bungalows de plein pied sont nichés au cœur de la propriété s'étendant entre les arbres tropicaux et les cours d'eau naturels. Ce cube de béton nu comprenant une chambre et une salle de bains est entièrement entouré d'une terrasse. Réduite à l'essentiel, l'architecture présente ici est une toile de fond discrète pour observer l'Océan Indien.

Het Hotel Resort Costa Lanta combineert oorspronkelijkheid met eigentijdse architectuur. Op een uitgestrekt grondstuk staan de twintig vrijstaande bungalows verspreid tussen tropische bomen en natuurlijke beekjes. Voor de sierbetonnen kubussen met slaapkamer en badkamer liggen met membraan bespannen terrassen. De sobere architectuur vormt de decente achtergrond voor het uitzicht op de Indische Oceaan.

Ron Arad developed the design for the painstaking restructuring of this hotel. He developed an entryway which opens out into the reception foyer in the shape of a vast and oversized ring in the center of the hotel. Like a lava flow, seats flow along the sides of the walls, not a rightangle in sight, everything fluid. Only the material for tables and chairs gives a whiff of the old Rimini: the bronze-colored surface is reminiscent of well-tanned skin.

Der Entwurf des aufwendigen Umbaues wurde von Ron Arad gestaltet. Er entwarf einen Eingang, der die Rezeption in Form eines übergroßen, unübersehbaren Ringes als Mittelpunkt des Hotels darstellt. Wie ein Lavastrom fließen die Sitzgelegenheiten an den Wänden entlang, nirgends rechte Winkel, alles zerfließt. Nur das Material von Tischen und Stühlen lässt einen Hauch des alten Riminis zurück: Die bronzefarbene Oberfläche erinnert an stark gebräunte Haut.

Ron Arad a développé les plans de la réhabilitation soigneuse de cet hôtel. Il a créé un hall d'entrée dont la réception est intégrée à un anneau géant, au centre de l'hôtel. Telles un flot de lave, les banquettes suivent les courbes des murs, sans jamais rencontrer aucun d'angle droit, en toute fluidité. Seul le matériau des tables et des chaises rappelle le vieux Rimini : cette surface de couleur bronze n'a d'égal que le hâle d'une peau dorée par le soleil.

Het ontwerp voor de kostbare verbouwing is van de hand van Ron Arad. Hij ontwierp een entree die de receptie, in de vorm van een enorme ring, tot middelpunt van het hotel maakt. De zitgelegenheden golven als een lavastroom langs de wanden. Nergens zijn rechte hoeken, alles vloeit in elkaar over. Alleen het materiaal van de tafels en stoelen herinnert vaag aan het oude Rimini. Het bronskleurige oppervlak doet denken aan een gebronsde huid.

The heart of this unmistakable hotel complex used to be a former iron foundry. The characteristic tile construction is encased in a modern architectural composition of glass, brick and steel. The construction combines solid historical architectonics with modern architectural design. An open construction with lounge spaces on various levels conveys a relaxed feeling of space, a sensation continued throughout the rooms of the hotel.

Eine historische Eisengießerei bildet das Herzstück des unverwechselbaren Hotel-Ensembles. Der markante Klinkerbau wird von einer modernen Gebäudekomposition aus Glas, Ziegel und Stahl umfasst. Die Anlage verbindet gekonnt historische Bausubstanz mit moderner Architektur. Eine offene Bauweise mit Aufenthaltszonen auf verschiedenen Ebenen vermittelt ein entspanntes Raumgefühl, das sich bis in die Hotelzimmer hinein fortsetzt.

Le cœur de cet immanquable complexe hôtelier n'est autre qu'une ancienne fonderie d'acier. Cette construction carrelée caractéristique est enceinte dans une composition moderne de verre, de briques et d'acier. Celle-ci combine des architectoniques historiques à un design architectural moderne. Cet édifice ouvert, constitué d'espaces salon sur différents niveaux procure un agréable sentiment d'espace, une sensation maintenue même dans les chambres de l'hôtel.

Een historische ijzergieterij vormt het hart van het karakteristieke hotelcomplex. Het markante bakstenen gebouw wordt omgeven door een moderne gebouwencompositie van glas, steen en staal. Het complex is een geslaagde verbinding van historische gebouwen met moderne architectuur. Een open bouwwijze met publieke ruimten op verschillende verdiepingen geeft een prettig ruimtelijk gevoel dat wordt voortgezet in de hotelkamers.

With its unique location, this hotel earns its name as a "hideaway". Situated on a peninsula which can only be reached by boat, the resort hides among verdant flora, spectacular rock formations and a white-sand beach. The buildings are constructed in a mix of modern and traditional Vietnamese architecture. The resort's 53 villas stand on the beach or are tucked into the hills, giving the guests that real Robinson Crusoe feeling.

Die Lage des Hideaway ist wirklich „hidden away". Auf einer Halbinsel, die nur per Boot erreichbar ist, versteckt sich das Resort zwischen grüner Vegetation, spektakulären Felsformationen und weißem Sandstrand. Die Gebäude sind in einer Mischung von moderner und landestypischer vietnamesischer Architektur eingerichtet. Die 53 Villen des Resorts sind am Strand oder in den Hügeln errichtet und verleihen den Gästen Robinson-Crusoe-Feeling.

Par son emplacement unique, cet hôtel a gagné son titre de « cachette ». Situé sur une péninsule accessible uniquement par bateau, le complexe se dissimule parmi une flore verdoyante, de spectaculaires formations rocheuses et une plage de sable fin. Les bâtiments mêlent architecture vietnamienne traditionnelle et moderne. Les 53 villas du complexe se trouvent sur la plage ou nichées dans les collines, faisant de ses hôtes de vrais Robinson Crusoé.

De locatie van het Hideaway is daadwerkelijk 'hidden away'. Op een schiereiland dat alleen per boot bereikbaar is, gaat het resort schuil tussen groene vegetatie, spectaculaire rotsformaties en witte zandstranden. De gebouwen zijn ingericht in een combinatie van moderne en typisch Vietnamese architectuur. De drieënvijftig villa's van het resort liggen aan het strand of in de heuvels en geven de gasten een Robinson-Crusoe-feeling.

Designer Philippe Starck presents his Buenos Aires masterpiece filled with poetry, glamour and elegance. The rooms are decorated with more than a touch of pomp, including curved divans, elegant groupings of natural leather armchairs, silk upholstery in ruby reds or purples – here sensuous beauty awaits the guest in a former grain storehouse over a century old. A place for the senses, stylish opulence of the very finest of course! A must for anyone who loves luxury, extravagance and design.

Voller Poesie, Prunk und Eleganz präsentiert der Designer Philippe Starck sein Glanzstück in Buenos Aires. Pompös eingerichtete Räume mit geschwungenen Diwanen, eleganten Ledersesselgruppen, Samtbezügen in schwerem Rubinrot oder Purpur – hier erwartet den Gast sinnliche Schönheit in einem über 100 Jahre alten ehemaligen Getreidespeicher. Ein Ort der Sinne, stilvoller Üppigkeit, und die nur vom Feinsten! Ein Muss für Freunde von Luxus, Extravaganz und Design.

Le Designer Philippe Starck présente son chef-d'œuvre de Buenos Aires, empreint de poésie, de glamour et d'élégance. Les chambres revêtent leurs plus beaux habits d'apparat : divans aux formes arrondies, ensembles élégants de fauteuils en cuir naturel, soieries pourpres ou rouge grenat – ici, une beauté voluptueuse attend l'hôte dans un ancien grenier à grains vieux de plus d'un siècle. Un lieu pour les sens, élégamment opulent et tout en finesse ! Un must pour quiconque aime le luxe, l'extravagance et le design.

Het pronkstuk van de designer Philippe Starck in Buenos Aires kenmerkt zich door een overvloed aan poëzie, pracht en elegantie. Weelderig ingerichte ruimten met sierlijke divans, elegante leren fauteuils, fluwelen bekledingen in diep robijnrood of purper – in dit hotel staat de gasten zinnelijke schoonheid in een meer dan honderd jaar oude voormalige graanschuur te wachten. Een betoverende, stijlvolle plek van een uitgelezen kwaliteit! Een must voor alle liefhebbers van luxe, extravagantie en design.

From the outside, this magnificent building, constructed in 1926, looks like an American office building from Chicago's Golden Twenties. This style is continued in the lobby with its heavy iron chandeliers. The decorative style inside the rooms is modern and matter-of-fact. A sensational roof terrace with pool offers a breathtaking view of the city both day and night.

Von außen wirkt der Prachtbau aus dem Jahr 1926 wie ein amerikanisches Firmengebäude der Golden Twenties in Chicago. Der Stil setzt sich in der Lobby mit ihren schweren Eisenlüstern fort. Auf den Zimmern dominiert ein sachlich-moderner Einrichtungsstil. Eine sensationelle Dachterrasse mit Pool bietet Tag und Nacht einen atemberaubenden Blick über die Stadt.

De l'extérieur, ce magnifique édifice construit en 1926 apparaît tel un bâtiment américain de l'âge d'or de Chicago. Ce style est perpétué dans le hall d'entrée au moyen de lourds chandeliers d'acier. La décoration intérieure des chambres est moderne et terre-à-terre. Un toit-terrasse sensationnel doté d'une piscine offre une vue surprenante sur la ville de jour comme de nuit.

Aan de buitenkant lijkt dit prachtige gebouw uit 1926 op een Amerikaans kantoorgebouw uit de Golden Twenties in Chicago. De stijl wordt voortgezet in de lobby met de zware ijzeren kroonkandelaars. Op de kamers overheerst een zakelijk-moderne stijl. Een sensationeel dakterras met zwembad biedt dag en nacht een adembenemend uitzicht op de stad.

From the outside, this building presents itself as a grandiose structure, from the basement with its glass-fronted bar and restaurant and four small designer boutiques to the upper levels with their large uniform window panes. Inside, however, the Greulich is laid out almost exclusively over a single level, the ground floor. The restaurant, bar and Cigar Lounge, the terrace and the hotel are all on one floor and open up to a courtyard complete with Japanese-inspired birch grove.

Nach außen präsentiert sich das Gebäude als imposante Einheit, vom Basement mit der Glasfront von Restaurant und Bar und den vier kleinen Design-Boutiquen bis hin zu den Stockwerken mit großen regelmäßigen Fensterflächen. Im Inneren findet das Greulich dagegen fast ausschließlich auf einer Ebene, dem Erdgeschoss, statt. Restaurant, Bar und Cigar Lounge, Terrasse und Hotel liegen auf einem Niveau und öffnen sich zum Innenhof mit seinem japanisch inspirierten Birkenhain.

De l'extérieur, ce bâtiment se présente comme une structure grandiose, depuis le rez-de-chaussée de verre accueillant bar et restaurant ainsi que quatre petites boutiques de créateurs, jusqu'aux étages supérieurs, habillés de larges baies vitrées. A l'intérieur, le Greulich s'étend presque exclusivement sur un seul étage, le rez-de-chaussée. Le restaurant, le bar et le Fumoir, la terrasse et l'hôtel sont regroupés sur un niveau, duquel s'ouvre une cour d'inspiration japonaise agrémentée de bouleaux.

Naar buiten toe presenteert het gebouw zich als een imposante eenheid, van de benedenverdieping met de glazen gevel van restaurant, bar en de vier kleine designboetiekjes tot de bovenverdiepingen met de grote, regelmatige raampartijen. Binnen heeft echter nagenoeg alles plaats op een etage, de begane grond. Restaurant, bar en cigar lounge, terras en hotel bevinden zich op een niveau en geven toegang tot de binnenplaats met zijn Japans geïnspireerde berkentuin.

The minimalist design of this hotel is based on the style of the 1960s and will appeal to guests searching for something "extravagant", who wish to escape the "everyday". The hotel's motif runs in a purist vein – no fussiness to distract from what really matters. The lobby itself is eye-catching with its mirrored ceiling from which six glittering disco balls are suspended. These reflect the sunlight and cast thousands of enchanting light effects onto the lobby's white walls in the evening. The building's exterior façade is designed like a shop window and changes colors every 30 seconds when it's dark outside.

Die minimalistische Einrichtung basiert auf dem Stil der 1960er Jahre und spricht Gäste an, die das „Extravagante", das „nicht Alltägliche" suchen. Die Linienführung im Hotel ist puristisch – kein Schnörkel, der vom Wesentlichen ablenken würde. Auffallend ist die Lobby mit verspiegeltem Plafond, an dem sechs glitzernde Discokugeln hängen. Diese reflektieren das Sonnenlicht und zaubern abends tausendfache Lichteffekte auf die weißen Flächen. Die Außenfassade des Hauses ist wie ein Schaufenster gestaltet und wechselt in der Dunkelheit alle 30 Sekunden die Farbe.

Le design minimaliste de cet hôtel est fondé sur un style années 60 et plaira aux hôtes à la recherche d'un peu « d'extravagance » désireux d'échapper au quotidien. La décoration de l'hôtel est ouvertement puriste : aucun chichi ne distrait du principal. Même le hall d'entrée attire l'attention, paré d'un plafond recouvert de miroirs d'où sont suspendues six boules à facettes scintillantes. Celles-ci reflètent les rayons du soleil et lancent des milliers d'éclats lumineux enchanteurs sur les surfaces blanches du hall. La façade extérieure du bâtiment ressemble à une vitrine de magasin et change de couleur toutes les 30 secondes à la nuit tombée.

De minimalistische inrichting is gebaseerd op de stijl van de jaren zestig en zal in de smaak vallen bij gasten die extravagantie verkiezen boven alledaagsheid. De lijnen in het hotel zijn sober – geen opsmuk leidt af van de essentie. Opvallend is de lobby met het gespiegelde plafond waaraan zes fonkelende discoballen hangen. Deze reflecteren het zonlicht en toveren 's avonds duizenden lichteffecten op de witte wanden. De voorgevel van het gebouw is ingericht als etalage en verandert in het donker om de dertig seconden van kleur.

The old Adlon was quickly proclaimed one of the world's most beautiful hotels after its opening in 1907. "Tout le monde" hailed it for its architecture, its artistic construction and its technical perfection. Guests from all over the world stayed here, including prominent contemporaries such as Thomas Mann, Enrico Caruso, Greta Garbo and Charlie Chaplin. Reopened in 1997, the new Hotel Adlon Kempinski is once again among the most beautiful, luxurious and famed hotels in the world. It is one of Berlin's premier addresses and is located on the famous Unter den Linden boulevard, looking out onto the Brandenburg Gate and right next to the Pariser Platz.

Das alte Adlon galt rasch nach seiner Eröffnung im Jahre 1907 als eines der schönsten Hotels der Welt. „Tout le monde" lobte es für seine Architektur, seine künstlerische Gestaltung und die technische Perfektion. Gäste aus aller Welt fanden sich ein, unter ihnen prominente Zeitgenossen wie Thomas Mann, Enrico Caruso, Greta Garbo und Charlie Chaplin. Das 1997 wiedereröffnete Hotel Adlon Kempinski ist eines der schönsten, luxuriösesten und bekanntesten Hotels weltweit. Es ist eine der ersten Adressen Berlins und liegt an der Straße Unter den Linden, in Sichtweite zum Brandenburger Tor direkt neben dem Pariser Platz.

L'ancien Adlon fut rapidement proclamé l'un des plus beaux hôtels du monde après son ouverture en 1907. Tout le monde acclama son architecture, sa conception artistique ainsi que sa perfection technique. Des clients du monde entier vinrent y séjourner, parmi lesquels des contemporains célèbres comme Thomas Mann, Enrico Caruso, Greta Garbo et Charlie Chaplin. Réouvert en 1997, le nouvel hôtel Adlon Kempinski est encore une fois parmi les plus beaux, les plus luxueux et les plus célèbres hôtels du monde. Il est l'une des adresses les plus courues de Berlin et se trouve sur le fameux Unter den Linden boulevard, faisant face à la porte de Brandebourg et situé juste à droite de la Pariser Platz.

Het oude Adlon Hotel gold al snel na zijn opening in 1907 als een van de mooiste hotels ter wereld. 'Tout le monde' prees het om zijn architectuur, zijn artistieke vormgeving en de technische perfectie. Gasten uit de hele wereld namen hun intrek in het hotel, onder hen prominente tijdgenoten als Enrico Caruso, Greta Garbo, Charlie Chaplin en Thomas Mann. Het in 1997 heropende Hotel Adlon Kempinski is tegenwoordig weer een van de mooiste, luxueuste en bekendste hotels wereldwijd. Het is een van de favoriete hotels van Berlijn en ligt in de straat Unter den Linden, vlakbij de Brandenburger Tor en de Pariser Platz.

This hotel is on the Bebelplatz in the center of Berlin near the famous Unter den Linden boulevard. The building, originally a municipal palace dating back to 1889, was stylishly renovated and the interior redone in an elegant modern design. Inside is a combination of neoclassical Berlin architectural elements and contemporary design features, in which glass and steel play a principal role. The visitor is greeted by two bright red-lacquered and oversized replicas of Farnese vases from Rome's Capitoline Museum.

Das Hotel befindet sich im Zentrum Berlins am Bebelplatz, in der Nähe von Unter den Linden. Das zugrunde liegende Haus, ein Stadtpalais von 1889, wurde stilvoll restauriert und innen mit einem modernen, eleganten Design versehen. Das Interieur setzt sich zusammen aus neoklassischen Berliner Architekturelementen und einer zeitgemäßen Einrichtung, in der Glas und Stahl eine gestalterische Rolle spielen. So wird der Besucher von zwei knallrot lackierten und extragroßen Kopien von Farnese-Vasen des Kapitolinischen Museums begrüßt.

Cet hôtel se trouve sur la Bebelplatz au centre de Berlin, près du fameux Unter den Linden boulevard. L'édifice, à l'origine bâtiment municipal construit en 1889, a été élégamment rénové et l'intérieur a été refait sur une idée chic et moderne. On y trouvera des éléments architecturaux néoclassiques berlinois combinés à un design et des matériaux contemporains, où dominent le verre et l'acier. Le visiteur est accueilli par deux répliques géantes des vases laqués de rouge de Farnèse, visibles au Musée du Capitole à Rome.

Het hotel bevindt zich in het centrum van Berlijn aan de Bebelplatz, vlakbij Unter den Linden. Het oorspronkelijke stadspaleis uit 1889 werd stijlvol gerestaureerd en binnen van een modern, elegant design voorzien. Het interieur bestaat uit een combinatie van neoklassieke Berlijnse architectuurelementen en een moderne inrichting, waarin glas en staal een decoratieve rol spelen. Zo wordt de bezoeker verwelkomd door twee knalrood gelakte en extragrote kopieën van Farnese-vazen van de Musei Capitolini te Rome.

The Marqués de Riscal was designed by architect Frank O. Gehry and is hailed as one of the most avant-garde and innovative hotels in the world. The structure's titanium facade glows in the distance like the wine for which this region is known: red and pink like the grapes which grow here, gold like the netting encasing a Rioja bottle and silver like its label. The complex is devoted to viniculture, the hotel remarkable both on inside and out for its flowing simple lines and iconographic design.

Das Marqués de Riscal wurde vom Architekten Frank O. Gehry entworfen und gehört zu den avantgardistischsten und innovativsten Hotels weltweit. Die Titan-Haut leuchtet schon von weitem so, wie der Wein aus dieser Region daherkommt: rot und rosa wie der Rebensaft, gold wie das Netz, das eine Rioja-Flasche überspannt, und silbern wie das Etikett. Der Komplex ist der Kultur des Weins gewidmet, das Hotel zeichnet sich sowohl von innen als auch von außen durch geschmeidige, einfache Linien und eine ikonografische Einrichtung aus.

Le Marqués de Riscal a été créé par l'architecte Frank O. Gehry et est tenu comme l'un des hôtels les plus avant-gardistes et innovants du monde. La structure en rubans de titane brille au loin, tel le vin faisant la renommée de la région : rouge et rosé comme le raisin poussant ici, doré comme la maille entourant chaque bouteille de Rioja et argenté comme son étiquette. Le complexe est dédié à la viniculture et l'hôtel est remarquable tant à l'intérieur comme à l'extérieur pour ses lignes simples et souples ainsi que pour son design iconographique.

Het Marqués de Riscal werd ontworpen door de architect Frank O. Gehry en behoort tot de meest avant-gardistische en innovatiefste hotels wereldwijd. De buitenkant van titanium licht al van verre op: rood en roze als de wijn uit deze regio, goud als het net waarmee een riojafles is omgeven en zilver als het etiket. Het complex is opgedragen aan de cultuur van de wijn en het hotel kenmerkt zich zowel aan de buiten- als aan de binnenkant door vloeiende, eenvoudige lijnen en een iconografische inrichting.

It shimmers like a mirage atop a hill on the edge of the Atlas mountains: over the course of the last seven years, the Kasbah Tamadot has been painstakingly renovated – with breathtaking results. With its secluded inner courtyards, roomy terraces and the eclectic mix of styles in its 18 rooms and suites, the Kasbah Tamadot gives its guests the feeling of staying in a private house rather than a hotel.

Sie thront wie eine Fata Morgana auf einem Hügel am Rande des Atlasgebirges: Im Laufe der letzten sieben Jahre wurde die Kasbah Tamadot mit großem Aufwand restauriert – und das Ergebnis ist atemberaubend. Mit seinen lauschigen Innenhöfen, großzügigen Terrassen und dem eklektischen Stilmix in den 18 Zimmern und Suiten gibt die Kasbah Tamadot ihren Gästen das Gefühl, eher in einem Privathaus denn in einem Hotel zu logieren.

Il apparaît comme un mirage au sommet de cette colline, à l'extrémité des montagnes de l'Atlas : durant les sept dernières années, le Kasbah Tamadot a été rénové avec soin, pour un résultat stupéfiant. Grâce à ses cours intérieures retirées, ses terrasses spacieuses et le mélange éclectique des styles de ses 18 chambres et suites, le Kasbah Tamadot offre davantage à ses hôtes le sentiment de séjourner chez l'habitant que dans un hôtel.

Het Kasbah Tamadot troont als een fata morgana op een heuvel aan de rand van het Atlasgebergte. De afgelopen zeven jaar werd het hotel grondig gerestaureerd – en het resultaat is adembenemend. Met de intieme binnenplaatsen, ruime terrassen en de eclectische stijlmix in de achttien kamers en suites roept het Kasbah Tamadot een huiselijke sfeer op.

This new and unique Maastricht hotel is the transformation of a former monastery. The nave, dating back to the 15th century, now houses a restaurant, bar and enoteca. The old glazing in the church windows has been painstakingly restored – just like the entire ensemble, which is protected under historical preservation status, allowing no major alterations.

In Maastricht wurde eine ehemalige Klosteranlage in ein neues und einzigartiges Hotel verwandelt. Das Kirchenschiff aus dem 15. Jahrhundert beherbergt zudem ein Restaurant, eine Bar und eine Vinothek. Die alte Verglasung der Kirchenfenster wurde aufwendig restauriert – ebenso das gesamte unter Denkmalschutz stehende Ensemble, in dem keinerlei Eingriffe vorgenommen werden durften.

Ce nouvel hôtel de Maastricht unique en son genre est issu de la transformation d'un ancien monastère. La nef, datant du XVe siècle, abrite désormais un restaurant, un bar et une œnothèque. Le vitrage ancien de l'église a été restauré avec assiduité, tout comme l'ensemble, aujourd'hui classé monument historique et n'acceptant plus aucune modification majeure.

In Maastricht werd een voormalig kloostercomplex tot een nieuw uniek hotel getransformeerd. Het schip van de kerk uit de vijftiende eeuw biedt bovendien onderdak aan een restaurant, een bar en een vinotheek. De oude ramen van de kerk werden grondig gerestaureerd – evenals het gehele onder monumentenzorg vallende complex waaraan geen aanpassingen mochten worden gedaan.

Located in the historic center of Puebla, this stunning hotel started life as a factory in the 19th century, used for water sanitation and for ice production. This tradition of clarity and purity is as evident in La Purificadora as ever. The exclusively black and white decoration is elegantly combined with original materials and the 26 rooms offer long-ranging views.

Im historischen Zentrum von Puebla gelegen, ist dieses umwerfende Hotel aus einer Fabrik des 19. Jahrhunderts hervorgegangen, die zur Wasserreinigung und Eisherstellung diente. Diese Tradition von Klarheit und Reinheit ist im La Purificadora nach wie vor offensichtlich. Die ausschließlich schwarz-weiße Ausstattung steht in eleganter Kombination zu originalen Materialien und die 26 Zimmer bieten weitläufige Ausblicke.

Situé dans le centre historique de Puebla, cet hôtel déroutant vit le jour au XIXᵉ siècle, sous les traits d'une usine d'assainissement des eaux et de fabrication de glace. Cette tradition de clarté et de pureté n'a jamais été aussi évidente que dans cet hôtel : la décoration exclusivement noire et blanche est élégamment mariée à des matériaux originaux et les 26 chambres offrent des vues imprenables.

Dit schitterende hotel in het historische centrum van Puebla verrees in een voormalige negentiende-eeuwse waterzuiveringsfabriek. Deze traditie in puurheid en reinheid komt ook in La Purificadora tot uiting. De uitsluitend zwart-witte inrichting vormt een elegante combinatie met de oorspronkelijke materialen en de zesentwintig kamers bieden mooie vergezichten.

This lodge, a recipient of multiple awards, contains 15 luxuriously furnished tent bungalows and is modeled after a safari camp. The tents are constructed on stilts and their furnishings tell tales of the early discovery of Australia. Offering gorgeous views of world-famous Uluru, or Ayers Rock, this unique ensemble is rounded off with a restaurant, bar, lounge and library.

Die mehrfach ausgezeichnete Lodge, die ihren Namen vom 131. Breitengrad hat, verfügt über 15 luxuriös eingerichtete Zeltbungalows und ist einem Safari-Camp nachempfunden. Die Zelte sind auf Stelzen errichtet und ihre Einrichtung erzählt Geschichten über die frühen Entdecker Australiens. Mit herrlichem Ausblick auf den weltberühmten Ayers Rock runden ein Restaurant sowie eine Bar, eine Lounge und eine Bibliothek das einmalige Angebot ab.

Ce Lodge, récompensé à multiples reprises, compte 15 bungalows-tentes luxueusement décorés et imite la structure des camps de safari. Des pilotis soutiennent les tentes, dont le mobilier raconte les premières expéditions en Australie. Offrant une vue somptueuse sur le mondialement connu Uluru, ou Ayers Rock, ce complexe unique comprend également restaurant, bar, salon et bibliothèque.

De meermaals onderscheiden lodge, die zijn naam dankt aan de 131e breedtegraad, beschikt over vijftien luxueus ingerichte tentbungalows en is ontworpen naar het voorbeeld van een safarikamp. De tenten staan op palen en de inrichting verhaalt over de vroege ontdekkers van Australië. Een restaurant, bar, lounge en bibliotheek ronden met een schitterend uitzicht op de wereldberoemde Ayers Rock het unieke geheel af.

Lute Suites is a uniquely designed luxury hotel on the urban edge of Amsterdam. The hotel is divided over seven small workers' cottages from the 18th century. Each apartment has the character of a private residence and is equipped for long-term guests with its own entryway, wireless LAN and, it goes without saying, all the amenities of a hotel – including breakfast brought right to your room.

Das Lute Suites ist ein individuell gestaltetes Luxushotel der besonderen Art am Stadtrand von Amsterdam. Das Hotel ist auf sieben kleine Arbeiterhäuser aus dem 18. Jahrhundert verteilt. Jedes der Apartments hat den Charakter eines Privathauses und ist für den dauerhaften Aufenthalt der Gäste mit eigenem Eingang, Wireless Lan und natürlich allen Annehmlichkeiten eines Hotels – einschließlich Frühstück auf dem Zimmer – ausgestattet.

Le Lute Suites est un hôtel luxueux de la périphérie urbaine d'Amsterdam. L'hôtel est divisé en sept petits pavillons ouvriers du XVIIIᵉ siècle. Chaque appartement a le caractère d'une résidence privée et est équipé pour des séjours à long terme, grâce à une entrée indépendante, réseau local sans fil et, cela va sans dire, toutes les commodités d'un hôtel (y compris le petit-déjeuner apporté dans la chambre).

Het Lute Suites is een uniek vormgegeven luxehotel aan de rand van Amsterdam. Het hotel bestaat uit zeven kleine arbeidershuisjes uit de achttiende eeuw. Elk appartement heeft een huiselijk karakter en is ingericht voor langdurig verblijf van de gasten met eigen opgang, wireless lan en uiteraard alle gemakken van een hotel – met inbegrip van ontbijt op de kamer.

The puristic Lux11 is perfect for big-city nomads who know the value of privacy. The rooms, with their refined and puristic designs, offer the peace and relaxation much needed after a long day in the city: plain walls made of concrete, warm colors and clear lines. The rooms are exceptionally large and furnished in an unusual way: besides the fax machine and flat-screen TV, there are also fully equipped kitchens.

Das puristische Lux11 ist genau das Richtige für Großstadtnomaden, die Privatsphäre schätzen. In den edel-puristisch gestalteten Räumen findet man die nötige Ruhe und Entspannung nach einem langen Metropolen-Tag: schlichte Wände aus Beton, helle Farben, klare Linien. Die Zimmer sind ausgesprochen groß und sehr bemerkenswert ausgestattet: Neben einem Fax und Flachbildfernseher gibt es auch komplette Küchen.

Le puriste Lux11 est tout approprié aux nomades des grandes cités connaissant la valeur de l'intimité. Les chambres au design raffiné et épuré, offrent la paix et le repos bien mérités après une longue journée à sillonner la ville : fines parois de béton, couleurs chaudes et lignes droites. Les chambres sont résolument spacieuses et habillées de manière inhabituelle : en plus du fax et de l'écran plat, les cuisines sont également équipées.

Kosmopolieten die prijs stellen op privacy zijn bij het puristische Lux11 aan het juiste adres. In de ingetogen vormgegeven ruimten vindt men de nodige rust en ontspanning na een lange dag in de metropool: sobere betonnen wanden, lichte kleuren en duidelijke lijnen. De kamers zijn buitengewoon groot en zeer opmerkelijk ingericht: naast een fax en televisie met platte beeldbuis beschikken enkele over een complete keuken.

You can have design – but nobody says you have to. The first designer hotel in the mountains also offers its guests designer suites which are a far cry from the nostalgic Alpine look. Located at the edge of the famed Ischgl ski resort, it offers a high standard of design and puristic architecture – and still a little something more. Here in the Hotel Madlein you have the opportunity not only to relax in the generously equipped wellness areas but also make use of a Zen garden as well as a fire room which brings the art of relaxation to a whole new level.

Design kann sein – muss aber nicht. Das erste Designhotel in den Bergen bietet seinen Gästen fernab aller Alpenromantik auch Designsuiten. Am Rand des berühmten Skifahrerorts Ischgl gelegen, bietet es einen hohen Designstandard und puristische Architektur – und noch ein bisschen mehr. Denn im Hotel Madlein kann man sich abends nicht nur in den großzügigen Wellness-Bereichen erholen, es gibt zudem einen Zen-Garten sowie einen Feuerraum, der Relaxen auf die etwas andere Art verspricht.

On peut avoir le design, mais qui a dit qu'il était obligatoire ? Le premier hôtel de designer dans les montagnes offre aussi à ses clients des suites de créateur fort éloignées du look alpin d'antan. Situé à l'extrémité de la station de ski d'Ischgl, il offre une décoration de haute qualité et une architecture épurée (et un peu plus encore). Pénétrez l'Hôtel Madlein et vous n'aurez pas seulement l'opportunité de vous relaxer dans des zones de bien-être généreusement équipées, mais vous pourrez aussi profiter du jardin zen ainsi que de la cheminée, élevant la relaxation à un niveau supérieur.

Design mag – maar hoeft niet. Het eerste designhotel in de bergen biedt zijn gasten designsuites zonder een spoortje Alpenromantiek. Het hotel aan de rand van de beroemde skiplaats Ischgl biedt een hoge designstandaard en sobere architectuur – en dat is niet alles. In hotel Madlein kunnen gasten 's avonds niet alleen in het ruime wellnesscentrum tot rust komen, het hotel beschikt tevens over een zentuin en een vuurkamer voor een andere manier van ontspanning.

A guest at Dhara Dhevi will get the feeling he's entering a Thai palace. To ensure that you feel like royalty inside as well, the various suites and residences have been decorated with precious woods and luxurious traditional silks. In the middle of the complex is a tropical garden with direct access from all rooms. Some rooms have their own private pools.

Im Dhara Dhevi wird dem Gast das Gefühl vermittelt, in einen thailändischen Palast einzutreten. Um sich auch im Inneren fürstlich zu fühlen, wurden die verschiedenen Suiten und Residenzen mit wertvollen Hölzern und traditionellen, luxuri-ösen Seidenstoffen ausgestattet. Inmitten der Anlage liegt ein tropischer Garten, zu dem alle Unterkünfte einen direkten Zugang haben, einige verfügen außerdem über einen privaten Pool.

L'hôte du Dhara Dhevi aura l'impression de pénétrer un palais Thaï. Afin d'assurer la longévité de cette noble sensation, les nombreuses suites et appartements sont décorés de bois précieux et de luxuriantes soies traditionnelles. Toutes les chambres ont accès au cœur de la propriété, où se cache un jardin tropical. Certaines chambres possèdent leur propre piscine privée.

In het Dhara Dhevi heeft de gast het gevoel binnen te treden in een Thais paleis. Ook het interieur biedt een vorstelijke aanblik dankzij het gebruik van waardevolle houtsoorten en traditionele zijden stoffen waarmee de verschillende suites en residenties zijn aangekleed. Midden in het complex bevindt zich een tropische tuin. Alle onderkomens hebben directe toegang tot de tuin en sommige beschikken bovendien over een privé-zwembad.

The Marataba Safari is a romantic hotel northwest of Johannesburg and the absolute epitome of all things African. It is not, however, a hotel in the classic sense: Guests stay in tent-like structures made from stone walls and fabric, with glorious views. The emphasis here has been placed on achieving the most authentic design possible, a design which harmonizes with the breathtaking landscape and untouched wilderness all around. Raw stone walls, dark woods, all the colors of the savanna and an elegant architecture all combine to achieve this end.

Das Marataba Safari ist ein romantisches Hotel nordwestlich von Johannesburg und der absolute Inbegriff von Afrika. Dabei gilt es nicht als Hotel im klassischen Sinne: Man logiert in zeltähnlichen Bauten, die Mauerelemente mit viel Stoff und einer herrlichen Aussicht verbinden. Hierbei hat man sehr viel Wert auf eine authentische Gestaltung gelegt, die mit der atemberaubenden Landschaft und der unberührten Natur harmoniert. Unverputzte Steinwände, dunkle Hölzer, die Farben der Savanne und eine elegante Architektur lassen dies gelingen.

Le Marataba Safari est un hôtel romantique au Nord-ouest de Johannesburg et la quintessence africaine absolue. Il n'est cependant pas un hôtel au sens classique : les hôtes sont hébergés dans des structures en dur couronnées d'un toit de tente, habillées de nombreux tissus et offrant des vues imprenables. Ici, un design des plus authentiques se fond dans des paysages à couper le souffle et dans la nature sauvage alentour. Des murs de pierres brutes, des bois sombres et tous les tons de la savane ainsi qu'une architecture élégante contribuent à cette authenticité.

Het Marataba Safari is een romantisch hotel ten noordwesten van Johannesburg en biedt een stukje onvervalst Afrika. Het is geen typisch hotel. De gasten verblijven in tentachtige onderkomens, die uit stenen muren en stof bestaan en een prachtig uitzicht bieden. Er is veel aandacht besteed aan authentieke vormgeving die uitstekend harmonieert met het adembenemende landschap en de ongerepte natuur dankzij de ongepleisterde muren, het donkere hout, de kleuren van de savanne en een elegante architectuur.

Architect Xavier Claramunt has taken great pains in restructuring the Maricel and traditional architectonic elements, such as the marble columns, have been maintained. The Maricel's rooms are constructed with three principles in mind: comfort, space and light. The hotel has been kept in a minimalist framework: sparse design but with a lot of warm colors. The terrace will captivate you with its wonderful views of the Mediterranean.

Das Maricel ist vom Architekten Xavier Claramunt aufwendig umstrukturiert worden. Die traditionell architektonischen Elemente, wie zum Beispiel Säulen aus Marmor, sind erhalten geblieben. Die Zimmer des Maricels sind mit drei Grundsätzen aufgebaut worden: Bequemlichkeit, Raum und Licht. Das Hotel ist minimalistisch gehalten: schlichte Ausstattung, aber viele warme Farben. Bestechend ist die große Terrasse mit einer wunderbaren Sicht über das Mittelmeer.

Restructurer le Maricel n'a pas été une tâche facile pour l'architecte Xavier Claramunt et certains éléments architecturaux traditionnels, comme les colonnes de marbre, ont été conservés. Les chambres du Maricel ont été créées sous trois conditions : confort, espace et lumière. L'hôtel a gardé un cadre minimaliste : un design épuré mais aux couleurs chaudes. La spacieuse terrasse vous captivera par ses splendides vues sur la Méditerranée.

De architect Xavier Claramunt heeft het Maricel grondig heringericht met behoud van de traditionele architectonische elementen zoals de marmeren zuilen. De kamers van het Maricel zijn gebaseerd op drie principes: comfort, ruimte en licht. De inrichting van het hotel is minimalistisch maar met veel warme kleuren. Het Maricel beschikt over een groot terras met een prachtig uitzicht op de Middellandse Zee.

The Hotel Mystique is located on the Greek island of Santorini, atop the famous cliffs of Oia. With its stunning location, the hotel offers breathtaking views of the sea, the volcano and the Aegean Caldera. 18 suites and villas enchant with their subdued elegance, created out of wood, native stone varieties and glass – a look enhanced by inlaid designs and Classical fabrics.

Auf der griechischen Insel Santorini, direkt an den berühmten Klippen von Oia gelegen, befindet sich das Hotel Mystique. Aufgrund seiner Lage bietet es einen atemberaubenden Blick auf das Meer, den Vulkan und auf die ägäische Caldera. 18 Suiten und Villen bestechen durch unaufdringliche Eleganz, sie sind aus Holz, einheimischen Steinarten und Glas gestaltet – in die Wände eingearbeitete Muster und antike Textilien runden das Design ab.

L'hôtel Mystique est situé sur l'île grecque de Santorin, au sommet des fameuses falaises d'Oia. Par sa situation étonnante, l'hôtel offre des vues époustouflantes sur la mer, le volcan et la Baie de la Caldera. 18 suites et villas enchanteresses à l'élégance discrète, habillées de bois, de variétés de pierres locales et de verre, dont l'apparence est parachevée par des motifs sculptés et des tissus anciens.

Op het Griekse eiland Santorini in de directe omgeving van de beroemde kliffen van Oia is het hotel Mystique gelegen. Dankzij zijn ligging biedt het hotel een adembenemend uitzicht op de zee, de vulkaan en de Egeïsche caldera. De achttien suites en villa's bekoren door hun decente elegantie. Ze zijn opgetrokken uit hout, inheemse steensoorten en glas en de in de wanden verwerkte patronen en antieke stoffen ronden het design af.

The shimmering walls of this hotel's foyer are bedecked with highly dramatic black and white photographs while ivory columns and avant-garde furniture add a modern and contemporary atmosphere. The Night Hotel is an impressive presence in its black and white and has the feeling of a private residence with the intimate and comfortable but also luxurious and cosmopolitan setting of midtown Manhattan.

Hochdramatische Schwarz-Weiß-Fotografien schmücken die schimmernden Wände der Eingangshalle, elfenbeinfarbene Säulen und avantgardistische Möbel sorgen für eine zeitgenössische Atmosphäre. Das Night ist eine beindruckende Präsenz in Schwarz und Weiß, es bietet das Feeling einer privaten Residenz mit intimer und komfortabler, doch luxuriöser und weltoffener Umgebung des Midtown Manhattan.

Les murs chatoyants du hall d'entrée de cet hôtel sont parés de photographies spectaculaires en noir et blanc, tandis que des colonnes d'ivoire et un ameublement avant-gardiste créent une atmosphère moderne et contemporaine. Les tons noirs et blancs donnent au Night une allure imposante; il crée le sentiment d'une résidence privée au cœur de Manhattan, intime, confortable, mais aussi luxueuse et cosmopolite.

Aangrijpende zwart-witfoto's sieren de zacht glanzende wanden van de entree en ivoorkleurige zuilen en avant-gardistische meubels zorgen voor een eigentijdse sfeer. Het Night Hotel is een imponerend hotel en biedt een huiselijke en comfortabele sfeer temidden van de luxueuze en wereldse omgeving van Midtown Manhattan.

Sur mes cahiers d'écolier   Sur mon

en las páginas

su le ginestre

windmill of   shadows

Liberty

на физическую   правду   пишу   твоё имя

Scrivo

The Puerta América hotel is unique. Behind the lamella façade it exhibits a wealth of various design concepts from various famous architects – a cross-section of contemporary architecture. Altogether, 19 of the hottest names in the international architecture and design scene had a hand in crafting the rooms. These include: Jean Nouvel, David Chipperfield, Arata Isozaki, Zaha Hadid, Sir Norman Foster and young designers such as Eva Castro and Holger Kehne of Plasma Studio.

Das Hotel Puerta América ist einzigartig. Hinter der Lamellenfassade zeigt es eine Fülle verschiedener Designkonzepte gegensätzlicher Stararchitekten – ein Querschnitt durch die Baukunst der Gegenwart: An der Gestaltung der Räume durften insgesamt 19 Stars der internationalen Architektur- und Designszene mitwirken. Mit dabei: Jean Nouvel, David Chipperfield, Arata Isozaki, Zaha Hadid, Sir Norman Foster sowie junge Designer wie Eva Castro und Holger Kehne von Plasma Studio.

L'hôtel Puerta América est unique en son genre. Derrière sa façade de lamelles sont regroupés différents concepts design pensés par différents architectes phares : c'est un échantillon d'architectures contemporaines. A l'unisson, 19 des plus grands designers et architectes de la scène internationale ont mis la main à la pâte. Au menu, Jean Nouvel, David Chipperfield, Arata Isozaki, Zaha Hadid, Sir Norman Foster ainsi que de jeunes designers comme Eva Castro et Holger Kehne de Plasma Studio.

Het hotel Puerta América is enig in zijn soort. Achter de lamellengevel vertoont het hotel een verscheidenheid aan uiteenlopende designconcepten van verschillende sterarchitecten – een overzicht van de hedendaagse bouwkunst. Aan de vormgeving van de ruimten mochten in totaal negentien sterren van de internationale architectuur- en designwereld meewerken, waaronder Jean Nouvel, David Chipperfield, Arata Isozaki, Zaha Hadid, Sir Norman Foster evenals jonge designers als Eva Castro en Holger Kehne van Plasma Studio.

415

The Berlin architecture office Graft has developed a hotel landscape in the truest sense of the word. Spatially formative elements such as ceilings, walls and floor dissolve and seem as if pleated, recreating the idea of space. Tilting surfaces act both as separating walls and usable furniture and the ground, rearing up, is a traffic space beneath the building's seemingly malleable skin. This principle infuses the entire structure, from the lobby to the rooms themselves.

Das Berliner Architekturbüro Graft hat eine Hotel-Landschaft im wahrsten Sinne des Wortes entwickelt. Raumbildende Elemente wie Decke, Wände und Fußboden lösen sich auf, wirken wie gefaltet und bilden den Raum neu. Geneigte Flächen sind gleichzeitig trennende Wand oder auch begehbares Möbel; der sich aufbäumende Boden ist Verkehrsfläche entstanden unter der als formbar begriffenen Haut des Hauses. Dieses Prinzip durchzieht das gesamte Gebäude, von der Lobby bis zu den Zimmern.

Le bureau d'architectes berlinois Graft a développé un paysage hôtelier, au sens le plus vrai du terme. Des éléments spatialement constitutifs, comme les plafonds, les murs et les sols se déstructurent et semblent mêlés, recréant ainsi le concept d'espace. Les surfaces inclinées servent à la fois de cloisons et de mobilier d'appoint ; le sol est un espace de circulation sous la peau apparemment malléable de l'édifice. Ce principe habite l'ensemble de la structure, du hall d'entrée aux chambres elles-mêmes.

Het Berlijnse architectenbureau Graft heeft een ultramodern hotel ontwikkeld. Ruimtebegrenzende elementen zoals plafonds, wanden en vloeren vervagen, lijken geplooid en definiëren de ruimten opnieuw. Hellende vlakken zijn tevens scheidswanden of ook begaanbare meubelstukken en de glooiende bodem is loopvlak. De buitenmuren van het hotel worden door de ontwerpers als vormbaar opgevat en dit principe komt in het hele gebouw tot uitdrukking, van de lobby tot de kamers.

The Farnham Hotel is both an elegant country home and an extravagant boutique hotel in the Georgian style. Its modern design fits flawlessly into the ambience of the 13th-century Farnham Estate. The hotel is located on a country estate of over 1235 acres (500 hectares) and is counted among the most beautiful resorts in Ireland.

Das Farnham Hotel ist ein gleichermaßen elegantes Landhotel wie ein extravagantes Boutiquehotel im georgianischen Stil. Sein modernes Design passt sich nahtlos an den Stil des aus dem 13. Jahrhundert stammenden Farnham Estate an. Das Hotel liegt in einem über 500 Hektar großen Landsitz und gilt als eines der schönsten Resorts Irlands.

Le Farnham Hotel est à la fois une élégante maison de maître et un hôtel-boutique extravagant de style géorgien. Son design moderne s'intègre harmonieusement à son apparence de style Farnham du XIIIe siècle. L'hôtel se situe sur une propriété de plus de 500 hectares et compte parmi les complexes les plus splendides d'Irlande.

Het Farnham Hotel is zowel een elegant landhotel als een extravagant boutiquehotel in Georgiaanse stijl. Het moderne design sluit naadloos aan bij de stijl van het dertiende-eeuwse Farnham Estate. Het hotel ligt op een landgoed van meer dan vijfhonderd hectare en geldt als een van de mooiste resorts van Ierland.

This exclusive resort consists of a complex totaling three hotels in the middle of a spacious garden plot. The complex includes an Omanian cultural center in which activities and exhibits are regularly offered and is a reflection of Oman's cultural heritage in architecture and design. The property is unique with the brown, barren and majestic mountains in the background, which appear to reach almost up to the hotel itself, and in the foreground a long white-sand beach and the azure sea.

Das exklusive Resort besteht aus einem Hotelkomplex von insgesamt drei Hotels inmitten einer großzügigen Gartenanlage. Zur Anlage gehört ein omanisches Kulturzentrum, in dem regelmäßig Aktivitäten und Ausstellungen geboten werden. Die Anlage spiegelt das kulturelle Erbe des Oman in Architektur und Design wider. Die Lage ist einmalig: Im Hintergrund die mächtigen, kargen und braunen Berge, die fast bis ins Hotel hineinzureichen scheinen, davor eine lange weiße Sandbucht und das tiefblaue Meer.

Ce luxueux complexe comprend au total trois hôtels au cœur d'un jardin spacieux, ainsi qu'un centre culturel omanien dans lequel se tiennent régulièrement activités et expositions. Le complexe est le reflet de l'héritage culturel de l'Oman en architecture et en design. Cette propriété unique est plantée dans un décor de majestueuses montagnes brunes et arides semblant presque atteindre l'hôtel, et bordée d'une longue plage de sable blanc léchée par les flots azurs.

Het exclusieve resort bestaat uit een hotelcomplex van in totaal drie hotels midden in een groot plantsoen. Tot het complex behoort een Omaans cultuurcentrum waar regelmatig activiteiten en tentoonstellingen worden georganiseerd. Het culturele erfgoed van Oman plaatst zijn stempel op de architectuur en het design van het complex. De ligging is uniek: op de achtergrond de indrukwekkende, kale, bruine bergen die het hotel lijken binnen te dringen en op de voorgrond een lange witte zandbaai met de diepblauwe zee.

The Six Senses Hideaway is located at the northernmost point of Koh Samui in Samrong Bay. It contains 64 private villas, every single one with a panorama view of the Gulf of Thailand and neighboring islands – most with a private pool. The Pool Villa Suite, with its spacious living room as well as several bathrooms and fenced-in outside shower, measures a luxurious 1880 square feet (175 square meters).

Am nördlichsten Punkt von Koh Samui in der Samrong-Bucht gelegen liegt das Six Senses Hideaway. Es umfasst 64 private Villen, jede einzelne mit einem Panoramablick auf den Golf von Thailand und die Nachbarinseln – die meisten davon mit privatem Pool. Luxuriöse 175 Quadratmeter schließlich misst die Pool Villa Suite, mit großem Wohnraum sowie mehreren Badezimmern samt umzäunter Außendusche.

Le Six Senses Hideaway se situe à l'extrême nord de Koh Samui, dans la baie de Samrong. Il contient 64 villas privées, chacune offrant une vue panoramique sur le Golfe de Thaïlande et les îles avoisinantes, dont la plupart donnent sur une piscine privative. La luxueuse suite, dotée d'un salon spacieux ainsi que de plusieurs salles de bain et d'une douche extérieure protégée, ne mesure pas moins de 175 mètres carrés.

Op het noordelijkste puntje van Koh Samui in de Baai van Samrong ligt het Six Senses Hideaway. Het complex omvat vierenzestig privé-villa's en elke villa heeft een panoramisch uitzicht op de Golf van Thailand en de omringende eilanden. De meeste villa's beschikken over een privé-zwembad. De Pool Villa Suite heeft een luxe afmeting van 175 vierkante meter en beschikt over een grote woonkamer en meerdere badkamers inclusief een omheinde buitendouche.

With views of mountains and olive grows and the beautiful Bay of Pollença in the distance, the hotel combines a respectfully restored 19th-century cloister with contemporary designs. Throughout the renovation, Classical architectonic elements were maintained and integrated into the newly transformed modern hotel. Behind the austere, monastical façade lies an ultramodern ambience: black floors, much dark wood, sparingly arranged design accents.

Mit Blick auf Berge und Olivenhaine sowie in der Ferne auf die herrliche Bucht von Pollença vereint das Hotel ein respektvoll restauriertes Kloster aus dem 19. Jahrhundert und eine zeitgenössische Einrichtung. Es wurde unter Beibehaltung der antiken architektonischen Elemente renoviert und in ein modernes Hotel verwandelt. Hinter der klösterlich strengen Fassade verbirgt sich ein ultramodernes Ambiente: schwarze Böden, viel dunkles Holz, sparsam gesetzte Design-Akzente.

Possédant une vue sur les montagnes, les champs d'oliviers et la splendide baie de Pollença, au loin, l'hôtel a su allier une thématique contemporaine au cadre d'un cloître du XIXe siècle, restauré avec cachet. Tout au long de la rénovation, les éléments architecturaux initiaux ont été conservés et intégrés à cet hôtel nouvellement transformé. Derrière l'austère façade monacale se cache une ambiance ultramoderne : sols noirs, bois sombres, design épuré savamment dosé.

Met uitzicht op de bergen en olijfbossen en een vergezicht op de prachtige baai van Pollença vereent het hotel een eerbiedig gerestaureerd negentiende-eeuws klooster met een eigentijds interieur. Het klooster werd gerenoveerd met behoud van de oude architectonische elementen en omgetoverd tot een modern hotel. Achter de kloosterlijk strenge gevel gaat een ultramoderne ambiance schuil: zwarte vloeren, veel donker hout en spaarzaam ingezette designaccenten.

Soneva Gili, with its imaginative water bungalows, is one of the North Male Atoll's romantic islands. This Robinson Crusoe paradise is situated in the centre of an enormous lagoon and surrounded by a coral reef. With an eye to personal privacy, the architects have managed to combine comfort, extravagance, creativity and environmentally conscious architecture in one single concept, a reflection of superior living and absolute harmony.

Soneva Gili ist mit seinen fantasievollen Wasser-Bungalows eine der romantischsten Inseln im Nordmale-Atoll. Das Crusoe-Paradies liegt inmitten einer riesigen Lagune, die von einem Korallenriff umgeben wird. Unter dem Motto „Privatsphäre" haben die Architekten es verstanden, Komfort, Extravaganz, Kreativität und umweltfreundliche Architektur in einem Konzept zu vereinen, das höchste Lebensqualität und Harmonie widerspiegelt.

Soneva Gili et ses bungalows aquatiques inspirés, est une des îles les plus romantiques de l'atoll Malé nord. Ce paradis pour Robinson Crusoé est situé au cœur d'un gigantesque lagon et entouré d'une barrière de corail. Tout en respectant le besoin d'intimité, les architectes ont réussi à allier confort, extravagance, créativité et une architecture respectueuse de l'environnement en un seul concept : l'image d'une qualité de vie supérieure et d'une harmonie absolue.

Soneva Gili is met zijn fantasievolle waterbungalows een van de meest romantische eilanden in de Noord-Malé Atol. Het Crusoeparadijs bevindt zich midden in een lagune die is omringd door een koraalrif. Onder het motto 'privé-sfeer' hebben de architecten comfort, extravagantie, creativiteit en milieuvriendelijke architectuur in een concept samengevat dat hoogste levenskwaliteit en harmonie weerspiegelt.

Worldwide, the name Pininfarina stands for outstanding automobile design, including icons such as Ferrari and Maserati. This is the first time that Paolo Pininfarina has put his mark on a hotel project, here in an historic building dating from 1890 in the Gaslamp quarter. The interior is characterized by elegant shapes, ergonomic arrangements and durable materials from the automotive industry, including aluminum, steel, leather and the classic Ferrari red.

Weltweit steht der Name Pininfarina für herausragendes Design automobiler Ikonen wie Ferrari und Maserati. Nun hat Paolo Pininfarina erstmalig seine Handschrift in ein Hotelprojekt eingebracht, umgesetzt in einem historischen Gebäude von 1890 im Herzen des Gaslamp-Viertels. So wird das Innere geprägt durch schnittige Formen, ergonomische Anordnungen und bewährte Materialien aus dem Automobilbau wie Aluminium, Stahl, Leder und klassisches Ferrari-Rot.

Dans le monde entier, le nom Pininfarina évoque un époustouflant design automobile, ayant forgé des icônes telles que Ferrari ou Maserati. C'est la première fois que Paolo Pininfarina appose sa marque à un projet hôtelier, ici sur un édifice historique datant de 1890 dans le quartier Gaslamp. L'intérieur se caractérise par des formes élancées, des aménagements ergonomiques et des matériaux issus de l'industrie automobile, comme l'aluminium, l'acier, le cuir et l'inimitable rouge Ferrari.

Wereldwijd staat de naam Pininfarina voor vooraanstaand design van automobieliconen als Ferrari en Maserati. Nu heeft Paolo Pininfarina voor het eerst zijn handtekening ingebracht in een hotelproject en wel in dit historische gebouw uit 1890 in het hart van de wijk Gaslamp. Het interieur wordt gekenmerkt door elegante vormen, een ergonomische inrichting en deugdelijke materialen uit de automobielindustrie zoals aluminium, staal, leer en klassiek Ferrari-rood.

KEATING

1890

Hidden behind a functional façade on Potsdamer Platz, the modern and elegant ambience of the Mandala hotel unfolds within. Despite its central location, you will find plenty of rest and relaxation in a structure which invites you to feel good about life with corner suites and interesting architectural details. In the Qiu-Lounch, Berlin night owls revel in the million spots of color cast by the art deco light effects and the flowing water in front of a golden Bisazza mosaic wall.

Verborgen hinter einer funktionalen Fassade am Potsdamer Platz entfaltet sich das moderne und elegante Ambiente des „The Mandala"-Hotels. Trotz seiner zentralen Lage findet man hier Ruhe und Erholung in einer Architektur, die mit Ecksuiten und interessanten räumlichen Details zum Wohlfühlen einlädt. In der Qiu-Lounge tummeln sich Berliner Nachtschwärmer zwischen Art-déco-Lichtspielen mit Millionen von Farbspielen und fließendem Wasser vor einer goldenen Bisazza-Mosaikwand.

Cachée derrière une façade fonctionnelle donnant sur la Potsdamer Platz, l'ambiance moderne et élégante de l'hôtel Mandala s'épanouit à l'intérieur. Malgré une situation en centre-ville, le repos et la relaxation sont au programme de cette structure invitant au bien-être, grâce à des suites spacieuses et d'intéressants détails architecturaux. Au Qiu-Lounge, les noctambules de Berlin se divertissent des millions de taches de couleur projetées par les effets de lumière art déco et de l'eau déferlant en cascade sur un mur de mosaïque dorée Bisazza.

Verborgen achter een functionele façade op de Potsdamer Platz, ontvouwt zich de moderne en elegante ambiance van het Mandala hotel. Ondanks de centrale ligging, is hier rust en ontspanning te vinden in een architectuur die het goede leven benadrukt, met rustige zithoeken en interessante architectonische details. In de Qiu-Lounge kunnen de liefhebbers van het Berlijnse nachtleven genieten van de miljoenen lichtpuntjes van de art-decolampen en het stromende water voor een gouden Bisazza-mozaïekwand.

This exclusive hotel is located in the northern part of the Krüger National Park in South Africa. Clear and simple lines are combined with aluminum elements, creating a unique style for this design hotel in the middle of the beautiful wilderness which surrounds it. The lodgings stand on stilts at the top of a hill, offering stately views over the Luvuvhu river. The highlight: at the edge of the balcony balustrade is a massive stone tub, an open invitation for bathing under the stars.

Das exklusive Hotel befindet sich im nördlichen Teil des Krüger National Parks in Südafrika. Einfache, klare Linien wurden mit Aluminium-Elementen kombiniert und schufen so den ganz eigenen Stil des Designhotels mitten in der Schönheit der Wildnis. Die Unterkünfte stehen auf Stelzen auf einem Hügel und bieten so einen imposanten Blick über dem Luvuvhu-Fluss. Das Highlight: Am Rande der Balkonbrüstung steht eine massive Steinwanne, die zu einem Bad unter freiem Himmel einlädt.

Cet hôtel huppé est situé au nord du Parc National Krüger, en Afrique du Sud. Des lignes nettes et simples se marient aux éléments en aluminium pour créer un style unique à cet hôtel en plein cœur de la nature sauvage qui l'entoure. Les chambres sur pilotis sont situées sur une colline, offrant une vue majestueuse sur le fleuve Luvuvhu. Le petit plus : en bordure du balcon se trouve une imposante baignoire de pierre invitant à la baignade sous les étoiles.

Dit exclusieve hotel bevindt zich in het noordelijk deel van het Kruger National Park in Zuid-Afrika. Eenvoudige, duidelijke lijnen werden gecombineerd met aluminiumelementen en creëerden zo de geheel eigen stijl van dit designhotel midden in de ongerepte wildernis. De onderkomens staan op palen op een heuvel en kijken uit op de Luvuhurivier. Troef: voor de balkonbalustrade staat een massief stenen bad dat uitnodigt een bad te nemen onder de vrije hemel.

The styles at Miss Sixty have been young fashion victims' cherished favorites for some time now. Now the label has opened its own hotel in the Italian beach town of Riccione. A veil with organic, retro-style apertures envelops this building from the 1950s. Thirty young artists were responsible for the interior; they let their imaginations run wild in the design of each accommodation. The rooms here glow in bold colors, the walls adorned with graffiti and unusual quotes.

Die Mode von Miss Sixty gehört schon lange zu den begehrten Lieblingsstücken junger Fashionvictims. Jetzt hat das Label auch sein eigenes Hotel im italienischen Badeort Riccione eröffnet. Eine Hülle mit organischen Öffnungen im Retrostil umschließt das Gebäude aus den 1950er Jahren. Im Inneren konnten dreißig junge Künstler ihre Ideen umsetzen und haben so individuelle Unterkünfte geschaffen. Die Räume erstrahlen in grellen Farben, mit Graffiti und ausgefallenen Zitaten an den Wänden.

Le style Miss Sixty est depuis quelques temps maintenant le chouchou des jeunes victimes de la mode. A présent, la marque a ouvert son propre hôtel dans la ville balnéaire italienne de Riccione. Une façade percée de formes organiques au style rétro pare cet édifice des années 50. L'intérieur a été confié à trente jeunes artistes ayant laissé libre cours à leur imagination. Ils ont décoré chacune des chambres de couleurs vives et ont orné les murs de graffitis et de messages décalés.

De stijl van Miss Sixty behoort al een tijd tot de favorieten van jonge modeliefhebbers. Nu heeft het merk een eigen hotel geopend in de Italiaanse badplaats Riccione. Een omhulsel met organische openingen in retrostijl omsluit het gebouw uit de jaren '50. Binnen hebben dertig jonge kunstenaars hun ideeën uitgewerkt en hebben zo individuele accommodaties gecreëerd. De kamers stralen in bonte kleuren, met graffiti en opmerkelijke citaten op de muren.

This Athens hotel did not pick the number 21 by chance: its street address, the number of its accomodations (16 rooms and five lofts) and even the name of the restaurant, are all 21. The dominant colors are muted: red, black and white. The unusual thing about the hotel is the wall decoration in its rooms: for this purpose, a sheet of wallpaper measuring about 750 square feet (70 square meters) was hand painted by an artist, then cut into 21 pieces, one piece adorning each room.

Die Zahl 21 kommt beim Athener Hotel Twentyone nicht von ungefähr: Hausnummer, die Anzahl der Unterkünfte, 16 Zimmer und fünf Lofts, sowie der Name des Restaurants lauten 21. Die vorherrschenden Farben sind gedeckt: Schwarz, Weiß und Rot. Das Besondere liegt in der Wandgestaltung der Zimmer. Hierfür wurde eine 70 Quadratmeter große Tapete von einem Künstler handbemalt, in 21 Teile geschnitten und an jeweils eine Wand pro Zimmer angebracht.

Cet hôtel d'Athènes n'a pas choisi le nombre 21 par hasard : son adresse, le nombre de ses suites (16 chambres et cinq lofts), mais aussi le nom du restaurant, tous forment le nombre 21. Les couleurs dominantes sont douces : rouge, noir et blanc. Le point remarquable de cet hôtel est la décoration murale des chambres : pour l'hôtel, un artiste a peint à la main une feuille de papier peint mesurant 70 mètres carrés, qui fut ensuite coupée en 21 pièces, chacune habillant une chambre.

Het getal 21 is bij het Atheense Hotel Twentyone niet uit de lucht gegrepen: huisnummer, het aantal onderkomens (zestien kamers en vijf lofts) en ook de naam van het restaurant luiden allemaal eenentwintig. De dominerende kleuren, zwart, wit en rood, zijn gedekt. Een bijzonder aspect vormt de aankleding van de wanden in de kamers. Hiervoor beschilderde een kunstenaar met de hand een stuk behang van zeventig vierkante meter. Het kunstwerk werd vervolgens in eenentwintig stukken verdeeld en aangebracht aan een wand in elke kamer.

The design of this hotel incorporates the façades of three office buildings which melt together into a synthesis of traditional and modern elements. Attractively shaped lamps radiate muted light from their positions on black lacquered tables. The minimalist rooms are also discreetly furnished. The walls are clad in precious zebrano wood, the seats as original as they are comfortable: an Oriental-looking burgundy cushion is the perfect place to dream a little, while the coquettish Eames rocking chair is an especially good spot for reading.

Bei der Gestaltung wurden die Fronten von drei Kontorhäusern zu einer Synthese aus traditionellen und modernen Elementen verschmolzen. Formschöne Lampen auf schwarzen Lacktischen verströmen gedämpftes Licht. Dezent auch die minimalistisch ausgestatteten Räume. Die Wände sind mit kostbarem Zebranoholz verkleidet, die Sitzmöbel sind ebenso originell wie bequem: Das orientalisch anmutende weinrote Sitzkissen lädt zum Träumen ein, während der kokette Eames-Schaukelstuhl sich besonders gut zum Lesen eignet.

Le design de cet hôtel comprend les façades de trois immeubles d'entreprise, se mêlant en une synthèse d'éléments traditionnels et modernes. Des lampes aux formes attrayantes émettent une lumière tamisée depuis leurs tables laquées noires. Les chambres minimalistes sont également meublées sans emphase. Les murs sont plaqués de zebrano et les fauteuils sont aussi originaux que confortables : un coussin en organdi d'inspiration orientale est un endroit propice à la rêverie, tandis que l'attirant fauteuil Eames se prête idéalement à la lecture.

Bij dit hotel gaan de voorgevels van drie koopmanshuizen een verbinding van traditionele en moderne elementen aan. Mooi gevormde lampen op zwartgelakte tafels verspreiden gedempt licht en ook de minimalistisch ingerichte ruimten zijn stemmig. De wanden zijn met kostbaar zebranohout bekleed en de zitmeubels zijn evenzo origineel als comfortabel: het Oriëntaals aandoende wijnrode zitkussen nodigt uit om weg te dromen, terwijl de kokette Eames-schommelstoel bijzonder geschikt is om te lezen.

Located in an historic building in the San Frediano district, this hotel offers a special experience. As the guest enters, he is greeted by an impressive flower mosaic, flowing over the ground, the reception area, the walls and up to the ceiling. The rest of the decorations are equally unusual: the Italian designer Fabio Novembre placed life-sized prints of Italian master-works in the halls and had Florentine coats of arms printed on the wallpaper of the dressing rooms.

In einem historischen Gebäude im Viertel San Frediano gelegen, verspricht das Hotel ein besonderes Erlebnis. Tritt der Gast ein, begrüßt ihn ein beeindruckendes Blumen-Mosaik, das sich über den Boden, die Rezeption, die Wände bis zur Decke ergießt. Auch die sonstige Gestaltung ist außergewöhnlich: Der italienische Designer Fabio Novembre platzierte lebensgroße Drucke italienischer Meister in den Fluren und ließ florentinische Wappen auf Tapeten in den Anziehräumen drucken.

Situé dans un bâtiment ancien du quartier San Frediano, cet hôtel permet une expérience unique. En arrivant à la réception, l'hôte est accueilli par une impressionnante mosaïque fleurie, courant du sol aux murs, voire au plafond. Le reste de la décoration est tout aussi spécial : le designer italien Fabio Novembre a placé dès l'entrée des chambres des reproductions grandeur nature de toiles de maîtres italiens et a fait imprimer des sceaux florentins au mur des dressings.

Het hotel dat is gehuisvest in een historisch gebouw in de wijk San Frediano is een bijzondere ervaring. Als de gast het hotel binnentreedt, wordt hij verwelkomd door een indrukwekkend bloemenmozaïek dat zich uitstrekt van de vloer, de receptie en de wanden tot aan het plafond. Ook de rest van het interieur is buitengewoon: de Italiaanse ontwerper Fabio Novembre plaatste levensgrote reproducties van Italiaanse meesters op de gangen en liet op het behang voor de kleedkamers Florentijnse wapens drukken.

The Viceroy is a modern version of old-fashioned Hollywood glamour, cinematically executed. The hybrid style preferred by movie divas and studio executives of the 1940s came to be known as "Hollywood Regency". The architects gave it a radical facelift when they transformed the park-like grounds and their small villas into southern California chic: a mix of op-art and neoclassicism, French salon style and modernist functionality.

Das Viceroy ist eine moderne Version alten Hollywood-Glamours, filmreif umgesetzt. „Hollywood Regency" nannte sich der Hybridstil, der von Filmdiven und Studiobossen in den 1940er Jahren bevorzugt wurde. Die Architekten verpassten ihm ein radikales Facelifting, indem sie die parkähnliche Anlage aus kleinen Villen in südkalifornischen Chic verwandelten: ein Mix aus Op-Art und Neoklassizismus, französischem Salon-Stil und modernistischer Funktionalität.

Le Viceroy est une adaptation moderne de l'ancien glamour hollywoodien des studios américains. Ce style hybride, plébiscité par les stars du grand écran et les patrons de studios des années 40, prit le nom de « Hollywood Regency ». Les architectes lui redonnèrent une nouvelle jeunesse lorsqu'ils dotèrent le parc et à ses petites villas d'un certain chic sud-californien : un mélange d'op-art et de néoclassicisme, de style salon français et de fonctionnalité moderniste.

Het Viceroy is een moderne versie van de oude Hollywoodglamour. De hybridestijl die bij de filmdiva's en studiobazen in de jaren veertig favoriet was, werd 'Hollywood regency' genoemd. De architecten gaven het hotel een radicale facelift door het parkachtige complex met de kleine villa's een Zuid-Californische elegantie te geven: een combinatie van op-art en neoclassicisme, Franse salonstijl en modernistische functionaliteit.

189

A totally unique mountain resort which can only be reached by cable car. The building's exterior elements are made exclusively of wood and glass, combined with clay and loam. The hotel snakes alongside a mountain ridge and gives the impression of being an enormous fallen tree. Matteo Thun has created a hotel here which combines desire for originality with respect for tradition, resulting in a style of "Alpine modernity".

Ein absolut einzigartiges Mountain Resort, welches nur mit einer Seilbahn zu erreichen ist. Die äußeren Elemente des Gebäudes sind ausschließlich aus Holz und Glas, ebenfalls zum Einsatz kamen Ton und Lehm. Das Hotel schlängelt sich auf einem Bergrücken entlang und vermittelt den Eindruck, als sei es ein riesiger, liegender Baum. Matteo Thun schuf hier ein Hotel, in dem er Lust auf Originäres und Respekt vor der Tradition zu einer „alpenländischen Modernität" miteinander verband.

On ne peut atteindre ce complexe de montagne, totalement incomparable, qu'en téléphérique. Les éléments extérieurs ne sont composés que de bois et de verre, complétés de terre et d'argile. L'hôtel serpente le long d'une crête et donne l'impression d'un immense arbre abattu. Matteo Thun a créé ici un hôtel combinant le désir d'originalité au respect de la tradition, résultant en un style de « modernité alpine ».

Een absoluut uniek mountain resort dat enkel bereikbaar is met een kabelbaan. De buitenste elementen van het hotel bestaan vrijwel uitsluitend uit hout en glas, maar ook klei en leem werden gebruikt. Het hotel slingert zich over een bergrug en doet denken aan een reusachtige, omgevallen boom. Matteo Thun heeft een hotel ontworpen waarin hij de hang naar originaliteit en respect voor de traditie samenvatte tot 'alpenlandschappelijke moderniteit'.

RESTAURANTS AND CAFES

GASTRONOMY

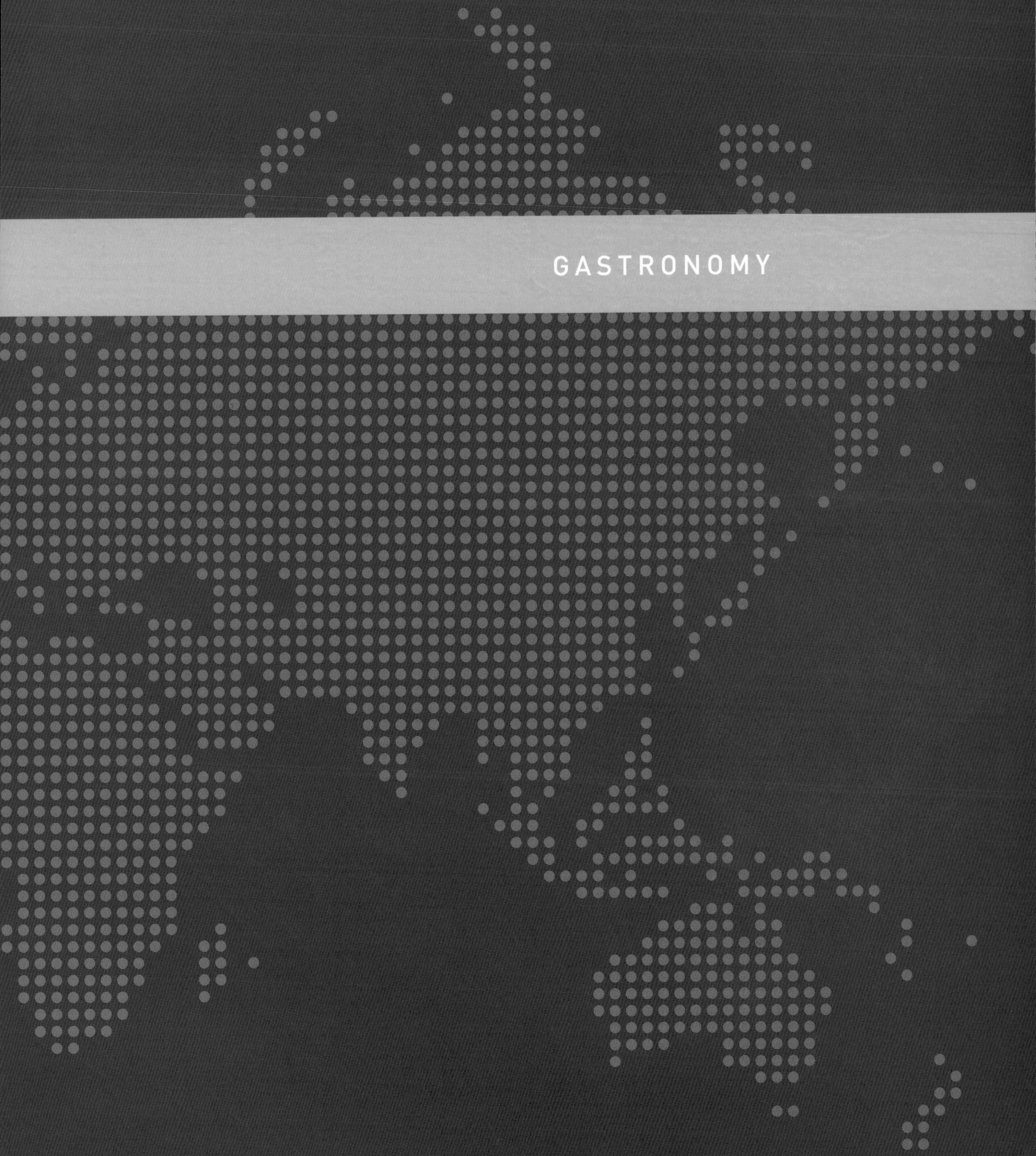

The Orient's cultural inheritance has been passed down and is now maintained and presented by local resorts such as the Al Hadheerah. It could be compared to a wonder from the Arabian Nights, surrounded by a glorious sandy desert at the edge of the Emirate of Dubai. With palpable love of detail, architecture and furnishings pay homage to a traditional image of the old mysterious Orient.

Das überlieferte Erbe des Orients wird von den Resorts vor Ort gepflegt und präsentiert, wie hier, das Al Hadheerah. Es liegt einem Wunder aus 1001 Nacht gleich im Herzen einer prachtvollen Sandwüste am Rande des Emirates Dubai. Mit spürbarer Liebe zum Detail huldigen Architektur und Ausstattung einem traditionellen Bild vom alten, oft geheimnisumrankten Orient.

L'héritage de la culture orientale a été transmis et est désormais préservé et mis en valeur par des complexes locaux tels que l'Al Hadheerah. On pourrait le comparer à une merveille sortie des Mille et une Nuits, entourée d'un désert de sable à la limite de l'Emirat de Dubaï. Cet amour apparent du détail, de l'architecture et du mobilier rend hommage à l'image traditionnelle de cet Orient mystérieux.

De overgeleverde erfenis van de Oriënt wordt door de plaatselijke resorts onderhouden en tentoongespreid, zoals ook in het Al Hadheerah. Het ligt, gelijk een wonder uit 1001 nacht, in het hart van een prachtvolle zandwoestijn aan de rand van het emiraat Dubai. De architectuur en inrichting vormen met een tastbare liefde voor detail een eerbetoon aan de traditionele, mysterieuze Oriënt.

Situated in an historic building in London, Blowfish achieves a successful combination of the old and the new. Walls and ceiling of a soft white and dark wood floors form the basis of this restaurant's interior design. Modern wood furniture, classic chandeliers and recessed green lighting complete the design. This restaurant's ambience enables classical dinner arrangements as well as a chic lounge atmosphere.

In einem historischen Londoner Gebäude gelegen, schafft das Blowfish eine gelungene Kombination von Altem und Neuem. Wände und Decken in sanftem Weiß und ein dunkler Holzboden bilden die Basis der Innenraumgestaltung. Moderne Holzmöbel, klassische Kronleuchter und grüne Lichtakzente komplettieren die Einrichtung. In diesem Ambiente ist eine klassische Dinner-Veranstaltung ebenso möglich und erwünscht wie eine schicke Lounge-Atmosphäre.

Situé dans un bâtiment historique de Londres, le Blowfish a combiné avec succès le mélange de l'ancien et du neuf. Les murs et le plafond d'un blanc doux et les sols de bois sombre sont la base de la décoration intérieure de ce restaurant. Le mobilier moderne en bois, les chandeliers classiques et l'éclairage vert dissimulé, complètent l'ensemble. L'ambiance de ce restaurant permet d'organiser des dîners classiques, ou de créer une atmosphère chic et lounge.

Het in een historisch Londens gebouw gehuisveste Blowfish is een geslaagde combinatie van oud en nieuw. Zacht witte wanden en plafonds en een donkere houten vloer vormen de basis van het interieur. Moderne houten meubels, klassieke kroonluchters en groene lichtaccenten vullen de inrichting aan. In deze ambiance is conventioneel dineren evenzo aan te bevelen als deftig loungen.

The owners' vision was to create a restaurant in which the best of British cuisine was combined with the best of British design. Canteen was designed as a democratic location with utilitarian yet elegant ambience. Designers Edward Barber and Jay Osgerby developed the no-frills furnishings with this purpose in mind. Warm wood elements, a good deal of white and light green accents complete the stark design.

Die Vision der Besitzer war es, ein Restaurant zu schaffen, in dem das Beste der britischen Küche mit dem Besten des britischen Designs kombiniert wird. Dabei sollte Canteen ein demokratisches Lokal mit einem zweckmäßigen und doch eleganten Ambiente werden. Dafür entwarfen die Designer Edward Barber and Jay Osgerby die schlichte Möblierung. Warme Holzelemente, viel Weiß und Akzente in hellem Grün komplettieren die reduzierte Gestaltung.

L'idée du propriétaire était de créer un restaurant combinant le meilleur de la cuisine et du design britanniques. Le Canteen a été pensé comme un lieu populaire à l'ambiance pragmatique bien qu'élégante. Dans cette idée, les designers Edward Barber et Jay Osgerby ont développé un mobilier sans prétention. Des éléments chauds en bois et une bonne dose de tons blancs et vert clair complètent ce design épuré.

De eigenaars hadden een restaurant voor ogen waarin het beste van de Britse keuken met het beste van het Britse design moest worden gecombineerd. Hiervoor moest Canteen een democratisch restaurant met een doelmatige en toch elegante sfeer worden. De designers Edward Barber en Jay Osgerby ontwierpen het sobere meubilair. Warme houtelementen, veel wit en accenten in lichtgroen vullen de gereduceerde vormgeving aan.

The Cantinella is a modern interpretation of an Italian wine bar. The design is characterized by massive hardwood paneling (barrel wood) and blackened steel (the barrel hoops), supplemented with handcrafted silk lights and modernist pre-cast trompe-l'œil murals.

Das Cantinella ist eine moderne Interpretation eines italienischen Weingeschäfts. Die Einrichtung wird geprägt durch Einbauten aus massivem Nussbaum (Fassholz) sowie geschwärztem Stahl (Fassring) und ergänzt durch handgefertigte Leuchten aus Seide und eine betonähnliche modernistische Trompe-l'œil-Malerei.

La Cantinella est l'interprétation moderne d'un bar à vin. Son design se caractérise par d'épais panneaux de bois (du chêne de tonneau) et de l'acier foncé (leur cerclage), rehaussés d'abat-jours en soie tissée main et de trompe-l'œil muraux.

Het Cantinella is een moderne interpretatie van een Italiaanse wijnzaak. Inbouwkasten van massief notenhout (van oude vaten) en zwart staal (ringen van de vaten) drukken een stempel op de inrichting. Deze wordt aangevuld met handgemaakte zijden lampen en een betonachtige modernistische trompe-l'œil.

This restaurant concentrates on black, white and transparent materials in its concept as a room within a room, separated by panes of glass. Tension and contrasts are highlighted, each of which beautifully enriches the atmosphere. The room design is rounded off with a glass-fronted wine rack, elegant plants and classical furnishings.

Als Raum im Raum, durch Glasscheiben getrennt, konzentriert sich das Restaurant konsequent auf weiße, schwarze und transparente Materialien. Thematisiert werden Spannung und Kontraste, von denen ein jeder die Atmosphäre aufs Vortrefflichste bereichert. Das Raumkonzept wird durch ein einsehbares Weinregal, dezente Pflanzen und Möbelklassiker abgerundet.

Ce restaurant allie les matériaux noirs, blancs et transparents pour nourrir le concept de pièce dans la pièce, toutes deux séparées par des cloisons de verre. La tension et les contrastes sont exacerbés, chacun enrichissant magnifiquement l'atmosphère. L'armoire de verre contenant des casiers à vin, les élégantes plantes et le mobilier classique achèvent le design de cette pièce.

Dit restaurant concentreert zich consequent op de kleuren zwart en wit en doorzichtige materialen om een ruimte in een ruimte te creëren. Spanning en contrast worden benadrukt, wat allebei prachtig bijdraagt aan de atmosfeer. Het ontwerp van de ruimte wordt afgerond door een wijnrek met een glazen voorkant, elegante planten en klassiek meubilair.

Minimalist furnishings made from precious materials are incorporated into a bare construction ambience completed by pipes and concrete. Details such as a leather-clad wall, secluded lamps and a cut-glass mirror behind the bar offer stark contrasts. The Asiatic style red and gold wallpaper draws your gaze inside from the covered terrace in the innermost of the five courtyards.

Hier findet sich eine minimalistische Möblierung aus edlen Materialien in einem Rohbauambiente mit Rohren und Beton wieder. Details wie eine mit Leder bezogene Wand, exklusive Lampen und geschliffenes Spiegelglas hinter der Bar bieten einen starken Kontrast dazu. Die orientalisch anmutende rot-goldene Tapete lenkt den Blick von der überdachten Terrasse – im Innenhof der Fünf Höfe – ins Innere.

Le mobilier minimaliste fait de matériaux précieux intègre une ambiance brute, véhiculée par des tuyaux et du béton. Des détails tels que le mur recouvert de cuir, l'éclairage faible et le miroir en cristal taillé derrière le bar offrent des contrastes saisissants. Le papier peint rouge et doré d'inspiration asiatique accompagne votre regard de la terrasse couverte aux tréfonds des cinq cours intérieures.

De minimalistische inrichting van het Comercial bestaat uit hoogwaardige materialen in een ruwbouwsfeer van buizen en beton. Details als een met leer beklede wand, exclusieve lampen en een geslepen spiegelwand achter de bar vormen een sterk contrast. Het oriëntaals aandoende rood-gouden behang verlegt de aandacht van het overdekte terras – op de binnenplaats van de Fünf Höfe – naar binnen.

The Cozmo is located on the edge of Beirut in a building reminiscent of a Spanish royal palace. To achieve its present size and volume, all the ceilings were removed from this historical manor house. White surfaces dominate the room, into which equally white furnishings and a kitchen have been skillfully integrated.

Das Cozmo ist in einem spanischen Adelspalast nicht unähnlichen Gebäude am Rande von Beirut untergebracht. In dem historischen Herrenhaus wurden alle Decken entfernt, um Größe und Volumen zu erreichen. Weiße Farben und Flächen dominieren den Raum, eine ebenfalls in Weiß gehaltene Möblierung sowie eine Showküche sind gekonnt integriert.

Le Cozmo se trouve à l'extrémité de Beyrouth, dans un bâtiment rappelant un palais royal espagnol. Afin d'atteindre sa taille actuelle, tous les plafonds de cette demeure historique ont dû être détruits. Des surfaces blanches dominent la pièce, dans laquelle le mobilier blanc et une cuisine ont été habilement intégrés.

Het Cozmo is ondergebracht in een op een Spaans paleis lijkend gebouw aan de rand van Beiroet. Alle plafonds in het historische herenhuis werden verwijderd om volume en ruimte te realiseren. Witte kleuren en vlakken dicteren de ruimte en het eveneens witte meubilair en de showkeuken zijn geslaagd opgenomen in het design.

Da Loretta is captivating with its contemporary interpretation of an Italian trattoria. The if-group's architects developed wallpaper patterns upon which stripes of brown, green and beige alternate with wood or lace decor, illuminated by hanging lamps made of industrial metal mesh. To promote communication among the guests, designer and proprietor Loretta Petti chose to incorporate wooden tables and benches into the design.

Da Loretta besticht durch seine zeitgemäße Interpretation einer italienischen Trattoria. Die Architekten der if-group entwarfen Tapetenmuster, auf denen sich Streifen in Braun, Grün und Beige mit welchen in Holz- oder Spitzendekor abwechseln, ausgeleuchtet von Hängelampen aus industriellem Metallgeflecht. Um die Kommunikation zwischen den Gästen zu fördern, entschieden sich Gestalter und Besitzerin Loretta Petti, lange Holztische und -bänke zu platzieren.

L'interprétation contemporaine qu'a fait Da Loretta d'une trattoria italienne est fascinante. Les architectes de l'if-group ont développé un concept de papier peint, dont les bandes de marron, vert et beige alternent avec du bois ou de la dentelle, l'ensemble étant mis en lumière par des suspensions faites de mailles d'acier industriel. Afin de faciliter la communication entre les clients, la designer et propriétaire Loretta Petti a choisi d'ajouter des tables en bois et des bancs.

Da Loretta bekoort door de eigentijdse interpretatie van een Italiaanse trattoria. De architecten van de if-group ontwierpen behang waarop bruine, groene en beige strepen worden afgewisseld door strepen met hout- en kantpatroon. Het geheel wordt verlicht door hanglampen met industrieel metaalvlechtwerk. Om de communicatie tussen de gasten te bevorderen kozen de ontwerpers en de eigenaresse Loretta Petti voor lange houten tafels en banken.

ogni tristo pensier caschi: facciam festa tuttavia. Chi vuol

This cosmopolitan brasserie and bar is situated on the second floor of the Hamburg mortgage bank's former lobby. Both massive, two-storey bank vaults are distinctive eye-catchers with their shimmering gold and silver paneling. These vaults house the cloakroom as well as select wines. Heavy cast-iron columns support the room, above which two glittering chandeliers hang, their Swarowski crystals catching the light and softening the room's original cold edge.

Die kosmopolitische Brasserie-Bar befindet sich im 1. Obergeschoss in den ehemaligen Kassenhallen der Hamburger Hypothekenbank. Die beiden kraftvollen, zweigeschossigen Tresorräume mit gold und silbern schimmernden Verkleidungen bilden einen markanten Blickfang im Raum. Die Tresore beherbergen Garderobe wie auch ausgewählte Weine. Schwere gusseiserne Säulen tragen den Raum und darüber schweben zwei strahlende Kronleuchter aus Swarowski-Kristallen und nehmen dem Raum seine ursprüngliche Strenge.

Ce bar/brasserie cosmopolite se trouve au deuxième étage de l'ancien hall d'entrée de la banque de prêt de Hambourg. Les deux coffres massifs de la banque attirent les regards par leurs panneaux chatoyants d'or et d'argent. Ces coffres accueillent le vestiaire ainsi que de grands crus. De lourdes colonnes d'acier soutiennent la salle, dominée par deux lustres scintillants dont les cristaux Swarowski retiennent la lumière et adoucissent le côté froid original de la pièce.

De kosmopolitische brasserie-bar bevindt zich op de eerste verdieping van het vroegere gebouw van de Hamburger Hypothekenbank. De twee solide hoge kluizen zijn in glanzend goud en zilver bekleed en vormen een markante blikvanger in de ruimte. In de kluizen bevindt zich de garderobe en worden uitgelezen wijnen bewaard. Zware gietijzeren zuilen dragen de ruimte en hoog in de ruimte zweven twee schitterende kroonluchters van Swarovski-kristal. Zij ontnemen de ruimte zijn oorspronkelijke strengheid.

This restaurant, situated in a wing of the Art Academy not far from Stockholm's historic city center, is one of the most popular addresses in the Swedish capitol today. The décor is modeled after Scandinavian design of the 1970s, with lamps shaped like champagne glasses dangling above the tables, long comfortable benches and subdued lighting.

Das in einem Flügel der Kunstakademie unweit des historischen Zentrums von Stockholm untergebrachte Restaurant F12 ist heute eine der angesagtesten Adressen der schwedischen Hauptstadt. Das Dekor ist dem skandinavischen Design der 1970er Jahre nachempfunden, mit Leuchten, die in Form von Champagnergläsern über den Tischen baumeln, langen, bequemen Sitzbänken und gedämpftem Licht.

Ce restaurant, situé dans une aile de l'Art Academy, à proximité du centre historique de Stockholm, est l'une des adresses actuelles les plus en vue de la capitale suédoise. Le décor s'inspire du style scandinave des années 70, avec ses lampes coniques suspendues au-dessus des tables, de longues banquettes confortables et un éclairage discret.

Het Restaurant F12, dat is gehuisvest in een vleugel van de kunstacademie in de buurt van het historische centrum, is tegenwoordig een van de meest geliefde etablissementen van de Zweedse hoofdstad. Het decor is geïnspireerd op het Scandinavische design uit de jaren zeventig met boven de tafels bungelende lampen in vorm van champagneglazen, lange comfortabele zitbanken en gedempt licht.

This postmodern restaurant is located on the top floor of the Pompidou Center and offers stunning views of the city. The interior is dominated by large amorphously shaped elements made of brushed aluminum and stainless steel. The inside is painted in various bright colors and houses intimate spaces here and there. The minimalist plastic chairs and the tables of sand-blasted glass complete the special ambience.

In der obersten Etage des Centre Pompidou und mit großartigem Blick über Paris findet sich dieses postmoderne Restaurant. Das Interieur wird dominiert von großen amorph geformten Elementen aus gebürstetem Aluminium und Edelstahl. Das Innere ist in verschiedenen hellen Farben gestrichen und beherbergt intime Bereiche. Die minimalistisch gestalteten Kunststoffstühle und Tische aus sandgestrahltem Glas vervollständigen das besondere Ambiente.

Ce restaurant postmoderne se situe au dernier étage du Centre Pompidou et offre une vue étonnante sur la ville. La décoration est dominée par de gigantesques éléments amorphes faits d'aluminium brossé et d'inox. L'intérieur est peint de diverses couleurs vives et abrite des espaces d'intimité ici et là. Les chaises en plastique minimalistes et les tables en verre dépoli complètent cette ambiance particulière.

Dit postmoderne restaurant bevindt zich op de bovenste verdieping van het Centre Pompidou en biedt een grandioos zicht over Parijs. Het interieur wordt bepaald door grote, amorfe elementen van geborsteld aluminium en roestvrij staal. Het interieur is in verschillende lichte kleuren geverfd en voorziet in intieme zithoekjes. De minimalistisch vormgegeven kunststofstoelen en de tafels van gezandstraald glas vullen de bijzondere sfeer aan.

Floating above a cliff, glass balconies and window frontage unite the restaurant with the natural world beyond. This elegant eatery is decorated in the cool greens and blues of the ocean. The guests relax in comfortable armchairs or dine with breathtaking views of the ocean.

Über einer Klippe schwebend schaffen Glasbalkone und Fensterfronten eine Einheit zwischen Restaurant und Natur. Das elegante Restaurant wurde in den kühlen grünen und blauen Farben des Ozeans gestaltet. Die Gäste entspannen in gemütlichen Sitzgruppen oder speisen mit atemberaubendem Blick auf den Ozean.

Flottant au-dessus d'une falaise, balcons de verre et baies vitrées unissent le restaurant à la nature environnante. La décoration de cet élégant restaurant se pare des verts et bleus froids de l'océan. Les hôtes peuvent se relaxer dans de confortables fauteuils ou dîner avec une vue époustouflante sur l'océan.

De glazen balkons en raampartijen scheppen een eenheid tussen het boven een klif zwevende restaurant en de natuur. Het restaurant werd uitgevoerd in de koele groene en blauwe tinten van de oceaan. De gasten komen tot rust in gezellige zithoeken of gebruiken de maaltijd met adembenemend zicht op de oceaan.

With its dark colors, the décor of this unique restaurant is reminiscent of an 18th-century opium den. The rooms are furnished with black leather sofas and Asiatic antiquities, including an opium table. Ceiling-high latticework screens with Oriental motifs separate the restaurant into different areas. The ambience is supplemented with contemporary accents such as minimalist upholstered furniture and illuminated floor panels.

Das Dekor dieses außergewöhnlichen Restaurants erinnert mit seinen dunklen Farben an eine Opium-Höhle des 18. Jahrhunderts. Möbliert sind die Räume mit schwarzen Ledersofas und asiatischen Antiquitäten, zu denen auch ein Opium-Tisch gehört. Raumhohe Paravents mit asiatischen Motiven unterteilen das Lokal in verschiedene Bereiche. Ergänzt wird das Ambiente durch zeitgemäße Akzente, wie minimalistisch gestaltete Polstermöbel oder beleuchtete Bodenplatten.

Paré de couleurs sombres, le décor de ce restaurant incomparable rappelle une fumerie d'opium du XVIIIᵉ siècle. Des banquettes de cuir noir, des antiquités asiatiques et des tables à opium meublent les chambres. De hauts panneaux treillagés ornés de motifs extrême-orientaux séparent le restaurant en différentes parties. Cette ambiance est affinée par les accents contemporains contenus dans le mobilier minimaliste et les dalles lumineuses.

Het decor van dit buitengewone restaurant doet met zijn donkere kleuren denken aan een achttiende-eeuws opiumhol. De ruimten zijn gemeubileerd met zwarte leren banken en Aziatische antiquiteiten waaronder ook een opiumtafel. Kamerhoge paravents met Aziatische motieven splitsen het restaurant in verschillende delen. De sfeer wordt aangevuld door eigentijdse accenten, zoals minimalistische, gestoffeerde meubels en verlichte vloerplaten.

The upper level of the emblematic Shanghai Art Museum is home to Kathleen's 5. The challenge to this modern construction was the task of harmonizing the glass atrium, elegant Orange Room and Terrace Bar with the museum's existing neoclassical architecture.

Im Dachgeschoss des emblematischen Shanghai Art Museum befindet sich das Kathleen's 5. Die Herausforderung des modernen Aufbaus war es, das Glas-Atrium, den eleganten Orange Room und die Terrace Bar in Einklang mit der neoklassizistischen Architektur des Museums zu bringen.

Le dernier étage de l'emblématique Shanghai Art Muséum abrite le Kathleen's 5. Le défi de cette construction moderne était d'harmoniser l'atrium de verre, l'élégante Salle Orange et le bar terrasse avec l'architecture néoclassique pré existante du musée.

Op zolder van het emblematische Shanghai Art Museum bevindt zich het Kathleen's 5. De uitdaging van de moderne opbouw bestond erin om het glasatrium, de elegante 'orange room' en de 'terrace bar' af te stemmen op de neoklassieke architectuur van het museum.

A new and unusual restaurant has been born in the Swiss Alps' oldest chalet. The principal architectural element here is a six-meter-high glass wall, containing a significant wine collection, which separates the restaurant's kitchen from its dance floor. Designer Patrick Jouin has offered a modern interpretation of traditional furniture and everyday objects, reinventing them for other uses. A terrace offers a breathtaking view of the surrounding Alpine landscape.

Im ältesten Berg-Chalet der Schweizer Alpen entstand ein neues ungewöhnliches Restaurant. Das elementare Gestaltungselement ist eine sechs Meter hohe Glaswand, in der eine bedeutende Weinsammlung Platz findet und die die Küche von den Restaurants und der Diskothek trennt. Traditionelle Möbel und Gebrauchsgegenstände wurden vom Designer Patrick Jouin modern interpretiert und erhielten neue Nutzungen. Eine Terrasse bietet einen atemberaubenden Blick in die umgebende Bergwelt.

Un restaurant exceptionnel est né dans le plus vieux chalet des Alpes suisses. Ici, le principal élément architectural est un mur de verre haut de six mètres, abritant un nombre important de grands crus, qui sépare la cuisine du restaurant de sa piste de danse. Le designer Patrick Jouin a réinterprété le mobilier traditionnel et d'autres objets en les réinventant pour des différents usages. La terrasse offre une vue époustouflante sur les paysages alpins environnants.

In het oudste bergchalet van de Zwitserse Alpen verrees een nieuw en bijzonder restaurant. Het belangrijkste vormelement is een zes meter hoge glaswand voor de aanzienlijke wijncollectie, die tevens de keuken van de restaurants en de discotheek scheidt. Traditionele meubels en gebruiksvoorwerpen werden door de designer Patrick Jouin modern geïnterpreteerd en kregen nieuwe gebruiksfuncties. Een terras kijkt uit op het omringende adembenemende berglandschap.

LOZOO RESTAURANT

NEW YORK | USA | GASTRONOMY

New York's Lozoo restaurant is laid out over six rooms on three different levels. The designers have created a unique ambience with the use of warm colors and materials. An imaginary timeline runs the length of the whole interior, placed at eyelevel. This characterizes the decisive "structural components" of the design and acts as a connection between floor and wall material, rounding the space off with a continuous felt bench and bar.

In sechs unterschiedlichen Räumen auf drei Ebenen präsentiert sich das New Yorker Restaurant Lozoo. Die Gestalter schaffen mit Hilfe warmer Farben und Materialien ein einzigartiges Ambiente. Eine gedachte Datumslinie in Augenhöhe zieht sich durch das gesamte Interieur. Sie kennzeichnet die maßgeblichen „Bauteile" des Designs, sie ist Verbindung zwischen Boden und Wandmaterial und bildet den Abschluss als durchgehende Filz-Bank und Bar-Ablage.

Le restaurant Lozoo de New York est réparti entre six pièces, sur trois différents niveaux. Ses designers ont créé une ambiance unique par l'usage de couleurs et de matières chaudes. Une ligne imaginaire, placée à hauteur du regard, court tout le long des murs. Celle-ci représente « les composantes structurelles » de base du design et a pour but de mettre en relation le matériau du sol et des murs, parfaisant cet espace par une banquette feutrée et un bar.

Het New Yorkse restaurant Lozoo bestaat uit zes verschillende ruimten op drie verdiepingen. De ontwerpers realiseerden met warme kleuren en materialen een unieke sfeer. Een denkbeeldige datumlijn op ooghoogte doorkruist het gehele interieur. Deze kenmerkt de belangrijkste componenten van het design, vormt een verbinding tussen vloer- en wandmateriaal en mondt uit in een doorlopende vilten bank en barblad.

A bright factory loft contains this sleek and popular sushi restaurant. Cord curtains veil the walls, simultaneously separating the restaurant into private dining area, lounge, bar and restaurant. A polished concrete floor, halogen lighting and stark furnishings compose the whole room.

Ein helles Fabrikloft beinhaltet ein schlichtes Sushi- wie angesagtes Szene-Restaurant. Schnurvorhänge verhüllen Wände und trennen gleichermaßen die einzelnen Bereiche wie Private-Dinning, Lounge, Bar und Restaurant. Ein polierter Betonboden, Halogenbeleuchtung und schlichtes Mobiliar bestimmen den gesamten Raum.

Un loft lumineux accueille ce restaurant de sushis soigné et très apprécié. Des rideaux de corde habillent les murs, séparant par la même occasion le restaurant entre espaces privés pour dîner, salon, bar et restaurant. Sol de béton poli, éclairage halogène et mobilier Stark sculptent la pièce.

Dit hippe restaurant in een lichte fabrieksloft serveert eenvoudige sushi. Kralen gordijnen verhullen de wanden en splitsen de ruimte in verschillende delen: privat dining, lounge, bar en restaurant. Een gepolijste betonvloer, halogeenverlichting en eenvoudig meubilair drukken een stempel op de gehele ruimte.

New York City is a true magnet for first-class cuisine. This is where Alain Ducasse – one of the greatest chefs and gastronomes in the world – had designer Patrick Jouin create his Mix restaurant. The reduced interior with its brick walls, old wood paneling and subdued lighting provides a stylish atmosphere.

New York City ist regelrecht ein Magnet für erstklassige Küche. So hat hier Alain Ducasse – einer der besten Meisterköche und Gastronomen der Welt – sein Restaurant Mix vom Designer Patrick Jouin gestalten lassen. Die reduzierte Innenausstattung mit Backsteinwänden, alte Holzdielen und einer reduzierten Beleuchtung sorgen für eine stilvolle Atmosphäre.

New York est un véritable aimant pour la grande cuisine. C'est là qu'Alain Ducasse, l'un des plus grands chefs et gastronomes au monde, a demandé au designer Patrick Jouin de créer son restaurant Mix. Les murs de briques, les vieux panneaux de bois et l'éclairage discret de cet intérieur épuré participent à la création d'une atmosphère élégante.

New York City is een ware magneet voor eersteklas koks. Zo heeft Alain Ducasse – een van de beste meesterkoks en gastronomen ter wereld – hier zijn restaurant Mix laten ontwerpen door de designer Patrick Jouin. De gereduceerde vormgeving van het interieur met stenen wanden, oude houten vloeren en spaarzame verlichting zorgt voor een stijlvolle sfeer.

Like pieces in a dreamscape, tables and stools in bright candy colors are arranged over the mosaic-like tiled floor of this cafe. The sophisticated lighting is controlled by a computer system which also projects pictures and films onto the walls, creating an ever-changing ambience each day.

Wie in einer Traumlandschaft verteilen sich in dem Café auf einem mosaikartig gefliesten Boden Hocker und Tische in bunten Bonbon-Farben. Ein computergesteuertes System ist für die raffinierte Beleuchtung verantwortlich, projiziert Bilder und Filme auf Wandflächen und erzeugt so täglich wechselnde Stimmungen.

Dignes d'un rêve d'enfant, les tables et tabourets parés de vives couleurs acidulées sont disposés sur le sol d'inspiration mosaïque de ce café. L'éclairage sophistiqué est contrôlé par un système électronique projetant également images et films sur les murs et créant une ambiance toujours nouvelle au fil des jours.

Als in een droomwereld staan in dit café krukken en tafels in bonte snoepjeskleuren verspreid over een mozaïekachtig betegelde vloer. Een computergestuurd systeem stuurt de geraffineerde belichting, projecteert beelden en films op de wanden en zorgt zo dagelijks voor een andere sfeer.

Anyone who wants to get noticed with a new restaurant in New York has to have something pretty good up his sleeve to reach an audience. Morimoto is one restaurant to have achieved this. Its cook, Masaharu Morimoto, is a TV star and both architect Tadao Ando as well as designer Ross Lovegrove are world renowned. The restaurant is characterized by geometric shapes, a style celebrated in materials such as concrete, glass and wood. In the bar and lounge one level below, a sculpture consisting of 17,000 (empty) Tynant water bottles acts as both eye-catcher and signpost.

Wer in New York mit einem neuen Restaurant Aufmerksamkeit erregen möchte, der muss sich schon einiges einfallen lassen, um sein Publikum zu finden. Beim Morimoto ist dies gelungen, der Koch Masaharu Morimoto ist ein TV-Star und Architekt Tadao Ando und Designer Ross Lovegrove sind weltbekannt. Das Restaurant wird von geometrischen Formen geprägt, sein Stil wird mit den Materialien Beton, Glas und Holz gekonnt zelebriert. Blickfang und Wegweiser in die eine Ebene tiefer gelegene Bar-Lounge ist eine aus 17.000 (leeren) Tynant-Wasserflaschen bestehende Skulptur.

Quiconque désire faire connaître son nouveau restaurant à New York doit avoir un concept qui tient la route pour attirer la clientèle. Le restaurant Morimoto y est parvenu. Son chef, Masaharu Morimoto est une star de la TV et l'architecte Tadao Ando, tout comme le designer Ross Lovergrove sont mondialement connus. Le restaurant se caractérise par des formes géométriques et un style concrétisé par des matériaux comme le béton, le verre et le bois. Dans le bar et le salon, un niveau plus bas, une sculpture constituée de 17 000 bouteilles d'eau (vides) Tynant attire tous les regards et sert également de poteau indicateur.

Wie in New York de aandacht wil vestigen op een nieuw restaurant, moet zijn uiterste best doen om publiek te trekken. Het Morimoto is hierin geslaagd. De kok Masaharu Morimoto is een tv-ster en de architect Tadao Ando en de designer Ross Lovegrove zijn wereldberoemd. Het restaurant wordt gekenmerkt door geometrische vormen en materialen als beton, glas en hout. Blikvanger en wegwijzer naar de een etage lager gelegen bar-lounge is een uit 17.000 (lege) Tynant-waterflessen opgebouwde sculptuur.

275

This restaurant was named after the nomads of Africa. It is arranged like a sultan's boudoir, with salon tables, large pillows and handcrafted curtains which separate the room. A fashionable location, where seeing and being seen is key. The sophisticated décor offers a unique ambience, enhanced by delicious food and delectable belly dancers – a flying carpet journey of a very special kind.

Dieses Restaurant wurde nach den Nomaden aus Afrika benannt. Es ist wie das Boudoir eines Sultans eingerichtet, mit Salontischen, großen Kissen und handgemachten Vorhängen, welche den Raum unterteilen. Ein modisches Lokal, Sehen und Gesehen werden ist hier das Motto. Die hochwertige Ausstattung bietet ein einzigartiges Ambiente, köstliches Essen und Bauchtänzerinnen – eine Fahrt auf einem fliegenden Teppich der ganz besonderen Art.

Ce restaurant tient son nom des nomades africains. Il est aménagé comme le boudoir d'un sultan, avec tables basses, larges coussins et rideaux tissés à la main séparant les espaces. Un endroit à la mode, où voir et être vu est la clé. Le décor sophistiqué offre une ambiance unique, sublimée par une nourriture délicieuse et de splendides danseuses du ventre : un voyage en tapis volant très spécial.

Dit restaurant werd vernoemd naar de nomaden uit Afrika. Het is ingericht als het boudoir van een sultan met salontafels, grote kussens en handgemaakte gordijnen die de ruimte indelen. Een modieus restaurant met als motto 'zien en gezien worden'. Het hoogwaardige restaurant biedt een unieke sfeer, heerlijk eten en buikdanseressen – kortom een uitstapje op een vliegend tapijt van bijzondere klasse.

Paris's Palais de Tokyo, constructed in 1937 for the World's Fair, today houses exhibition spaces for contemporary culture. In this industrial memorial you will find the Tokyo Eat restaurant, famed for its original design. Large-scale portraits cover the windows, giant pink-colored lights with built-in speakers hang from the ceiling, and the classic chairs are individually painted.

Der zur Weltausstellung 1937 errichtete Palais de Tokyo beherbergt heute Ausstellungsräume für zeitgenössische Kultur. In diesem Industriedenkmal befindet sich das Restaurant Tokyo Eat, das berühmt ist für sein originelles Design. Große Porträts verdecken die Fenster, von den Decken hängen riesige, rosafarbene Leuchten, in die Lautsprecher integriert sind, und die klassischen Stühle wurden individuell bemalt.

Le Palais de Tokyo à Paris, édifié en 1937 pour l'Exposition Universelle, abrite aujourd'hui des espaces d'exposition destinés à la culture contemporaine. C'est dans ce monument industriel que se trouve le restaurant Tokyo Eat, renommé pour son design original. De larges portraits couvrent les fenêtres, des suspensions roses géantes intégrant des haut-parleurs descendent du plafond et la décoration de chaque chaise est unique.

Het voor de Wereldtentoonstelling in 1937 opgerichte Palais de Tokyo herbergt tegenwoordig tentoonstellingsruimten voor hedendaagse cultuur. In dit industriemonument bevindt zich het restaurant Tokyo Eat dat vermaard is om zijn originele design. Grote portretten verhullen de ramen, aan de plafonds hangen reusachtige, roze lampen waarin luidsprekers zijn geïntegreerd en de klassieke stoelen werden afzonderlijk beschilderd.

Optically, the Plateau is perhaps the most beautiful restaurant on Canary Wharf, London's new financial center east of Tower Bridge (Manhattan on the Thames). The restaurant, designed by Sir Terence Conran, is competely glassed in and offers a dreamlike view over the new skyscrapers and manicured green spaces of the former harbor.

Das Plateau ist optisch wohl das schönste Restaurant von Canary Wharf, Londons neuem Zentrum der Finanzwelt östlich der Tower Bridge (Manhattan an der Themse). Das von Sir Terence Conran entworfene Restaurant ist rundum verglast und bietet einen traumhaften Blick auf die neuen Wolkenkratzer und gepflegten Grünflächen des ehemaligen Hafens.

Esthétiquement, Plateau est peut-être le plus beau restaurant de Canary Wharf, le nouveau centre financier de Londres, à l'est de Tower Bridge (le Manhattan de la Tamise). Ce restaurant, pensé par Sir Terence Conran, est totalement entouré de verre et offre une vue de rêve sur les nouveaux gratte-ciels et les espaces verts manucurés de l'ancien port.

Het Plateau is optisch waarschijnlijk het mooiste restaurant van Canary Wharf, het nieuwste financiële centrum van Londen ten oosten van de Tower Bridge (Manhattan aan de Theems). Het door Sir Terence Conran ontworpen restaurant is rondom voorzien van glas en biedt een schitterend zicht op de nieuwe wolkenkrabbers en verzorgde plantsoenen van het voormalige havengebied.

The bar and restaurant of this superior Parisian hotel are captivating in their design, incorporating contemporary creations into the existing Baroque elements. Wooden wall panels and parquet floors form the backdrop for the predominantly silver-colored, Baroque-style furniture creations. A chandelier is suspended above the gray marble mantel, veiled by a translucent silver mesh.

Bar und Restaurant des Pariser Nobelhotels bestechen durch ihre Einrichtung, so werden die bestehenden barocken Elemente gekonnt mit zeitgemäßem Design kombiniert. Hölzerne Wandvertäfelungen und Parkettböden bilden die Kulisse für die meist silberfarbenen, barock anmutenden Möbelkreationen. Über dem grauen Marmor-Kamin hängt ein Kronleuchter, umhüllt von einer transluzenten silbernen Folie.

Le design du bar et du restaurant de cet hôtel parisien de grand standing est captivant, incorporant des créations contemporaines aux éléments baroques pré-existants. Des panneaux de bois muraux et du parquet servent de toile de fond au mobilier baroque de créateur, où domine l'argenté. Un lustre est suspendu au-dessus de la cheminée de marbre gris, voilé d'un maillage d'argent.

De bar en het restaurant van het Parijse luxehotel bekoren door de inrichting. De bestaande barokke elementen werden kundig gecombineerd met eigentijds design. Houten lambriseringen en parketvloeren vormen de achtergrond voor de veelal zilveren, barokachtige meubelcreaties. Boven de grijze marmeren schouw hangt een kroonluchter die is gehuld in een doorschijnende zilveren folie.

This historic building dating from 1906 now houses an out-of-the-ordinary restaurant. Neogothic elements such as gilded molding, opulent mosaics and artificial marble dominate the interior design. Crystal lamps, white table cloths and candle-light provide an interesting contrast with their subdued colors, illuminated floor and sparse furnishings.

Das historische Gebäude aus dem Jahr 1906 beherbergt ein ungewöhnliches Restaurant. Neogotische Elemente, wie vergoldeter Stuck, opulente Mosaike und künstlicher Marmor dominieren die Gestaltung des Innenraums. Kristallleuchter, weiße Tischdecken und Kerzenlicht bilden mit zurückhaltenden Farben, leuchtenden Böden und reduzierten Möbeln einen interessanten Kontrast.

Cet édifice historique de 1906 accueille désormais un restaurant peu commun. Des éléments néogothiques tels que des dorures, d'opulentes mosaïques et du marbre artificiel dominent le design intérieur. Lampes de cristal, nappes blanches et bougies apportent un contraste intéressant par des couleurs discrètes, des dalles lumineuses et un mobilier épuré.

Het historische gebouw uit 1906 herbergt een bijzonder restaurant. Neogotische elementen, zoals gulden stucwerk, weelderige mozaïeken en kunstmarmer, domineren het interieur. Kristallen kroonluchters, witte tafelkleden en kaarslicht vormen met de ingetogen kleuren, glanzende vloeren en spaarzame meubilering een interessant contrast.

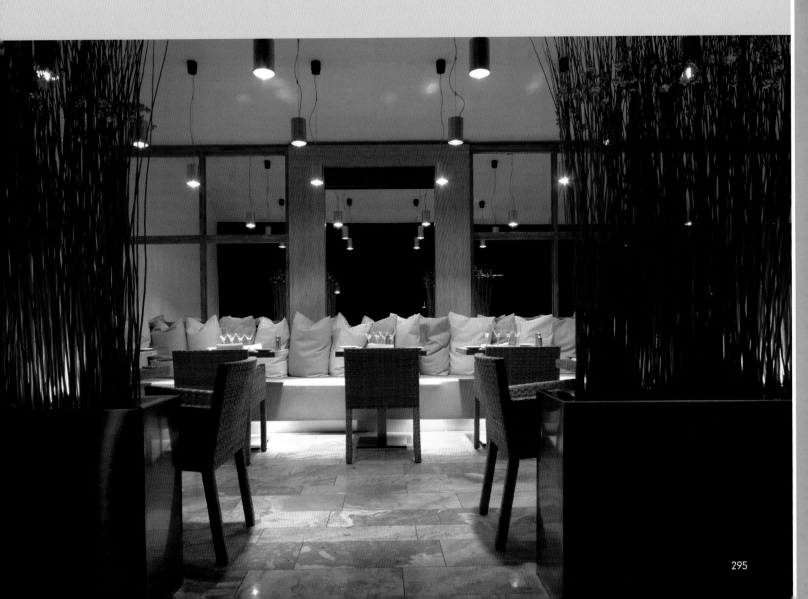

The cardinal elements air, light, fire and water are responsible for the look of this bakery café. With water running out of a sunken fountain and a fireplace in the visible bakery, architect Claudio Silvestrin reminds us that bread was once baked in actual wood-burning ovens.

Die Elemente Luft, Licht, Feuer und Wasser bestimmen die Charakteristik des Princi Bakery Café. Wasser rinnt aus einem eingelassenen Brunnenstein und mit einer Feuerstätte in der einsehbaren Backstube erinnert Architekt Claudio Silvestrin daran, dass Brot ursprünglich im Holzofen gebacken wurde.

Les quatre éléments, l'air, la lumière, le feu et l'eau sont à l'origine du style de ce café-boulangerie. Par l'eau coulant d'une fontaine encastrée et par l'âtre visible de la boulangerie, l'architecte Claudio Silvestrin nous rappelle que le pain était jadis cuit dans de vrais fours à bois.

De elementen lucht, licht, vuur en water bepalen het karakter van het Princi Bakery Café. De architect Claudio Silvestrin her-innert de bezoeker er met een stookplaats in de open bakkerij aan dat brood oorspronkelijk in houtovens werd gebakken.

After thorough renovation of Bremen's venerable courthouse, a modern refuge for optical purists and culinary connoisseurs was created. Installations and alterations dominate in the rambling, high-ceilinged room. Exposed concrete bars and dividers, colorfully accented seats in the lounge and restaurant area.

Nachdem das ehrwürdige Bremer Gerichtshaus generalsaniert wurde, ist hier ein modernes Refugium für optische Puristen und kulinarische Genießer geschaffen worden. In dem hohen und weitläufigen Raum dominieren Ein- und Umbauten: Tresen und Abtrennungen aus Sichtbeton, farblich akzentuierte Sitzmöbel im Lounge- und Restaurantbereich.

Après une rénovation complète du vénérable tribunal de Brême, un refuge moderne pour les esthètes et gastronomes puristes a été créé. Installations et transformations dominent cette pièce irrégulière et haute de plafond, décorée de barres et cloisons apparentes en béton ainsi que de fauteuils colorés dans le salon et le restaurant.

Nadat het eerwaardige gerechtsgebouw in Bremen geheel was gerestaureerd, verrees hier een modern toevluchtsoord voor optische puristen en culinaire fijnproevers. De hoge, grote ruimte wordt gedicteerd door in- en ombouwconstructies: bar, scheidingswanden van sierbeton en zitmeubels met kleuraccenten in het lounge- en restaurantgedeelte.

Shumi can be found between the exclusive men's clubs of London high society on St. James Street. Long, typical London escalators bring the guest into the bar. Decorated in a noble white and beige, furnished with discreet arm chairs, it is nothing like its neighbors and radiates its own cultivated atmosphere. Plate-sized stainless steel lamps bathe both the bar and restaurant in a pleasant light.

Zwischen den exklusiven Herren-Clubs der britischen Society findet sich auf der Londoner St. James Street das Shumi. Lange, für die britische Hauptstadt typische Rolltreppen führen den Gast ins Innere der Bar. Edel in Weiß und Beige, bestuhlt mit schlichten Polsterstühlen, steht es seinen Nachbarn in nichts nach und strahlt eine gediegene Atmosphäre aus. Tellergroße Leuchten aus gebürstetem Edelstahl tauchen Bar und Restaurant in ein angenehmes Licht.

Le Shumi cohabite avec les cercles masculins très privés de la haute société londonienne, sur St. James Street. De longs escalators typiques mènent l'hôte jusqu'au bar. Habillé de blanc et de beige, meublé de fauteuils discrets, il ne ressemble en rien à ses voisins et diffuse sa propre atmosphère. Des lampes plateaux en inox baignent à la fois le bar et le restaurant d'une lumière agréable.

Tussen de exclusieve herenclubs van de Britse society in de Londense St. James Street bevindt zich ook het Shumi. Lange roltrappen, die kenmerkend zijn voor de Britse hoofdstad, brengen de gast naar de bar. Het Shumi doet met zijn edele witte en beige tinten en de sobere, gecapitonneerde stoelen niet onder voor zijn buren en straalt een degelijke sfeer uit. Schotelvormige lampen van geborsteld roestvrij staal hullen de bar en het restaurant in een aangenaam licht.

Seeing and being seen is an integral part of the concept here. The design principle in this restaurant is the interplay of transparency, translucence and clarity. The asymmetric seats, upholstered in purple leather, act as connecting element. The decoration is a symbol of the overall architecture – it is just as multifunctional as the room itself.

Sehen und Gesehen werden ist Bestandteil des Konzepts. Kern der Gestaltung ist das Spiel mit Transparenz, Ein- und Durchblicken. Verbindendes Element sind die asymmetrischen Sitzmöbel in lila Leder. Die Ausstattung ist ein Symbol für die gesamte Architektur – sie ist genauso multifunktional wie der Raum selbst.

Voir et être vu est ici partie intégrante du concept. Le principe de base de ce restaurant est l'interaction entre le transparent, le translucide et la clarté. Les fauteuils asymétriques recouverts de cuir mauve servent de liens. La décoration symbolise l'ensemble de l'architecture : elle est aussi multifonctionnelle que la pièce elle-même.

Zien en gezien worden is onderdeel van het concept. Essentie van de vormgeving is het spel met transparantie en in- en doorkijkjes. Verbindend element zijn de asymmetrische zitmeubels in lila leer. De inrichting is een symbool voor de gehele architectuur – hij is even multifunctioneel als de ruimte zelf.

"Change" is the guiding principle here. The walls are clad in variable, colored and flowing sheets of flexible fiberglass. These are continued from room to room, simultaneously integrating the seating assemblies. True to the overall concept, the music, menu, light and décor of this popular café change on a daily basis.

Das Leitmotiv lautet Veränderung. Variable, farbige und fließend anmutende Wandverkleidungen aus biegsamem Fiberglas durchziehen die Räume und integrieren gleichzeitig die Sitzgelegenheiten. Getreu dem Gesamtkonzept ändern sich Musik, Menü, Licht und Einrichtung in der angesagten Cafeteria täglich.

Ici, la ligne directrice est le « changement ». Les murs sont revêtus de feuilles souples en fibre de verre, ondulantes et colorées. Celles-ci habillent toutes les pièces venant ainsi s'intégrer aux banquettes. Fidèles au concept général, la musique, le menu, la lumière et le décor de ce café populaire changent quotidiennement.

Het leidmotief luidt verandering. Variabele, kleurrijke en vloeiende wandbekledingen van buigzaam fiberglas komen in alle ruimten terug en integreren tegelijkertijd de zitplaatsen. Overeenkomstig het totaalconcept verandert de muziek, het menu, de belichting en inrichting dagelijks in het zeer populaire eetcafé.

The design of this sushi restaurant in the recently renovated Kurashiki quarter emphasizes Japan's traditional sushi culture, while implementing an unambiguous and formal innovative motif. Every detail, including the floor, walls and their decorations has been harmonized with all others, creating a powerful overall impression.

Die Gestaltung dieses Sushi-Restaurants, in dem vor kurzem restaurierten Viertel Kurashiki, bezieht sich auf die traditionelle japanische Sushi-Kultur, setzt aber gleichzeitig auf eine formell innovative und klare Designlinie. Alle Details wie Boden, Wände, Dekoration wurden sorgfältig aufeinander abgestimmt, was zu einem starken Gesamteindruck führt.

Le design de ce restaurant de sushis situé dans le quartier de Kurashiki, récemment rénové, insiste sur la culture traditionnelle japonaise du sushi, tout en apportant une touche ambigüe et hautement innovante. Chaque détail, sol, murs et leurs décorations compris, s'harmonise avec tous les autres, créant une puissante impression générale.

De vormgeving van dit sushirestaurant in de recentelijk gerestaureerde wijk Kurashiki verwijst naar de traditionele Japanse sushicultuur maar streeft tevens naar een formeel innovatieve en duidelijke designlijn. Alle details zoals vloeren, wanden, decoratie werden zorgvuldig op elkaar afgestemd, hetgeen een geweldige totaalindruk oplevert.

The Loft is one of Sydney's most popular locations, located at the north end of the fashionable King Street Wharf. The rooms are dominated by dark, subdued colors and shimmering honey-gold lighting which enhances an exuberantly Oriental décor. The Loft is arranged in such a manner that its guests can stay comfortable throughout the entire evening.

The Loft ist eine der angesagtesten Locations Sydneys und liegt am nördlichen Ende der Ausgehmeile King Street Wharf. Die Räume werden beherrscht durch dunkle, gedeckte Farben und eine honiggolden schimmernde Beleuchtung, die eine überbordend orientalisch wirkende Ornamentik aufgreift und verstärkt. The Loft ist darauf ausgelegt, dass sich die Gäste wohlfühlen, und das möglichst die ganze Nacht.

Le Loft est un des lieux les plus en vue de Sydney, situé à l'extrémité nord du très fréquenté King Street Wharf. Les pièces sont dominées par de discrètes couleurs sombres et un éclairage jaune doré chatoyant, à même de relever un décor oriental exubérant. Le Loft est conçu de manière à ce que ses hôtes puissent rester confortablement installés tout au long de la soirée.

The Loft is een van de geliefdste etablissementen van Sydney en ligt aan het noordelijk uiteinde van het uitgaansgebied King Street Wharf. De ruimten worden overheerst door donkere, gedekte kleuren en een goudgele belichting die de weelderige oriëntaals aandoende versiering accentueert. Gasten moeten zich in het Loft prettig voelen en dat liefst de hele nacht.

As the name says, this place is all about wine. A long, narrow room is decorated entirely in fine, dark wood. The motif: wine, as far as the eye can see, and to try as many different types as possible in one evening. You can order wine flights for this purpose: three half glasses containing various wines, such as three different rosés, three whites or three dessert wines. Then you order more of whichever one hit the spot.

Wie der Name bereits sagt, hier dreht sich alles um Wein. Ein langer, schmaler Raum ist komplett in edlem, dunklem Holz gehalten. Das Konzept: Wein, so weit das Auge reicht, um an einem Abend so viele Weine wie möglich zu probieren. Dazu kann man „Flights" bestellen: drei halbe Gläser mit verschiedenen Weinen, also drei verschiedene Rosés, drei Weiße oder drei Dessertweine. Was am besten schmeckt, bestellt man einfach nach.

Comme son nom l'indique, cet endroit est dédié au vin. Cette pièce longue et étroite est décorée de bois sombres et raffinés. Le thème : le vin, à perte de vue, et d'une diversité maximum en une soirée. A cet effet, il est possible de commander un assortiment : trois demi-verres contenant divers vins, comme trois différents rosés, trois blancs ou trois vins sucrés, vous permettant ensuite de commander celui qui vous aura séduit.

Zoals de naam al aangeeft, draait hier alles om wijn. De lange, smalle ruimte is compleet uitgevoerd in hoogwaardig donker hout. Het concept: wijn zo ver het oog reikt om op een avond zo veel mogelijk wijnen te proeven. Daartoe kan de gast 'Flights' bestellen: drie halve glazen met verschillende wijnen, dus drie verschillende rosés, drie witte wijnen of drie dessertwijnen. En de lekkerste wijn, bestelt men eenvoudig weer.

At first sight, you might think you're at the wrong address. But behind the walls of the historic Shikumen building, constructed in 1928, the diner will be greeted by some of the best Shanghai cuisine in a lovely ambience. Select antiquities and a carefully chosen mixture of lighting and material colors lend the large, high room a light yet sophisticated atmosphere.

Im ersten Moment wähnt man sich an der falschen Adresse. Aber hinter den Mauern des historischen Shikumen-Gebäudes aus dem Jahre 1928 wird man von bester Shanghai-Küche in einem schönen Ambiente empfangen. Ausgewählte Antiquitäten, eine sorgfältig abgestimmte Mischung der Licht- und Materialfarben verleihen dem großen und hohen Raum eine leichte und dennoch kostbare Grundstimmung.

A première vue, vous pourriez penser vous être trompé d'endroit. Mais derrière les murs de l'historique bâtiment Shikumen, édifié en 1928, l'hôte affamé appréciera l'une des meilleures cuisines de Shanghai, dans une ambiance plaisante. Des antiquités rares et un mélange soigneusement étudié de lumières et de couleurs confèrent à cette pièce large et haute, une atmosphère lumineuse et sophistiquée.

Aanvankelijk denkt men op het verkeerde adres te zijn, maar achter de muren van het historische Shikumengebouw uit 1928 wordt men verwelkomd door de beste keuken van Shanghai in een mooie ambiance. Prachtige antiquiteiten en een zorgvuldig afgestemde combinatie van licht- en materiaalkleuren verlenen de grote en hoge ruimte een lichte maar tevens dure sfeer.

BARS, LOUNGES, AND CLUBS

NIGHTLIFE

The emphasis of this Berlin club is on relaxing in comfort. You don't sit around ordinary tables here, but recline on a white field of cushions. Absolutely everything is presented in white or silver; the White Bar is the perfect place for an after-work cocktail or the end to a long night of partying. You can dance the night away in the Silver Room while the atmospherically lighted terrace is inviting for those private moments.

Bequem relaxen ist das Motto des Berliner Clubs. Hier wird nicht an herkömmlichen Tischen gegessen, sondern liegend auf den weißen Bettenwiesen. Überhaupt ist alles in Weiß und Silber gehalten: die White Bar ist der perfekte Ort für einen Feierabend-Cocktail oder den Abschluss einer langen Partynacht. Im Silver Room kann die ganze Nacht getanzt werden und die stimmungsvoll beleuchtete Terrasse lädt zu privaten Momenten ein.

Ce club de Berlin ne vise que votre confort. Ici vous ne vous asseyez pas autour d'une table banale, mais vous allongez sur une «blanche prairie de coussins ». Tout est blanc ou argenté, sans exception ; le White Bar est l'endroit parfait pour un cocktail after-work ou pour clore une longue nuit de fête. Vous pouvez danser toute la nuit dans la Salle d'Argent, tandis que la terrasse au clair de lune vous invite à des moments privés.

Comfortabel relaxen luidt het motto van deze club in Berlijn. Hier wordt niet gegeten van gebruikelijke tafels maar liggend op de witte banken. De gehele club is in wit- en zilvertinten uitgevoerd: de 'white bar' is de perfecte plek voor een cocktail na werktijd of een afsluitend drankje na een lange nacht stappen. In de 'silver room' kan de hele nacht worden gedanst en het sfeervol verlichte terras nodigt uit voor intieme onderonsjes.

Way up in the highest house in Switzerland, a place has been developed for the senses, a place of passion and desire. The guest here will enjoy a breathtaking view of the city of Basel. The interior, with its red leather sofas, plush pillows and red lighting provides an intimate atmosphere.

Ganz oben, im höchsten Haus der Schweiz, wurde ein Ort der Sinne, der Leidenschaften und der Sehnsüchte geschaffen. Von hier genießt der Gast einen atemberaubenden Ausblick auf die Stadt Basel. Das Interieur mit roten Ledersofas, Plüschkissen und der ebenso roten Beleuchtung schafft eine intime Atmosphäre.

Au sommet du plus haut immeuble de Suisse, cet endroit a été créé pour les sens : un lieu de passion et de désir. Ici, les hôtes jouissent d'une vue époustouflante sur Basel. A l'intérieur, l'atmosphère est intime grâce aux canapés de cuir rouge, aux coussins moelleux et à la lumière rouge.

Helemaal boven, in het hoogst gelegen huis van Zwitserland werd een plek van zinnelijke levensvreugde, passies en hunkeringen geschapen. Hier geniet de gast van een adembenemend uitzicht op de stad Basel. Het interieur met rode leren banken, kussens van pluche en de eveneens rode belichting zorgen voor een intieme sfeer.

This new bar and lounge has been conceived as a large entry and consultancy zone on the ground floor of a bank building – with its own unique design. The large room, up to 15.75 feet (4.8 meters) high in places and equipped with a glass façade, has been created with the use of ceiling-high cubes upholstered with artificial leather.

Das neue Lokal mit Bar- und Loungebereich wurde als Teil der großen Eingangs- und Beratungszone im Erdgeschoss eines Bankgebäudes konzipiert, jedoch eigenständig gestaltet. Aufgrund des großen und bis zu 4,80 Meter hohen Raumes mit Glasfassade wurde dies mit raumhohen, gepolsterten und mit Kunstleder bespannten Kuben realisiert.

Ce nouveau bar et lounge a été conçu comme une large zone de passage et de rencontre au rez-de-chaussée d'un immeuble financier au design unique. La large salle, haute de 4,8 mètres en certains endroits et dotée d'une large façade vitrée, est habillée jusqu'au plafond d'une structure de cubes recouverts de cuir synthétique.

Dit nieuwe etablissement met bar- en loungegedeelte maakt deel uit van de grote ontvangstruimte op de begane grond van een bankgebouw, maar is op geheel eigen wijze vormgegeven. Vanwege de grote en tot wel 4,80 meter hoge ruimte met glazen voorgevel werd dit gerealiseerd met kamerhoge scheidingswanden van met kunstleer beklede kubussen.

During the day only the metal façade is visible, appearing as a single-level circular concrete disk. When evening falls, the hydraulic roof lifts up, letting in light and air and the guest steps down the stairs into the subterranean club. The white concrete floor is an attractive contrast to the dark wooden furnishings and the walls draped with red lengths of fabric. The red-upholstered sofas and chairs are all equipped with folding backrests.

Tagsüber ist nur die Metall-Fassade sichtbar, die sich ebenerdig in eine kreisrunde Betonscheibe zu drücken scheint. Wird es Abend, fährt das hydraulische Dach auf, lässt Licht und Luft hinein und der Gast gelangt über eine Treppe in den unterirdischen Club. Der karge Betonboden ist ein reizvoller Kontrast zu den Möbeln in dunklem Holz und den mit roten Stoffbahnen verkleideten Wänden.

De jour, seule la façade de métal est visible, apparaissant telle un disque de béton. Lorsque la nuit tombe, le toit hydraulique s'élève, laissant entrer l'air et la lumière et l'hôte peut alors descendre dans le club souterrain. Le sol de béton blanc contraste magnifiquement avec le mobilier de bois sombre et les murs drapés de laies de tissus rouge. Les sofas et fauteuils tapissés de rouge sont tous équipés de dossiers rabattables.

Overdag is enkel de metalen buitenkant zichtbaar die zich gelijkvloers in de cirkelvormige betonschijf lijkt te persen. Zodra de avond valt, gaat het hydraulische dak omhoog, laat licht en lucht binnen en de gast kan via de trap in de onderaardse club afdalen. De sobere betonnen vloer vormt een mooi contrast met de meubels van donker hout en de met rode stofbanen beklede wanden. De rood beklede banken en fauteuils hebben allen een opklapbare rugleuning.

This club is a veritable labyrinth of various lounging areas, bars and karaoke rooms, arranged over various roomy spaces. Public and private zones offer the right ambience for any offbeat wish its guests might have. Red and gray are the dominant colors here, shiny surfaces reflecting the numerous lights on the ceilings and walls.

Der Club gestaltet sich als Labyrinth aus verschiedenen Aufenthaltszonen, Bars und Karaoke-Räumen, die in verschieden große Bereiche gegliedert sind. Öffentliche und private Zonen bieten für jeden ausgefallenen Wunsch der Gäste das richtige Ambiente. Rot und Grau sind die vorherrschenden Farben, hochglänzende Oberflächen reflektieren die zahlreichen Lichter an Decken und Wänden.

Ce club est un véritable labyrinthe de salons, de bars et de karaokés divers et variés, tous abonnés à des pièces spacieuses. Des zones publiques et privées permettent de trouver l'ambiance désirée, selon les envies. Les couleurs dominantes sont le rouge et le gris et des surfaces brillantes reflètent les multiples sources lumineuses du plafond et des murs.

De club is een doolhof van verschillende verblijfsruimten, bars en karaokezalen, die zijn ingedeeld in verschillend grote zones. Voor elke excentrieke wens van de gasten voorzien de publieke en privé-zones in de juiste ambiance. De dominerende kleuren zijn rood en grijs en de hoogglanzende oppervlakken reflecteren de talrijke lichten aan de plafonds en wanden.

This casino is a stately structure even from the outside; inside it is the quintessence of Las Vegas's glamorous image combined with the most modern technology. An oversized artificial waterfall can be seen behind the reception desk, rushing down the wall in front of a red backdrop. The golden dome is a throwback to legendary casinos such as the Bellagio. The gaming rooms are also decorated in a combination of historical interiors and modern design.

Schon von außen ist das Casino ein imposantes Gebäude, im Inneren wurde auf das glanzvolle Image von Las Vegas in Kombination mit modernster Technik gesetzt. Hinter der Rezeption befindet sich ein überdimensionaler Wasserfall, der vor einem roten Hintergrund von der Wand herabrauscht. Und die goldene Kuppel erinnert an legendäre Casinos wie das Bellagio. Auch die Spielräume sind mit einer gelungenen Kombination aus historischem Interieur und moderner Ausstattung bestückt.

Ce casino est une structure imposante, même de l'extérieur ; à l'intérieur explose la quintessence du glamour de Las Vegas combinée à la technologie la plus moderne. Une cascade artificielle démesurée habille la réception et se déverse devant un pan de mur rouge. Le dôme doré fait référence aux casinos légendaires comme le Bellagio. Les salles de jeu sont également décorées en mêlant les grands classiques du genre au design moderne.

Al aan de buitenkant is het casino een imposant gebouw en binnen wordt het luisterrijke imago van Las Vegas gecombineerd met de modernste techniek. Achter de receptie bevindt zich een buitensporig grote waterval die voor een rode achtergrond naar beneden klatert. De gouden koepel herinnert aan legendarische casino's zoals het Bellagio. Ook de speelzalen zijn ingericht in een geslaagde combinatie van historisch interieur en moderne uitrusting.

A mixture of hospital, pharmacy and laboratory await the socialite here in the Clinic Club. Guests can enjoy their meals in an unusual ambience – sitting in wheelchairs at operating tables. Large surgical lamps provide the right kind of light. The food is appropriately presented in kidney-shaped bowls while the Morphine Bar serves up drinks in test tubes or IV packs.

Eine Mischung aus Krankenhaus, Apotheke und Labor erwartet den Szenegänger im Clinic Club. In diesem außerge-wöhnlichen Ambiente wird in Rollstühlen an Operationstischen gegessen und getrunken. Große OP-Leuchten sorgen für das richtige Licht. Das Essen wird stilgerecht in Nierenschüsseln serviert, die Drinks an der Morphine Bar kommen aus Reagenzgläsern oder Infusionsbeuteln.

Un savant mélange d'hôpital, de pharmacie et de laboratoire attend le noctambule au Clinic Club. Les hôtes consomment ici dans une ambiance inhabituelle : assis à une table d'opération, dans un fauteuil roulant. De larges lampes chirurgicales fournissent la lumière idoine. Les plats sont servis dans des bassinets en haricot tandis que le Morphine Bar administre les boissons dans des tubes à essai ou des poches de perfusion.

In de Clinic Club staat de gasten een kruising van ziekenhuis, apotheek en laboratorium te wachten. In deze bijzondere ambiance eten de gasten in rolstoelen aan operatietafels. Grote OK-lampen zorgen voor de verlichting en het eten wordt geheel in stijl opgediend in nierbekkens. De drankjes aan de 'morphine bar' worden geschonken in reageerbuisjes of infuuszakjes.

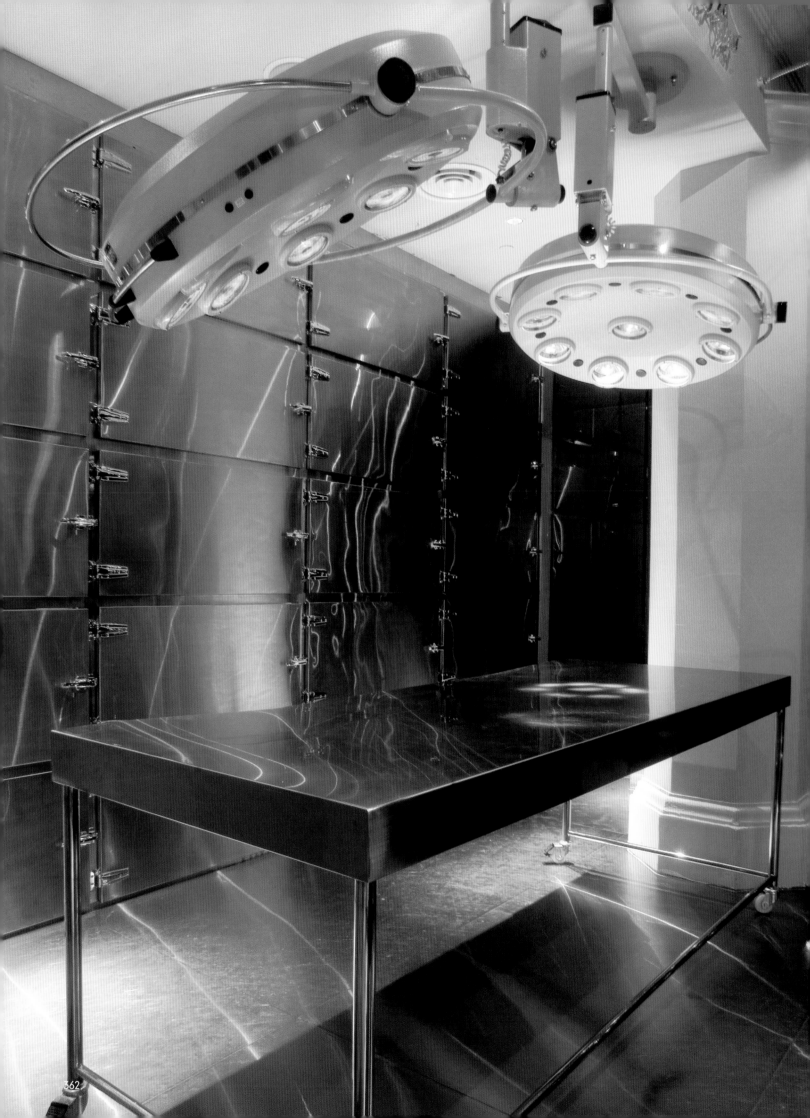

The atmosphere of this night club and restaurant has an almost sacred air. Developed by the architects at the Suppose Design Office, Camellia boasts dramatic lighting with the use of carefully placed light sources. Napped and perforated steel walls provide sophisticated acoustics by reverberating whatever music is playing without interrupting conversation.

Fast schon sakral anmutend ist die Atmosphäre des Nachtclubs und Restaurants Camellia. Der von den Architekten des Suppose Design Office entworfene Club wird durch gezielt eingesetzte Lichtquellen dramatisch beleuchtet. Perforierte und aufgeraute Stahlwände sorgen für eine ausgeklügelte Akustik, indem sie die gespielte Musik widerhallen lassen, ohne dabei die Konversation der Gäste zu stören.

L'atmosphère de ce night club et restaurant tient presque du sacré. Développé par les architectes du Suppose Design Office, le Camellia se targue d'un éclairage spectaculaire par la disposition soigneuse des sources de lumière. Des murs d'acier perforé permettent une acoustique sophistiquée en répartissant la musique de manière à pouvoir converser.

De sfeer van de nachtclub en het restaurant Camellia doet haast heilig aan. De door de architecten van de Suppose Design Office ontworpen club wordt door gericht ingezette lichtbronnen dramatisch verlicht. Geperforeerde en opgeruwde stalen wanden zorgen voor een geraffineerde akoestiek, doordat ze de gespeelde muziek laten weerklinken zonder hierbij de conversaties van de gasten te storen.

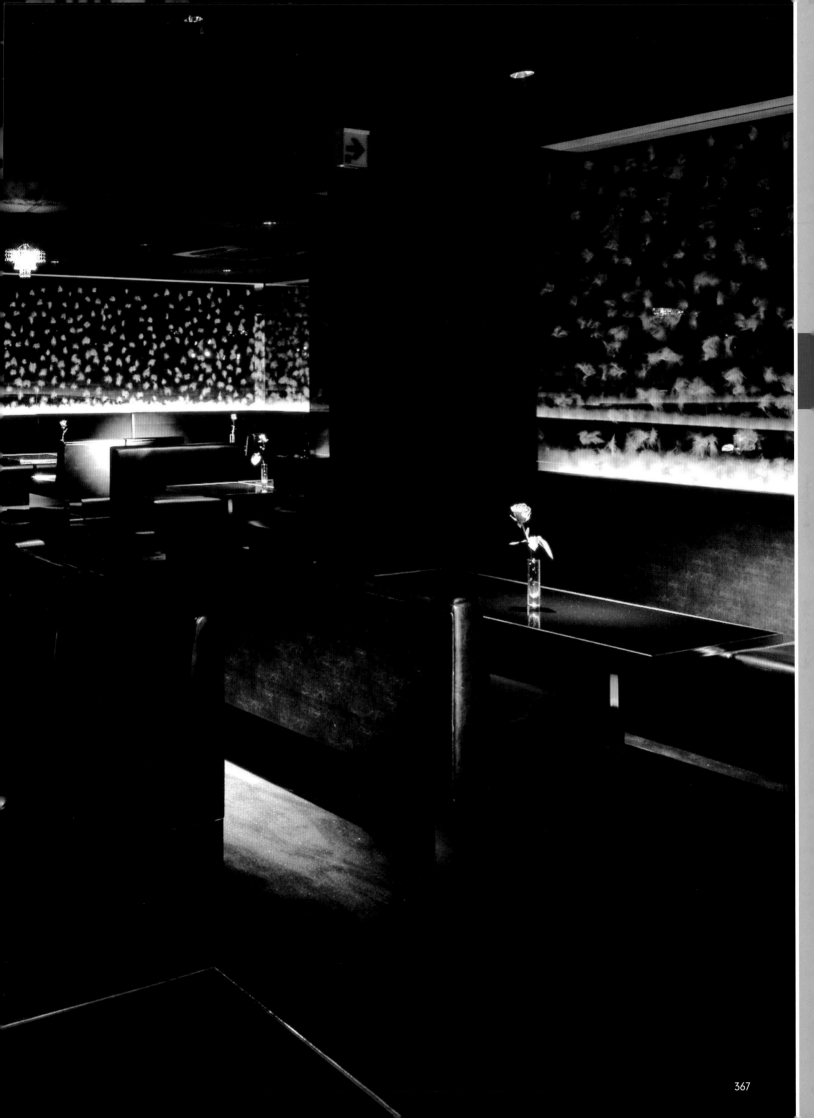

The amorphous shapes in this Bucarest club present a modern interpretation of embryonic human development. The club's walls as well as its seats have been designed in imitation of cell membranes and the curving red architectural elements inspire associations with that elixir of life. The intense light effects, part of the club's overall concept, are reflected in the white, epoxied resin floor, the white walls and furniture and offer a diverse backdrop for those nights of dancing.

Die amorphen Formen dieses Bukarester Clubs zeigen eine moderne Interpretation der menschlichen embryonalen Entwicklung. So erinnern Wände und Sitzgelegenheiten an Zellmembranen und die rot geschwungenen Geländer wecken Assoziationen mit dem Lebenselixier. Die schrillen Lichteffekte, die zum Konzept des Clubs gehören, werden vom weißen Epoxydharzboden, den weißen Wänden und Möbeln reflektiert und bieten eine abwechslungsreiche Kulisse für durchtanzte Nächte.

Les formes irrégulières de ce club de Bucarest présentent une interprétation moderne du développement embryonnaire humain. Les murs et les fauteuils de ce club imitent le tissu cellulaire et les éléments architecturaux rouges et arrondis créent des associations d'idée autour de la vie. Les effets lumineux intenses, partie intégrante du concept du club, sont réfléchis par le sol de résine époxy blanche, les murs et le mobilier immaculés, mais offrent aussi différentes toiles de fond pour des nuits dansantes ininterrompues.

De amorfe vormen van deze club in Boekarest tonen een moderne opvatting van de ontwikkeling van het menselijk embryo. De wanden en zithoeken roepen associaties op met celmembranen. De schelle lichteffecten die tot het concept van de club behoren, worden door de witte vloeren van epoxyhars, de witte wanden en meubels gereflecteerd en bieden een gevarieerde achtergrond voor een hele nacht dansen.

The Cocoon Club fuses architecture, graphic arts and web design into a successful harmony. The most striking element is the main room's perforated wall panels, reminiscent of cell membranes. Visitors enter through openings in these 'membranes'. Amorphous, capsule-shaped rooms poke through this wall, to form a kind of 'cocooning' whenever you wish to withdraw from the club's action.

Im Cocoon Club verschmelzen Architektur, grafisches Programm sowie Medien- und Webdesign zu einer gelungenen Einheit. Das auffälligste Element sind die perforierten Wandflächen des Hauptraumes, die an Zellmembranen erinnern und durch deren Öffnungen der Besucher eintritt. Kapselartige, amorph geformte Räume durchstoßen diese Wand und ermöglichen „cocooning", den Rückzug aus dem aktiven Club-Geschehen.

L'harmonie du Cocoon Club est née de la fusion de l'architecture, des arts graphiques et du web design. Les éléments les plus notables sont des panneaux muraux perforés, rappelant le tissu cellulaire. Les visiteurs entrent par des ouvertures dans ce « tissu », constitué également de pièces en forme de capsules irrégulières, offrant un « cocon » pour se retirer hors de l'activité du club lorsque le besoin s'en fait sentir.

In de Cocoon Club versmelten architectuur, grafisch programma en media- en webdesign tot een geslaagde eenheid. Het opvallendste element zijn de geperforeerde wandvlakken van de hoofdruimte die aan celmembranen doen denken en waardoor de gasten de club betreden. Kokerachtige, amorf gevormde ruimten doorbreken deze wand en maken 'cocooning' mogelijk, het terugtrekken uit het actieve clubgebeuren.

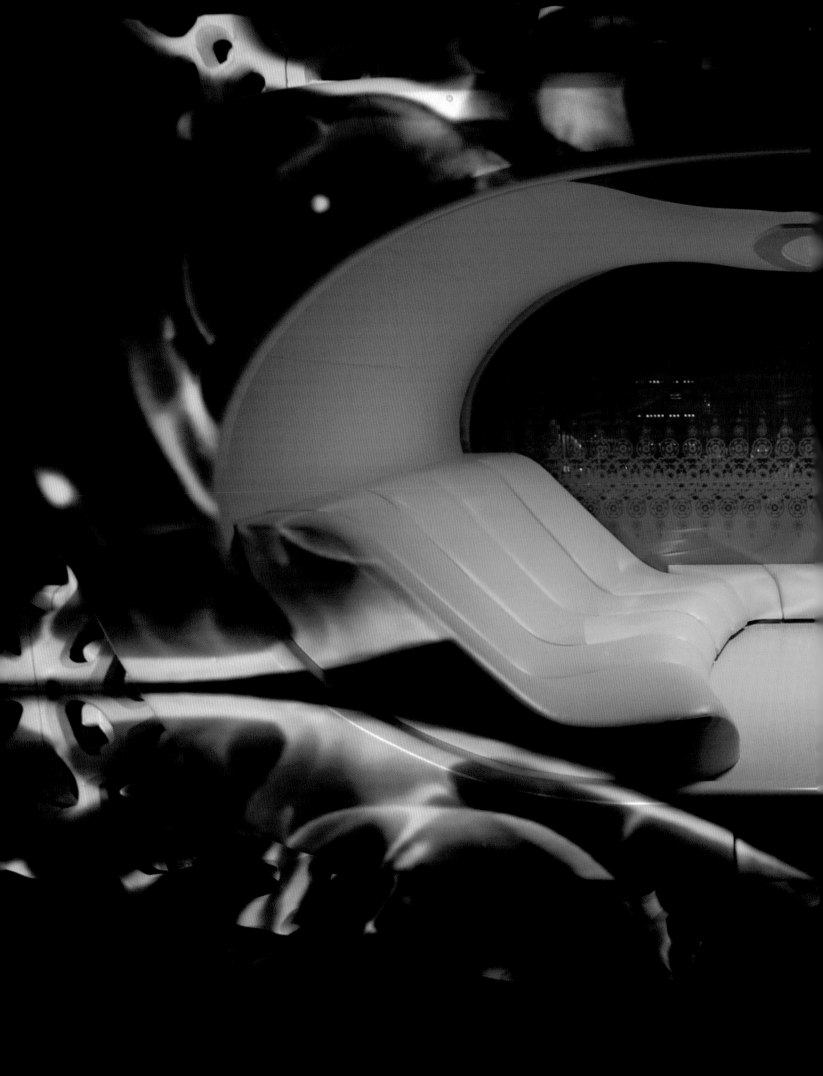

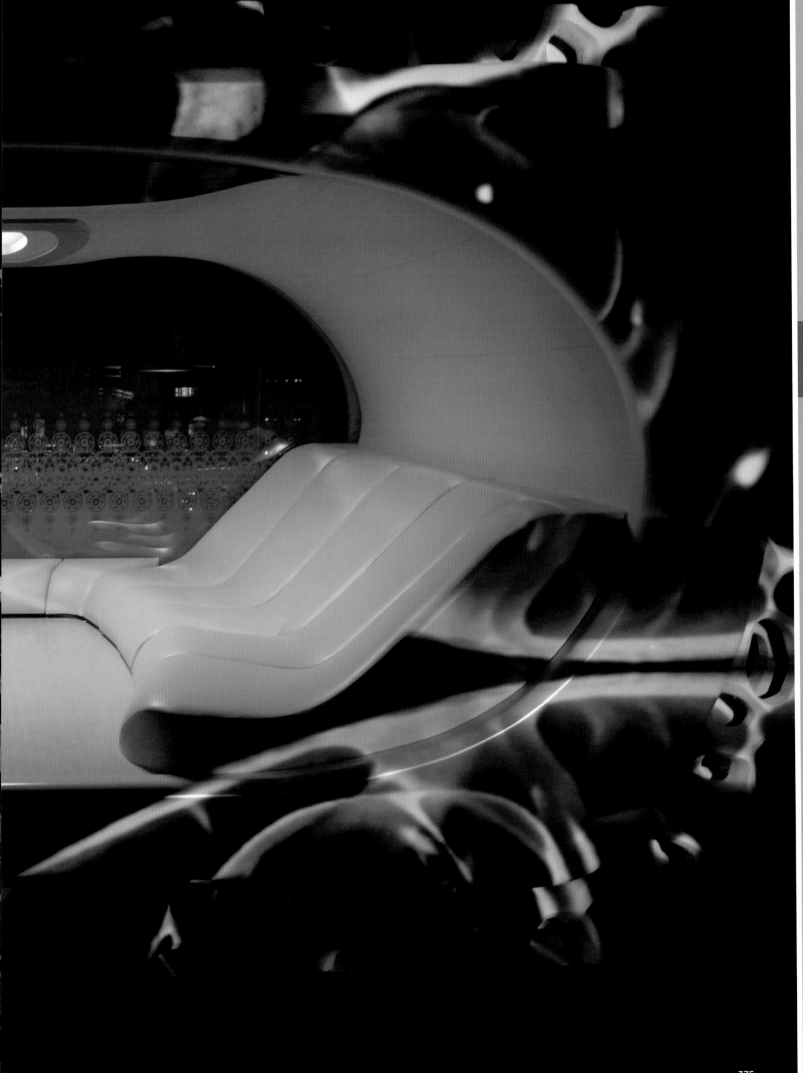

This fascinating newcomer to the Melbourne club scene captivates both with its choice of building and the design within. The club is housed in a turn-of-the-century building whose walls and doors glow in a brilliant white and whose interior is composed of a combination of antique furnishings and unique, custom-made design elements by Sawaya & Moroni.

Dieser faszinierende Neuling in der Melbourner Clubszene besticht durch die Wahl des Gebäudes und das Innendesign. Der Club ist in einem Gebäude der Jahrhundertwende untergebracht, dessen Wände und Türen in strahlendem Weiß leuchten und dessen Interieur aus einer vielschichtigen Kombination antiken Mobiliars und eigens angefertigter Einrichtungsunikate von Sawaya & Moroni gestaltet wurde.

Ce nouvel arrivant fascinant sur la scène nocturne de Melbourne captive à la fois par le bâtiment choisi que par sa décoration. Le club est abrité par un bâtiment fin de siècle dont les murs et les portes luisent d'un blanc brillant et dont l'intérieur est composé d'un mélange de mobilier antique et de pièces uniques faites sur commande par Sawaya & Moroni.

Deze fascinerende nieuwkomer in het uitgaansleven van Melbourne bekoort door de keuze van het gebouw en het interieur. De club is gehuisvest in een gebouw van rond de eeuwwisseling. De wanden en deuren zijn stralend wit en het interieur bestaat uit een complexe combinatie van antiek meubilair en door Sawaya & Moroni vervaardigde originele inrichtingsstukken.

The El Otro is not just a grandiose bar, but is also quite out of the ordinary in a city where minimalist modern design is hard to find. Despite the cool ambience, its guests are not at all pretentious. You will be won over by the first-class drinks selection, the friendly service and an appealing mix of music.

Das El Otro ist nicht nur eine grandiose Bar, sondern auch ungewöhnlich in einer Stadt, in der minimalistisch modernes Design eher selten zu finden ist. Trotz des coolen Ambientes sind die Gäste recht unprätentiös. Überzeugend sind die erstklassige Getränkeauswahl, das freundliche Personal und eine anspruchsvolle Musikmischung.

Le El Otro n'est pas qu'un bar grandiose, il sort aussi de l'ordinaire dans une ville où le design moderne minimaliste est quasi inexistant. En dépit d'une ambiance froide, ses clients ne sont pas du tout prétentieux. Vous serez gagné par une sélection de boissons de grande qualité, un service chaleureux et un mix musical bien léché.

De El Otro is niet alleen een geweldige bar, maar het is ook een uitzondering in een stad waar minimalistisch modern design bijna niet te vinden is. Ondanks de hippe uitstraling, hebben de gasten niet te veel pretenties. De keuze aan eersteklas drankjes, het vriendelijke personeel en de aansprekende muziek zijn overtuigend.

After its restructuring, the old Allianz Villa, so rich in tradition, now shines with fresh luster. Whether over coffee in one of the comfortable salons, after shopping or in the evening with friends, this club offers the right ambience for any time of day. Its 7530 square feet (700 square meters) unite historic charm with modern design. In the financial quarter, vis-à-vis the old Opera, rooms have been created the likes of which have never been seen in Frankfurt before.

Nach Umgestaltung der alten Allianz-Villa erstrahlt nun die traditionsreiche Bausubstanz in neuem Glanz. Ob bei einem Kaffee in einem der bequemen Salons, ob nach dem Einkauf oder am Abend mit Freunden, der Club bietet für jede Tageszeit das passende Ambiente. Auf 700 Quadratmetern vereint sich historischer Charme mit modernem Design. Im Bankenviertel, vis-a-vis der Alten Oper, wurden Räume geschaffen, wie es sie in dieser Form in Frankfurt bisher nicht gab.

Après sa restructuration, l'ancienne Allianz-Villa, si riche de traditions, brille d'un nouvel éclat. A l'heure du café après du shopping, dans un des confortables salons, ou le soir, entre amis, ce club permet une ambiance adaptée à tout moment de la journée. Ses 700 mètres carrés unissent le charme historique au design moderne. Au quartier des affaires, face à l'Opéra, est apparu un club que Francfort n'avait encore jusque-là jamais imaginé.

Na de herinrichting van de oude Allianz Villa schittert het traditierijke gebouw in nieuwe glorie. Of nu voor een kopje koffie in een van de comfortabele salons, voor een drankje na het winkelen of 's avonds met vrienden, de club biedt op elk tijdstip van de dag de juiste sfeer. Op 700 vierkante meter vereent de club historische charme met modern design. In de financiële wijk, tegenover de oude opera, werden interieurs gecreëerd die in Frankfurt tot nu toe ongekend waren.

Slow dining is the catch phrase of this harmonically arranged place of quiet, with an emphasis on beige and earth tones. A place which seems like a dusky cloister, enchanting with its mystical character. Blooming Japanese cherry trees pop up as a motif on the walls, the floor and the tabletops.

Slow dining ist das Motto dieses harmonisch gegliederten Ortes der Ruhe, in dem Beige und natürliche Töne dominieren. Ein Ort, der wie ein dämmeriges Kloster mit mystischem Charakter wirkt. Blühende japanische Kirschbäume tauchen als Motiv an den Wänden, auf dem Fußboden und den Tischplatten auf.

« Prendre le temps » est le slogan de cet harmonieux lieu de silence, aux tonalités de beiges et de couleurs terriennes. Voici une sorte de cloitre aux tons mats et enchanteur par son caractère mystique. Les murs, le sol et les tables sont parés de branches de cerisiers du Japon en fleurs.

Slow dining is het motto van deze harmonisch ingedeelde plek van rust, waar beige en natuurlijke tinten overheersen. Een plek die aandoet als een schemerig klooster met mystiek karakter. Bloeiende Japanse kersenbomen verschijnen als motief aan de wanden, op de vloer en de tafelbladen.

Everything in this club is white: walls, floors, furniture and lamps. Rounded window apertures and space-age curves define the futuristic design. The entry area is decorated with a spacious aquarium filled with Japanese carp. Inside, three different bars and a dance floor await the guest.

Alles in diesem Club ist weiß: Wände, Böden, Möbel und Lampen. Abgerundete Fensteröffnungen und eine geschwungene Linienführung zeichnen das futuristische Design aus. Der Eingangsbereich wird von einem großzügigen Aquarium mit japanischen Karpfen geschmückt. Im Inneren erwarten den Gast drei verschiedene Bars und eine Tanzfläche.

Tout dans ce club est blanc : murs, sols, mobilier et lampes. Des fenêtres arrondies et des courbes futuristes définissent son design avant-gardiste. L'entrée est décorée d'aquariums spacieux habités par des carpes japonaises. A l'intérieur, trois bars et une piste de danse attendent le visiteur.

Alles in deze club is wit: wanden, vloeren, meubels en lampen. Afgeronde raamopeningen en vloeiende lijnen kenmerken het futuristische design. De toegang tot de club wordt versierd door een groot aquarium met Japanse karpers. Binnen staat de gast drie verschillende bars en een dansvloer te wachten.

This club's essential characteristic is its backdrop. Amorphous silver-gray lines and bubble shapes run along the walls, exuberantly Oriental patterns reach up to the ceiling while an illuminated wall of drinks greets you from behind the bar. Walls, décor, shapes and surfaces coalesce in a stimulating ambience, the effect of which is enhanced by the dramatic lighting.

Charakteristisches Merkmal dieses Clubs ist die Hintergrundkulisse. Silbergraue amorphe Linien und Blasen ziehen sich an den Wänden entlang, überbordend orientalische Muster ragen zur Decke hoch und hinter der Bar betört eine beleuchtete Getränkewand. Wände, Einrichtung sowie die Flächen und Formen verdichten sich zu einem aufregenden Ambiente, dessen Wirkung durch die dramatische Beleuchtung noch verstärkt wird.

La caractéristique essentielle de ce club est sa toile de fond. Des lignes irrégulières gris-argenté et des bulles courent le long des murs, des motifs orientaux exubérants montent jusqu'au plafond, tandis qu'un mur de bouteilles illuminées derrière le bar vous invite à la fête. Murs, décor, formes et surfaces s'unissent en une ambiance stimulante, dont l'effet est accentué par un éclairage bien particulier.

Karakteristiek kenmerk van deze club is de achtergrond. Zilvergrijze amorfe lijnen en bellen verdelen zich over de wanden, weelderige oriëntaalse patronen stijgen op tot het plafond en achter de bar betovert een verlichte drankwand. De wanden, de inrichting en ook de vlakken en vormen versterken elkaar tot een opwindende ambiance en het effect wordt door de dramatische verlichting nog geïntensiveerd.

This eminent club offers a casual dinner experience and the new interpretation of an English gentlemen's club. The elegant interior design combines clear modern lines with sensuous materials such as silk, leather and solid wood surfaces. The whole club stretches over a single level and is dominated by exceptional pieces such as the illuminated horse by Front Design.

Dieser besondere Club bietet ein legeres Dinner-Erlebnis und die Neuinterpretation eines englischen Herren-Clubs. Das elegante Innendesign kombiniert klare moderne Linien, mit sinnlichen Materialien wie Seide, Leder und Oberflächen aus Massivholz. Der gesamte Club erstreckt sich über eine Etage und wird von ausgefallenen Objekten, wie das beleuchtete Pferd von Front Design dominiert.

Ce club réputé offre une expérience dinatoire désinvolte ainsi qu'une réinterprétation du cercle masculin à l'anglaise. Cette élégante décoration intérieure combine des lignes modernes nettes à des matériaux voluptueux tels que la soie, le cuir et d'imposantes surfaces en bois. Le club s'étend sur un étage et présente des pièces exceptionnelles, telles que ce cheval illuminé de Front Design.

Deze bijzondere club staat in voor een ongedwongen dinerbelevenis en is een moderne interpretatie van een Engelse herenclub. Het elegante interieur combineert duidelijke lijnen met moderne en zinnelijke materialen als zijde, leer en oppervlakken van massief hout. De club beslaat een verdieping en wordt gedicteerd door excentrieke voorwerpen zoals het verlichte paard van Front Design.

"Food, art and music" – a successful combination. The owners have transformed an 18th-century townhouse in London's city center into an avant-garde address of the first order. Here you will find restaurants, bars and an art gallery. The interior design is bold and extravagant, with a décor in the Louis XVI style, unique LED installations and plastic coffee stains on the staircase. Particular highlights are the toilet stalls underneath a glass ceiling in the shape of dinosaur eggs.

„Food, Art and Music" – eine gelungene Kombination. Die Inhaber haben ein Stadthaus aus dem 18. Jahrhundert in Londons Innenstadt in eine Avantgarde-Adresse erster Klasse verwandelt. Hier befinden sich Restaurants, Bars und eine Kunstgalerie. Die Innenausstattung ist extravagant und schrill, Interieur im Stil Ludwigs XVI., einzigartige LED-Installationen oder Plastik-Kaffeeflecken auf der Treppe. Besonderer Clou sind die Toilettenkabinen unter dem Glasdach in Form von Dinosaurier-Eiern.

« Nourriture, art et musique » : une recette à succès. Les propriétaires ont transformé cette maison de ville du XVIIIe siècle du centre de Londres en une adresse avant-gardiste de premier choix. Ici vous trouverez des restaurants, des bars et une galerie d'art. La décoration intérieure est audacieuse et extravagante : style Louis XVI, installations de LED et tâches de café en plastique dans les escaliers. Les toilettes en forme d'œufs de dinosaure trônant sous un plafond de verre sont remarquables.

'Food, art and music' – een geslaagde combinatie. De eigenaars hebben een stadshuis uit de achttiende eeuw in de Londense binnenstad getransformeerd tot een eersterangs avant-gardeadres. Het omvat restaurants, bars en een kunstgalerie. De inrichting is extravagant en schril: interieur in de stijl van Lodewijk XVI, unieke led-installaties en plastic koffievlekken op de trap. Klapstuk zijn de toilethokjes onder het glazen dak in de vorm van dinosauruseieren.

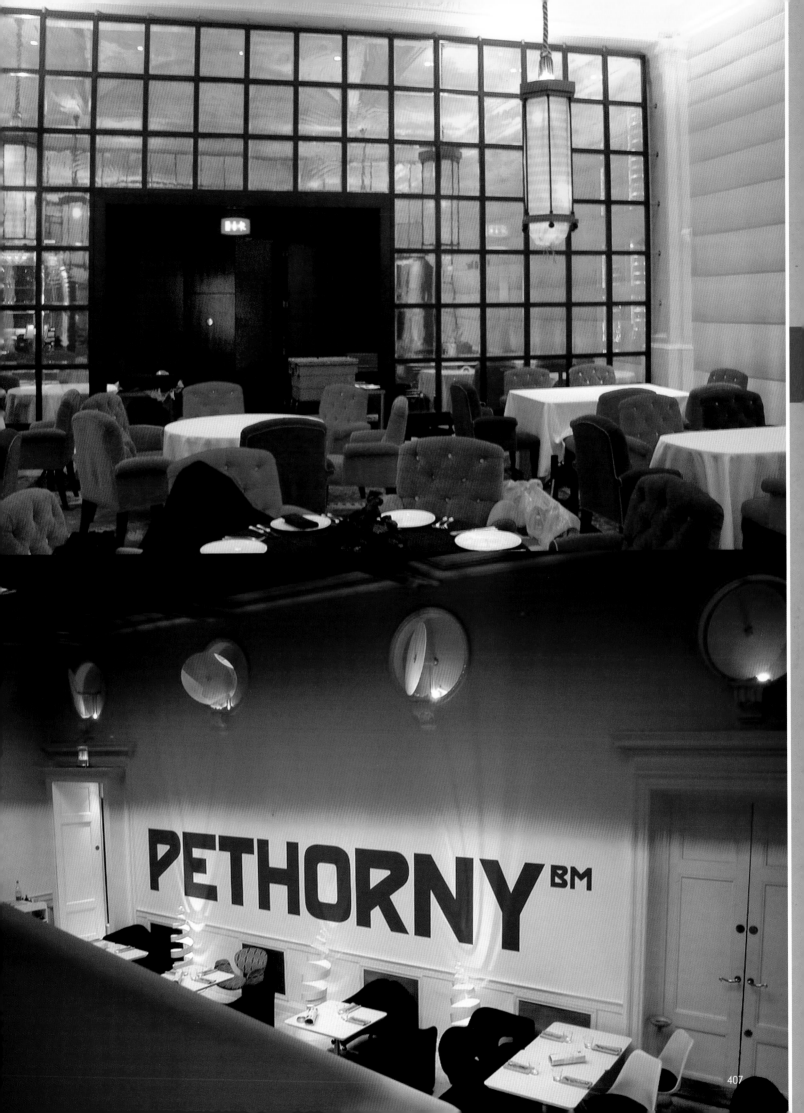

Right in the heart of Berlin, the 17th floor of a 1970s highrise offers grandiose views over the German capital. Its guests relax in roomy sofas or on top of swinging benches. A winding staircase leads from the lounge into the restaurant below. Cream-white upholstered chairs, cloth lampshades and dark wood present a refined dining atmosphere.

Im Herzen Berlins bietet sich von der 17. Etage eines in den siebziger Jahren erbauten Hochhauses ein grandioser Blick über die Stadt. Die Gäste entspannen in großzügigen Sofa-Landschaften oder Schaukeln. Eine Wendeltreppe führt von der Lounge ins darunter gelegene Restaurant. Gepolsterte Stühle in Cremeweiß, mit Stoff bezogene Lampenschirme und dunkles Holz bieten ein klassisches Dinner-Ambiente.

En plein cœur de Berlin, le 17ème étage d'un building des années 70 offre une vue grandiose sur la capitale allemande. Ses hôtes peuvent se relaxer sur de spacieuses banquettes ou de confortables balançoires. Un escalier en colimaçon mène du salon au restaurant. Les chaises crème, les abat-jours de tissu et le bois sombre y forment une atmosphère raffinée.

In hartje Berlijn kijkt de zeventiende verdieping van een in de jaren zeventig gebouwde flatgebouw prachtig uit over de stad. De gasten komen tot rust op ruime banken of schommels. Een wenteltrap voert van de lounge naar het onder gelegen restaurant. Crèmekleurig beklede stoelen, stoffen lampenkappen en donker hout verlenen de interieurs een klassieke sfeer.

Architect Matthias Müller topped the "Kaiser Turm" (Kaiser's Tower) monument with a glass cube during its renovation. Lovers of nightlife will find a new meeting place here. The lounge greets its guests with a flood of light and a unique view. Clear design in glass, steel and white furnishings is deftly combined with cool-colored sofa arrangements.

Dem Industriedenkmal „Kaiser Turm" setzte der Architekt Matthias Müller bei der Sanierung einen Glaskubus auf. In diesem findet sich ein neuer Treffpunkt der Nachtschwärmer. Lichtdurchflutet und mit einzigartigem Rundumblick präsentiert sich die Lounge den Gästen. Klares Design in Glas, Stahl und weißen Möbeln wird mit Sofa-Landschaften in kühlen Farben geschickt kombiniert.

Lors de la rénovation de la Kaiser Turm (La tour du Kaiser), l'architecte Matthias Müller l'a coiffé d'un cube de verre. Les gens de la nuit y trouveront un nouveau lieu de rencontres. Le salon accueille ses hôtes par un flot de lumière et une vue imprenable. La décoration de verre, acier et mobilier blanc est adroitement combinée à la disposition des banquettes aux couleurs chaudes.

De architect Matthias Müller liet tijdens de restauratie van het industriemonument 'Kaiser Turm' een glazen kubus plaatsen. Hierin bevindt zich een nieuwe ontmoetingsplek voor nachtbrakers. De lichte lounge biedt unieke vergezichten. Helder design met glas, staal en witte meubels worden kundig gecombineerd met banken in koele kleuren.

Many consider this to be the greatest club in the world. Supper clubs are far more than mere restaurants. Anyone who dines here will be presented with all the latest from the worlds of art, cuisine, fashion, music, style and performance – all at the same time. From the outside, the club looks like a gigantic metal air bubble and from the inside it's pure "2001 – a Space Odyssey", and all of it is bathed in blue and pink light – this is how you experience the Bed Supperclub.

Für viele gilt er als der beste Club der Welt. Supperclubs sind mehr als Restaurants. Wer hier diniert, dem werden die neuesten Formeln für Essen, Kunst, Mode, Musik, Performance und Style präsentiert. Und das alles auf einmal. Der Club sieht von außen aus wie eine gigantische Luftblase aus Metall, jetzt noch innen die Optik von „2001 – Space Odyssey" dazu und das alles in blaues und rosa Licht getaucht – so hat man den Bed Supperclub vor Augen.

Pour certains, c'est le meilleur club du monde. Les Supper Clubs sont bien plus que des restaurants. Quiconque y dîne rencontrera la crème des mondes de l'art, de la cuisine, de la mode, de la musique, du style et de la performance. Et tous ensembles. De l'extérieur, ce club ressemble à une gigantesque bulle d'air en métal, tandis qu'à l'intérieur se joue « 2001, l'odyssée de l'espace », baigné dans une lumière bleue et rose. Voilà ce qu'est l'expérience Bed Supperclub.

Voor velen geldt deze club als de beste ter wereld. Zoals het een echte supperclub betaamt, krijgt men hier de nieuwste formules voor eten, kunst, mode, muziek, performance en style voorgeschoteld – en weliswaar allemaal tegelijk. De club ziet er aan de buitenkant uit als een enorme luchtbel van metaal, daarbij komt een voorkomen als in de film '2001: A Space Odyssey' en het geheel gehuld in blauw en roze licht – zo moet men zich het Bed Supperclub voorstellen.

Even starting with the name, this club is closely connected with Theodor Heuss Street and inspires numerous associations with the German President and the eponymous Party Mile. These are also reflected in the club's interior design. Both the furniture and installations are in solid black and white. The tarred floor and black plank walls are illustrated with contrasting white graphics.

Dieser Club ist schon vom Namen her eng mit der Theodor-Heuss-Straße verbunden und weckt zahlreiche Assoziationen mit dem Bundespräsidenten und der gleichnamigen Partymeile. Diese finden sich auch in der Gestaltung der Innenräume wieder. Ausschließlich in Schwarz-Weiß gehaltene Möbel und Einbauten wurden hier verwendet. Der geteerte Boden und die schwarzen Bretterwände werden von plakativen weißen Grafiken bespielt.

Par son seul nom, ce club est étroitement lié à la Theodor Heuss Street et inspire de nombreuses associations entre le président allemand et la « rue de la nuit » éponyme. Elles sont également présentes dans la décoration intérieure. Le mobilier et les installations sont parés de noir et de blancs profonds. Le sol goudronné et les murs de planches noires sont illustrés de motifs blancs contrastés.

Deze club is al door de naam nauw verbonden met de Theodor-Heuss-Strasse en roept talrijke associaties op met de bondspresident en het gelijknamige uitgaansgebied. Deze komen ook terug in de vormgeving van de interieurs. Er werden uitsluitend zwart-witte meubels en inbouwconstructies gebruikt. De geteerde vloer en het zwarte plankenbeschot zijn getooid met opvallende, witte grafische kunstwerken.

Light, floors, walls and overall design are presented in harmonized tones of violet. The challenge was to dramatize the materials, passageways and different levels. Together with the purposefully whimsical design and the hand-crafted wallpaper, the club offers a wealth of contrasts and is vaguely reminiscent of an off-the-wall western saloon.

Licht, Böden, Wände und Design sind in aufeinander abgestimmten und violetten Farbtönen gehalten. Die Herausforderung war, Materialien, Übergänge und verschiedene Stockwerke zu dramatisieren. Zusammen mit der ausgewählt skurrilen Einrichtung und den handgefertigten Tapeten bietet der Club somit eine Fülle an Kontrasten und erinnert einen an einen – durchgeknallten – Westernsalon.

Lumières, sols, murs et design dans son ensemble forment un camaïeu de violet. Le challenge était de théâtraliser les matériaux, les couloirs et les différents étages. Le design intentionnellement fantasque et le papier peint artisanal permettent à ce club de provoquer les contrastes et de rappeler vaguement un excentrique saloon de western.

Licht, vloeren, wanden en design zijn uitgevoerd in op elkaar afgestemde paarse kleurtinten. De uitdaging bestond erin om materialen, overgangen en verschillende verdiepingen te dramatiseren. Samen met de onmiskenbaar zonderlinge inrichting en het handgemaakte behang biedt de club een verscheidenheid aan contrasten en herinnert aan een – gesjeesde – westernsaloon.

425

In 1916 a neoclassical shopping paradise was constructed at the prominent "Three on the Bund" address, which, after extensive renovation, now boasts three of the best clubs and restaurants in the city. The club can be seen as a successful fusion of art deco and traditional Chinese elements. Exclusive materials give the room an atmosphere of luxury and glamour.

An der prominenten Adresse „Three on the Bund" entstand 1916 ein neoklassizistisches Shopping-Paradies, das aufwendig renoviert, drei der besten Clubs und Restaurants der Stadt vorweist. Der Club versteht sich als eine gelungene Fusion des Art déco mit traditionellen chinesischen Elementen. Exklusive Materialien verleihen den Räumen eine Atmosphäre von Luxus und Glamour.

En 1916, un paradis néoclassique du shopping fut construit à cette adresse appartenant à « Three on the Bund », qui, après une rénovation considérable peut se targuer aujourd'hui de regrouper trois des meilleurs clubs et restaurants de la ville. Le club est une fusion épatante d'art déco et de tradition chinoise. Les matériaux exclusifs donnent à la pièce une atmosphère évoquant luxe et glamour.

Op het prominente adres 'Three on the Bund' ontstond in 1916 een neoklassiek winkelparadijs dat grondig werd opgeknapt en drie van de beste clubs en restaurants van de stad te bieden heeft. De club is bedoeld als een geslaagde fusie tussen art deco met traditionele Chinese elementen. Exclusieve materialen verlenen de vertrekken een sfeer van luxe en glamour.

MALLS AND STORES

SHOPPING

The 3Retail provides its fastidious Shanghai clientele with exclusive fashion labels, shoes and cosmetics. Large, freestanding changing rooms look like oversized cocoons in the middle of the room, suggesting that you have changed more than just your outfit when you emerge.

Im 3Retail werden exklusive Modelabels, Schuhe und Kosmetik einer verwöhnten Shanghaier Klientel angeboten. Große, frei im Raum platzierte Umkleidekabinen wirken wie übergroße Kokons, in denen die Anprobe als Akt der Verwandlung inszeniert wird.

Le 3Retail fournit à sa clientèle huppée de Shanghai les marques, chaussures et cosmétiques dernier cri. Au beau milieu du magasin, les spacieuses cabines d'essayage ressemblent à des cocons surdimensionnés, laissant penser qu'en en sortant, on y a changé bien plus que sa tenue.

In het 3Retail worden exclusieve modelabels, schoenen en cosmetica aangeboden aan een verwend Sjanghais clientèle. Grote, vrij in de ruimte geplaatste paskamers doen denken aan grote cocons, waarin het passen van kleding tot een metamorfosehandeling verwordt.

The visitor must walk through the so-called "fog wall" to enter this futuristic lounge under the ownership of an Austrian cell phone provider. The lounge's glass façade is filled with an artificial mist, an electronic control system continuously altering its density. The interior contains tables which, equipped with LCDs, appear to glow from within. The integrated displays show real and planned products. A ramp takes the visitor past holograms of future products and up to the cafe and lounge on the second floor.

Um ins Innere der futuristischen Lounge eines österreichischen Mobilfunkanbieters zu gelangen, muss die so genannte fog wall passiert werden. Zwischenräume der Glasfassade sind mit künstlichem Nebel gefüllt, dessen Dichte elektronisch gesteuert werden kann. Im Innenraum stehen Tische, die, ausgestattet mit LCDs, von innen heraus zu leuchten scheinen. Die integrierten Displays zeigen reale und geplante Produkte. Eine Rampe bringt den Besucher, vorbei an Hologrammen zukünftiger Produkte, in das Obergeschoss mit Café und Lounge.

Il faut traverser un « écran de fumée » pour pénétrer dans ce salon futuriste, tenu par un fournisseur de téléphonie mobile autrichien. La façade de verre du salon est teintée d'un brouillard artificiel dont l'opacité est contrôlée de manière continue par un système électronique. A l'intérieur, les tables équipées d'écrans LCD semblent rayonner de l'intérieur. Les écrans intégrés présentent des produits en vente ou au stade de la conception. Une rampe conduit le visiteur, à travers des hologrammes des projets à venir, vers le second étage où se trouvent le café et le restaurant.

Om de futuristische lounge van een Oostenrijkse mobiele telefoonaanbieder te betreden, moet men eerst de zogeheten fog wall passeren. De tussenruimten van de glasfaçade zijn gevuld met kunstmist en de dichtheid wordt elektronisch gestuurd. De tafels binnen, die zijn uitgerust met lcd's, lijken van binnenuit te stralen. De geïntegreerde displays tonen bestaande en geplande producten. Een platform brengt de bezoeker, via hologrammen van toekomstige producten, naar de bovenverdieping met café en lounge.

a1 lounge

og bar
   conference
eg news
ug shop

↖ bar
   conferen

439

The footwear brand's hometown is now the home of a shop which puts the legendary retro sneaker into a contemporary framework. The display, fitting room and retail area are all in one area, there are no permanent installations and the products are presented on large-scale tables. Shoes are attached to mobile wall elements without any visible supports. The secret: magnets. The visitor enters the retail area, located in a former garage, without having to negotiate any threshold.

In der Geburtstadt der Originals-Kollektion wurde jetzt ein Shop eröffnet, der den Mythos der Retro-Sneaker zeitgemäß umsetzt. Das Ausstellen, Anprobieren und Kaufen findet an einem Ort statt, es gibt keine festen Einbauten, und das Angebot wird auf großformatigen Tischen präsentiert. An den mobilen Wandelementen sind die Waren ohne eine sichtbare Tragstruktur mit Magneten befestigt. Der Kunde betritt den in einer ehemaligen Garage untergebrachten Verkaufsraum ohne eine Schwelle zu überwinden.

La ville natale de la marque de sport compte désormais une boutique intégrant la légendaire chaussure retro dans un cadre contemporain. Un espace unique abrite les articles et les cabines d'essayage : il n'y a aucun présentoir permanent et les articles sont posés sur de larges tables. Les chaussures sont attachées à des panneaux mobiles par des supports invisibles. Le secret ? Des aimants. Le visiteur pénètre dans la boutique, située dans un ancien garage, sans avoir à passer de porte.

In de geboortestad van de originals-collectie is nu een winkel geopend die de mythe van de retrosneaker eigentijds vertaalt. De presentatie van de producten, het aanpassen en de aankoop vinden plaats in dezelfde ruimte. De producten worden op grote tafels uitgestald of met magneten aan de mobiele wandelementen bevestigd. De klant betreedt de in een voormalige garage gehuisveste verkoopruimte zonder over een drempel te hoeven stappen.

The New York designer's modern and innovative design concept casts the right kind of spotlight on the Alessi line. A clever display system presents the Italian dishes, glasses and household appliances. Sensationally illuminated crevices in the white walls and ceiling accentuate this snazzy image. For the caffeine-deprived, an espresso bar awaits in the back of the store.

Das moderne und innovative Designkonzept der New Yorker Gestalter rückt die Alessi-Produktpalette ins richtige Licht. Ein ausgeklügeltes Steck-System präsentiert die italienischen Schalen, Gläser und Haushaltsgeräte. Effektvoll beleuchtete Risse in den weißen Wänden und Decken akzentuieren das gelungene Konzept. Im hinteren Bereich des Ladens findet sich eine Espressobar.

Le nouveau concept de design moderne et innovant du créateur New Yorkais met réellement en valeur la ligne Alessi. Un système intelligent d'écrans présente les plats, verres et articles de maison italiens. Des fissures dans les murs et le plafond blancs, éclairées magistralement, accentuent cette image très sympathique. Un bar à expresso attend les accros à la caféine au fond du magasin.

Het moderne en innovatieve designconcept van de New Yorkse ontwerpers plaatst het productaanbod van Alessi in het juiste licht. Op het geraffineerde schappensysteem staan de Italiaanse schalen, glazen en huishoudelijke voorwerpen geëtaleerd. De effectvol verlichte scheuren in de witte wanden en plafonds accentueren het geslaagde concept. Achterin de winkel bevindt zich een espressobar.

Simple shapes, clear lines and an elegant selection of materials: these were all prerequisites for this Japanese flagship. The façade is divided in two: above, brushed stainless steel panels clad the renovated office building while unframed, ceiling-high windows look out at street level. These allow you a glimpse of the spectacular winding glass staircase inside the store. This draws the visitor in and up to the second level with its presentation areas, bar and conference room.

Einfache Formen, klare Linien und eine elegante Materialauswahl, das waren die Vorgaben für den japanischen Flagship-store. Die Fassade ist zweigeteilt: Oben verkleiden Paneele aus gebürstetem Edelstahl das renovierte Bürogebäude, auf Straßenniveau stehen rahmenlose, raumhohe Fensterbänder. Diese erlauben einen flüchtigen Blick ins Innere auf die spektakuläre Glas-Wendeltreppe. Diese zieht den Besucher hinein und führt ihn in das Obergeschoss mit Präsentations-flächen, einer Bar und Konferenzraum.

Des formes simples, des lignes épurées et une élégante sélection de matières étaient les seuls besoins de ce représen-tant japonais de la marque. La façade est divisée en deux : au-dessus, des panneaux d'inox brossé recouvrent le bâtiment rénové tandis que des baies vitrées sans cadre permettent l'entrée par la rue. Celles-ci permettent de jeter un coup d'œil au spectaculaire escalier tournant de verre dans le magasin, conduisant le visiteur jusqu'au second étage et ses espaces de vente, son bar et sa salle de conférence.

Eenvoudige vormen, duidelijke lijnen en een elegante materiaalkeuze waren de uitgangspunten voor de Japanse flagship-store. De gevel is in tweeën gedeeld: boven verhullen panelen van geborsteld roestvrij staal het gerenoveerde kantoorge-bouw en op straatniveau bevindt zich een reeks kamerhoge, smalle vensters. De ramen maken het mogelijk een vluchtige blik naar binnen te werpen op de spectaculaire glazen wenteltrap. De trap lokt de bezoeker naar binnen en voert hem naar de bovenverdieping met de tentoongespreide collectie, een bar en een conferentieruimte.

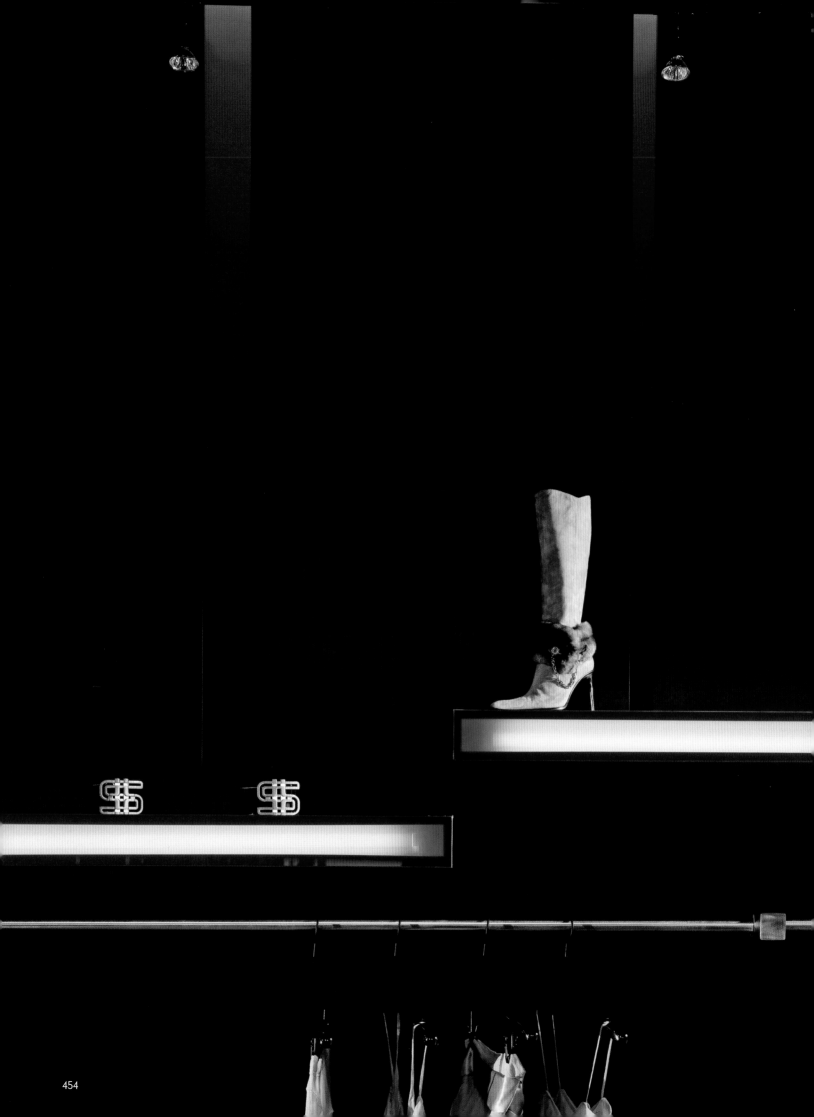

B8 Couture is a popular boutique in the heart of Paris. The offbeat interior design in blacks and purples is sensationally shown off by the use of well-chosen lighting. The perfect platform for the fashionable creations of designers J. Lindeberg, Julien MacDonald and Stella Cadente.

B8 Couture ist eine angesagte Boutique im Herzen von Paris. Das ausgefallene Innendesign in violetten und schwarzen Farben wird durch geschickt plazierte Lichtquellen eindrucksvoll in Szene gesetzt. Eine ideale Bühne für die modischen Artikel der Designer J. Lindeberg, Julien MacDonald, Stella Cadente.

B8 Couture est une boutique populaire située au cœur de Paris. La décoration intérieure originale en noir et violet est incroyablement mise en valeur par un éclairage savamment choisi. C'est la plateforme parfaite aux créations tendance des designers J. Lindeberg, Julien MacDonald et Stella Cadente.

B8 Couture is een geliefde boetiek in hartje Parijs. Het aparte interieurdesign met paarse en zwarte kleuren wordt door de geraffineerd opgestelde lichtbronnen indrukwekkend gearrangeerd. Een ideale schouwplaats voor de modieuze artikelen van de designers J. Lindeberg, Julien MacDonald en Stella Cadente.

The architects responsible for Bellucci succeeded in connecting two existing retail spaces. The midsection, where the changing rooms are located, symmetrically divides the store and separates it into a men's and women's department. This also explains the choice of materials and colors: on one side dark masculine hues prevail while the other is warmer and more feminine.

Zwei bestehende Ladenflächen wurden von den Architekten zusammengefügt. Der Mittelteil mit seinen Umkleidekabinen macht den Laden symmetrisch und trennt ihn gleichzeitig in einen Frauen- und Männerteil. So ist dann auch die Auswahl der Materialien und Farben zu verstehen: einerseits männlich hart und andererseits weiblich warm.

Les architectes en charge du Bellucci ont réussi à connecter deux magasins pré-existants. La section intermédiaire, où sont situées les cabines d'essayage, divise symétriquement la boutique et la sépare en deux départements homme et femme. Ceci explique également le choix des matériaux et des couleurs : d'un côté des tonalités sombres et masculines, de l'autre, des tons plus chauds et féminins.

Twee bestaande winkels werden door de architect samengevoegd. Het middelste gedeelte met de kleedkamers maakt de winkel symmetrisch en scheidt hem tevens in een vrouwen- en mannengedeelte. En zo moet ook de keuze voor de materialen en kleuren worden opgevat: aan de ene kant mannelijk hard en aan de andere kant vrouwelijk warm.

Like all Bisazza's showrooms, this Paris flagship store displays various kinds of ambience, all clad in the new mosaic collection. Select design objects and individual pieces from the new Bisazza Home line complete the atmosphere. The exhibition space is reminiscent of a theater which gives free rein to the company's creativity and the mosaic's aesthetic quality.

Wie alle Showrooms von Bisazza präsentiert sich auch der Flagshipstore in Paris mit unterschiedlichen Wohnambienten, die alle mit den neuen Mosaikkollektionen verkleidet sind. Ausgewählte Designobjekte und Einzelstücke aus der neuen Linie Bisazza Home vervollständigen das Ambiente. Der Ausstellungsraum erinnert an ein Theater, das die kreative Ader des Unternehmens und die ästhetische Qualität des Mosaiks zur Geltung kommen lässt.

Comme tous les showrooms Bisazza, ce flagship store de Paris présente différents types d'ambiances, toutes revêtues de la nouvelle collection de mosaïques. Des objets design de choix et des éléments individuels de la nouvelle ligne Bisazza Home complètent l'atmosphère. L'espace d'exposition rappelle un théâtre, donnant libre cours à la créativité de la marque et aux qualités esthétiques des mosaïques.

Zoals alle showrooms van Bisazza presenteert ook de flagshipstore in Parijs verschillende woonstijlen die allen zijn aangekleed met de nieuwe mozaïekcollecties. Uitgelezen designobjecten en afzonderlijke stukken van de nieuwe lijn 'Bisazza Home' vullen de sfeer aan. De expositieruimte doet denken aan een theater dat het creatieve talent van de onderneming en de esthetische kwaliteit van het mozaïek tot zijn recht laat komen.

This shop is characterized by the interplay of raw materials and fine details. The boxes installed in the shop achieve a room-inside-a-room configuration which offers the visitor a stimulating walk through the store's inventory. Select classic furniture and natural materials enhance the collection's character and create an intriguing context with shiny, polished surfaces.

Der Shop wird durch das Zusammenspiel von roher Materialität und feinen Details charakterisiert. Eingestellte Boxen bewirken eine Raum-in-Raum-Konstellation, die dem Kunden einen spannungsreichen Parcours durch die Warenwelt bereitet. Ausgewählte Möbelklassiker und in ihrer Natürlichkeit belassene Materialien verstärken den Charakter der Kollektion und bilden in Kombination mit lackierten Flächen und glänzenden Oberflächen einen spannungsvollen Kontext.

Ce magasin se caractérise par l'interaction des matériaux bruts et des détails fins. Les box constituant la boutique créent une constellation de « pièces dans la pièce » offrant au visiteur un parcours stimulant à travers les collections. Un mobilier classique de choix et des matériaux bruts donnent du cachet aux produits et les surfaces brillantes et polies créent un contexte fascinant.

De winkel wordt gekenmerkt door het samenspel van ruwe stoffelijkheid en fijne details. De in de ruimte opgestelde boxen brengen een constellatie van 'ruimte in de ruimte' teweeg en leveren voor de klant een boeiend parcours op door de winkel. Uitgelezen meubelklassiekers en natuurlijke materialen versterken het karakter van de collectie en vormen in combinatie met gelakte vlakken en glanzende oppervlakken een spannende context.

The Camper shop is an exceptional locale with its mixture of Baroque and sleek elements in red, black, white and gold. The furniture pieces you see were specially conceived and handcrafted for the store: wooden tables with sculpted legs, terracotta lamps with innovative finishes and chairs with enormous backrests.

Die Mischung aus barocken und schlichten Elementen in Rot, Schwarz, Weiß und Gold machen den Camper-Shop zu einem ungewöhnlichen Ort. So wurden Möbelstücke speziell für den Shop konzipiert und handgefertigt: Holztische mit verschiedenen Beinen, Lampen aus Terrakotta mit einer neuartigen Oberfläche und Stühle mit überdimensionierten Lehnen.

Cette boutique Camper est un lieu exceptionnel, mêlant Baroque et éléments épurés rouges, noirs, blancs et dorés. Les meubles visibles ici ont été spécialement conçus et fabriqués pour la boutique : tables de bois aux pieds sculptés ; lampes en terre cuite aux finitions innovantes et fauteuils aux dossiers surdimensionnés.

De combinatie van barokke en sobere elementen in rood, zwart, wit en goud maken van de Camper-shop een ongebruikelijke plek. De meubels werden speciaal voor Camper ontworpen en met de hand gemaakt: houten tafels met verschillende poten, lampen van terracotta en stoelen met enorme leuningen.

This flagship store is located in a somber industrial building in the center of Tokyo. The goal of architect Hideo Yasui was to implement the design symbolic of the D Grace brand while emphasizing his concept of transparence, reduction and clarity. The design had to be integrated into the existing spaces and was created using glass, steel and light.

Dieser Flagshipstore befindet sich in einem nüchternen Industriegebäude im Zentrum von Tokio. Der Architekt Hideo Yasui hatte sich zum Ziel gesetzt, das Design, das die Marke D Grace symbolisiert, umzusetzen und sein Konzept wie Transparenz, Reduktion und Klarheit zu unterstreichen. Dies musste in bereits bestehende Räumlichkeiten integriert werden und wurde mit Glas, Stahl und Licht umgesetzt.

Ce flagship store se trouve dans un sombre bâtiment industriel du centre de Tokyo. Le but de l'architecte Hideo Yasui était de conserver le design symbolique de la marque D Grace tout en insistant sur son concept de transparence, minimalisme et clarté. Le design devait pouvoir s'intégrer aux espaces existants et fut réalisé à l'aide de verre, d'acier et de lumière.

Deze flagshipstore bevindt zich in een sober industriegebouw in het centrum van Tokyo. De architect Hideo Yasui had zich tot doel gesteld om het design, dat het merk D Grace symboliseert, te vertalen in transparantie, reductie en helderheid. Dit concept moest in reeds bestaande ruimten worden geïntegreerd en werd gerealiseerd met glas, staal en licht.

A presentation platform for internationally active interior brands was created under the name Design Post. The latest products and collections for living and working are displayed in the historic building which once was a post office. The seven monumental halls from 1913 were renovated into an airy and modern exhibition building, while not forgetting their historic significance.

Unter dem Namen Design Post wurde eine Präsentationsfläche für international agierende Interieurmarken geschaffen. In dem historischen Gebäude der ehemaligen Post werden die neusten Produkte und Kollektionen für Wohnen und Arbeiten gezeigt. Die sieben monumentalen Hallen aus dem Jahr 1913 wurden unter Beachtung der historischen Bedeutung zu einem modernen und leichten Ausstellungsgebäude umgebaut.

Une plateforme de présentation destinée aux marques d'intérieur internationales porte le nom de Design Post. Les produits et collections les plus récents dans le domaine de l'art de vivre et du travail sont présentés dans ce bâtiment historique qui fut autrefois une poste. Les sept halles monumentales datant de 1913 ont été rénovées et forment à présent un bâtiment d'exposition aéré et moderne, tout en ne dénaturant pas l'histoire dont elles sont chargées.

Onder de naam Design Post is een presentatieplatform voor internationaal actieve merken opgericht. De nieuwste producten en collecties voor leven en werken worden getoond in een historisch gebouw dat ooit dienst deed als postkantoor. De zeven monumentale hallen uit 1913 zijn gerenoveerd tot een modern en licht expositiegebouw, met behoud van de oorspronkelijke betekenis.

Like the proverbial red band, a strip of red fiberglass winds its way through the showroom. It rises up from the ground, turns into a table, rises again, then falls into the restaurant area, where it becomes a bar for drinks. This is contrasted by the other, more subdued, space-defining elements, such as the transparent glass panes separating the various areas. Satined steel furniture, upholstered with soft translucent textiles, ensures a well-balanced whole.

Wie der sprichwörtliche rote Faden windet sich ein dynamisches, rotes Band aus Fiberglas durch den Showroom. Es erhebt sich vom Boden, wird zum Tisch, steigt weiter an, sinkt im Restaurantbereich wieder, schließt sich und wird zur Bartheke. Die übrigen raumbildenden Elemente dagegen präsentieren sich zurückhaltend: Transparente Glasflächen trennen die verschiedenen Bereiche. Möbel aus satiniertem Stahl, bezogen mit weichem, transluzentem Textil, sorgen für ein ausgewogenes Gesamtbild.

Tel un fil rouge, une bande rouge en fibre de verre serpente dans le showroom. Elle s'élève du sol, se transforme en table, s'élève à nouveau pour retomber dans le restaurant et terminer sa course au bar. Le contraste est marqué, par d'autres éléments, plus discrets, de définition de l'espace, comme les panneaux de verre séparant les différentes zones. Un mobilier d'acier satiné, recouvert de textiles translucides assure un équilibre à l'ensemble.

Zoals de spreekwoordelijke rode draad baant een dynamisch, rood lint van fiberglas zich een weg door de showroom. Het verheft zich van de vloer, wordt tafel, stijgt weer omhoog, daalt neer in het restaurantgedeelte en wordt bar. De overige ruimtelijke elementen daarentegen zijn ingetogen: transparante glazen wandvlakken scheiden de verschillende gedeelten en meubels van glanzend staal, overtrokken met soepel, doorschijnend textiel, zorgen voor een evenwichtig totaalbeeld.

485

Elegance, purism and understatement are the values this Italian label opts for, as witnessed in the design of its shop. The interior is presented in a raw and natural look, reduced to a few select colors and materials arranged in bold, clear lines.

Eleganz, Purismus und Understatement sind Werte, die das italienische Label auch im Design seines Shops vermittelt. Die natürliche, auf wenige Farben und Materialien reduzierte Innenausstattung ist in klaren Linien arrangiert und wie maßgeschneidert für die präsentierte Damen- und Herrenmode.

Élégance et discrétion sont les valeurs dont la marque italienne peut se targuer, comme le prouve le design de sa boutique. La décoration intérieure est brute et naturelle, réduite à quelques couleurs bien choisies et à des matériaux utilisés dans des lignes épurées.

Elegantie, purisme en understatement zijn waarden die het Italiaanse label ook in het design van zijn winkel tot uiting brengt. De natuurlijke, op enkele kleuren en materialen gereduceerde inrichting is in duidelijke lijnen gearrangeerd.

This store is part of the Premium fashion fair, and it's no wonder you'll find such a great selection of high-end international labels, including Scandinavian designers such as Mads Norgaard, Unconditional from England and France's April 77. The "made in Berlin" theme can now also be found in the interior's street design. Jewelry boxes, seat cushions and coffee table books sit atop stacks of wooden palettes. The jeans display is equally far-out: the pants hang from the ceiling like fallen angels – only much more symmetrical.

Der Laden gehört zur Modemesse Premium, entsprechend findet man eine feine Auswahl gehobener internationaler Labels, so skandinavische Designer wie Mads Norgaard, Unconditional aus England und April 77 aus Frankreich. Mittlerweile gilt „Made in Berlin" auch für das Street-Design in der Inneneinrichtung. So ruhen die Schmuck-Kästen, Sitzpolster und Bildband-Auslagen auf ausrangierten Holzpaletten. Ebenso ausgefallen die Jeans-Auslage: wie gefallene Engel hängen die Hosen von der Decke – nur viel symmetrischer.

Cette boutique fait partie du Salon de la mode Premium ; il n'est donc pas étonnant d'y trouver une grande sélection de marques internationales, celles des stylistes scandinaves comme Mads Norgaard, anglais comme Unconditional et français, comme April 77. Le thème « Made in Berlin » est aussi présent dans la décoration urbaine. Boîtes à bijoux, coussins et beaux livres trônent sur des palettes de bois empilées. La présentation des jeans est aussi extravagante : les pantalons tombent du ciel tels des anges déchus- mais de manière plus symétrique.

De winkel behoort tot de 'Modemesse Premium' en we treffen hier dan ook een verfijnde selectie van hoogwaardige internationale labels aan, zoals Scandinavische designers als Mads Norgaard, Unconditional uit Engeland en April 77 uit Frankrijk. Intussen is 'Made in Berlin' ook van toepassing op het streetdesign van het interieur. Zo leunen de sieradenkasten, de zitkussens en de uitstalvlakken voor de fotoboeken op afgedankte houten palets. Ook de presentatie van de spijkerbroeken is bijzonder: de broeken hangen als gevallen engelen aan het plafond – maar dan veel symmetrischer.

Nine "noses" form a kaleidoscope of the perfumer's craft. Frederic Malle, the brains behind Editions de Parfums, has come up with some very clever ideas. Case in point: the nine parfumeure or "scented pods", the smelling boxes which professional perfumers use to better judge their olfactory creations and which are normally reserved for their eyes only (or noses, as the case may be). You can find them in the small Paris shop on the Rue de Grenelle. The result is Andrée Putman's avant-garde gem.

Neun „Nasen", die ein Kaleidoskop der Parfumeurskunst ausmachen. Frederic Malle, der Kopf hinter den Editions de Parfums, hatte eine sehr clevere Idee. Man nehme neun Parfumeure, „scented pods", die Riechboxen für Profis, die normalerweise den Kreateuren selber vorbehalten sind, um ihre Kreationen besser beurteilen zu können, sowie einen kleinen Pariser Laden in der Rue de Grenelle. Das Ergebnis ist ein von Andrée Putman gestaltetes Kleinod der Avantgarde.

Neuf « nez » forment un kaléidoscope de l'art du parfumeur. Frédéric Malle, le cerveau des Éditions de Parfums, a apporté des idées remarquablement brillantes. Un exemple : les neuf parfumeurs ou « cosses parfumées », les boîtes à odeur que les professionnels utilisent pour mieux vérifier leur création et normalement réservés à eux seuls (ou plutôt à leur nez). Vous les trouverez dans la petite boutique de Paris, rue de Grenelle. Le résultat est une petite merveille avant-gardiste signée Andrée Putman.

Negen 'neuzen' die een caleidoscoop van de parfumkunst vormen. Frédéric Malle, het brein achter de Editions de Parfums, had een zeer geraffineerd idee. Men neme negen parfumeurs, scented pods (de reukflacons die normaal gesproken zijn voorbehouden aan de parfumeurs zelf zodat ze hun creaties beter kunnen beoordelen) en een klein Parijs winkeltje in de Rue de Grenelle. Het resultaat is een door Andrée Putman vormgeven juweeltje van de avant-garde.

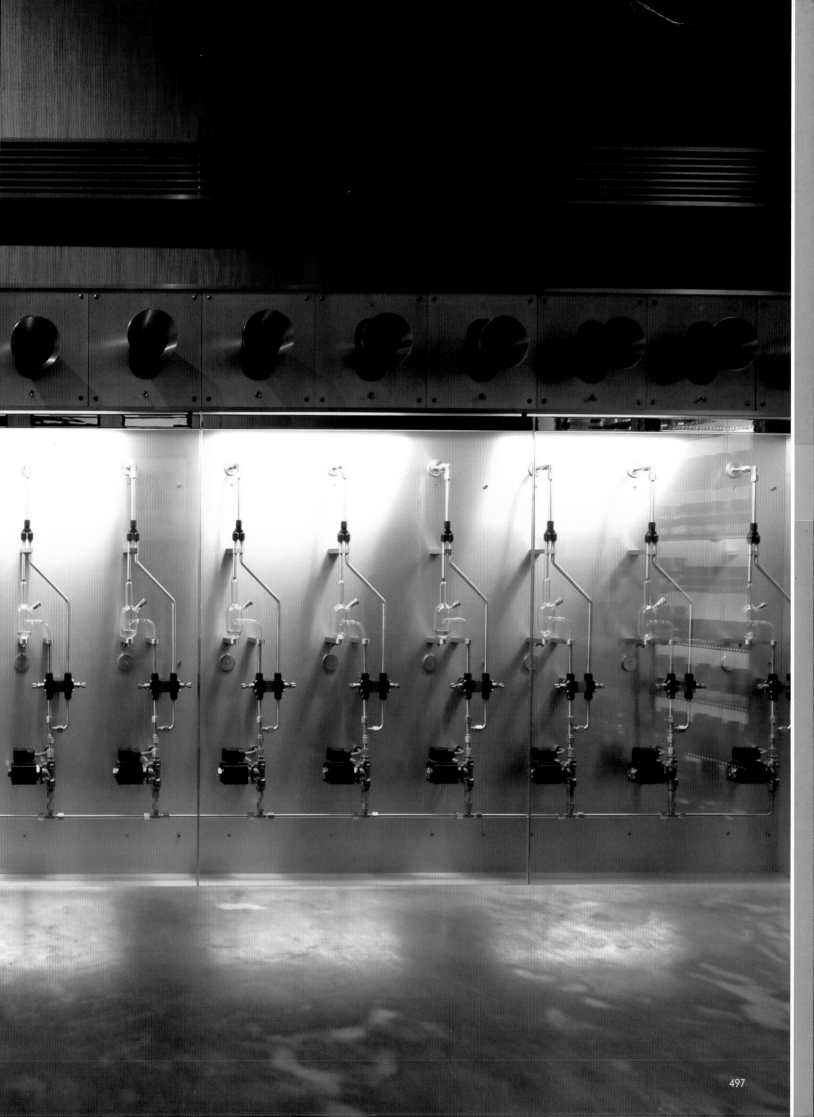

The Freitag brothers have created bags out of used car covers, seat belts and airbags. Each product, from purses to shoulder bags, is unique, created from a different piece of synthetic material. To display this character and their original idea on the outside as well, the flagship store has been constructed from of some nine shipping containers stacked together. Inside you will find countless packaged models from which entire walls have been formed.

Die Gebrüder Freitag erfanden Taschen aus gebrauchten LKW-Planen, Sicherheitsgurten und Airbags. Jedes Produkt, von der Tasche bis zum Boxsack, ist aus einem anderen Stück Kunststoff hergestellt und somit einzigartig. Um den Charakter und die ursprüngliche Idee auch nach außen hin darzustellen, wurde der Flagshipstore aus bis zu neun ausrangierten Containern gestapelt. Im Inneren finden sich unzählige verpackte Modelle, auch diese zu ganzen Wänden aufgebaut.

Les frères Freitag ont créé des sacs à partir de vieilles housses de voitures, de ceintures de sécurité et d'airbags. Chaque produit, du sac à main à la besace, est unique et constitué de différentes pièces de matière synthétique. Afin de représenter cette caractéristique ainsi que l'originalité de leur idée, leur flagship store a été construit à partir de neuf containers empilés. Vous y trouverez des murs entiers recouverts d'innombrables modèles emballés.

De gebroeders Freitag ontwerpen tassen van gebruikt vrachtwagenzeil, veiligheidsgordels en airbags. Elk product, van de tas tot de boxzak, is vervaardigd van een ander stuk kunststof en daarmee uniek. Om het karakter en de oorspronkelijke idee ook naar buiten toe uit te dragen, werd de Flagshipstore opgebouwd uit negen afgedankte, opgestapelde containers. Binnen bevinden zich ontelbare verpakte modellen die eveneens hoog zijn opgestapeld.

This "zero room" was developed for the German fashion label, a reducted space which does without colors or illusory spectacles. The focus here is a wall-length mirror, constructed from 5,000 reflective panes. Round shapes constitute the main style characteristic of the store's design concept, including round changing rooms and a bench of lunar-like gold leather. The motif of roundness is a reflection of the sensuality and femininity of the store's clients, with an eye towards warmth and charm.

Für das deutsche Modelabel konnte dieser reduzierte und auf Farbe und spektakuläre Illusionswelten verzichtende „Zero-Raum" verwirklicht werden. Im Fokus steht ein wandumspannender Spiegel aus 5000 aufgesetzten Spiegelscheiben. Runde Formen bilden ein Hauptstilmerkmal im Entwurfskonzept, rund sind daher auch die Kabinen sowie eine Bank aus mondgoldenem Leder. Das Rund greift die Sinnlichkeit und Weiblichkeit der Kundinnen auf, warm und charmant erwünscht.

Cette « navette spatiale » a été développée pour la marque allemande; c'est un espace réduit, sans couleurs ni fioritures. La pièce maîtresse est ici un mur de miroirs, constitué de 5000 panneaux réfléchissants. Les formes rondes constituent la principale caractéristique stylistique du concept de ce magasin : cabines d'essayage rondes et une banquette de cuir doré d'inspiration lunaire. Ces rondeurs rappellent la sensualité et la féminité des clientes du magasin et inspirent la chaleur et le charme.

Voor het Duitse modelabel werd deze gereduceerde 'zero-ruimte', zonder kleuren en spectaculaire illusionaire werelden, geschapen. Het middelpunt wordt gevormd door een wandgrote spiegel van 5000 spiegelstukjes. Het centrale stijlkenmerk in het ontwerpconcept zijn ronde vormen en daarom zijn ook de paskamers en de maangouden lerenbank rond van vorm. De ronde vormen omarmen de vrouwelijkheid en de zinnelijkheid van de vrouwelijke klanten.

You will be forgiven for thinking you've been beamed into the future when you see this shop's organic honeycomb structures, its twenty-foot-high amorphous sculptures entitled "genetics" and its arched white concrete walls. A showroom and label store are awaiting visitor and customer alike in an oversized glass cube, also containing an academy space with training rooms for conferences and seminars, a design lab for product development and a chill-out zone with its own bar.

Mit den organischen, wabenartigen Strukturen, mit den „genetics" – sechs Meter hohe, amorphe Skulpturen – und den gewölbten, weißen Betonwänden glaubt man sich mit der Zeitmaschine in die Zukunft transferiert. Besucher und Kunden erwartet im glass cube ein Showroom und Markenshop, ein Academy-Bereich mit Schulungsräumen für Seminare und Tagungen, ein Design Lab für die Produktentwicklung und eine Chill Zone mit Bar.

On vous pardonnera de penser avoir été télé-transporté dans le futur en voyant les structures alvéolaires de ce magasin, ses sculptures irrégulières de 6 mètres de haut appelées « génétique » et ses murs de béton blanc arrondis. Un showroom et un magasin multimarques attendent le visiteur et le client, dans un cube de verre démesuré, contenant également un espace de formation destiné aux conférences et séminaires, un laboratoire de design dédié au développement de produits et une zone de repos, dotée de son propre bar.

Met de organische, honingraatachtige structuren, de 'genetics' – zes meter hoge, amorfe sculpturen – en de gewelfde, witte betonwanden waant de bezoeker zich in een futuristische wereld. Bezoekers en klanten staan in de 'glass cube' een showroom en winkel met merkartikelen te wachten. Verder is er een 'academy zone' met conferentiezalen voor seminars en congressen, een 'design lab' voor de productontwikkeling en een 'chill zone' met bar.

Seoul's Myeongdong district is home to the brand-new Lotte Department Store, offering a wealth of international luxury brands over five levels. The label store also contains three cinemas, an entire spa level and a restaurant with a roof terrace. The retail area is characterized by its hand-spun cord walls and its 164-foot-long (50-meter-long) wall sculpture, which the architects created out of traditional Korean tiles.

In Seouls Myeongdong-Viertel liegt der allerneueste Lotte Department Store und bietet auf fünf Stockwerken eine Fülle an internationalen Luxusmarken. Weiterhin beinhaltet der Brandstore drei Kinos, eine SPA-Etage und ein Restaurant mit Dachterrasse. Der Verkaufsraum wird geprägt durch seine von Hand gesponnenen Schnurwände sowie eine 50 Meter lange Wandskulptur, von den Architekten aus traditionellen koreanischen Fliesen erstellt.

Le quartier Myeongdong de Séoul vient d'accueillir le tout nouveau magasin Lotte, offrant une multitude de marques de luxe, sur cinq niveaux. Le magasin multimarques regroupe également trois cinémas, un spa sur tout un étage et un restaurant sur les toits, avec terrasse. L'espace de vente se caractérise par des cloisons de corde tissées à la main et par une sculpture murale de 50 mètres de long, que l'architecte a pensée à partir de carrelage coréen.

In de wijk Myeongdong in Seoul bevindt zich de allernieuwste Lotte Department Store en deze biedt op vijf verdiepingen een verscheidenheid aan internationale luxemerken. Verder omvat de brandstore drie bioscopen, een spa-afdeling en een restaurant met dakterras. De verkoopruimte wordt gekenmerkt door de handgemaakte draadwanden en een vijftig meter lange, door de architect ontworpen wandsculptuur van traditionele Koreaanse tegels.

The "Seduction Shop" offers lingerie, negligées and corsets as well as a separate home collection with its own seductively designed motifs. This is a designer who combines sensuous lingerie with haute couture and presents this combination in the design of a shop viewed simultaneously as a private and public lifestyle statement.

Der „Shop der Verführung" bietet Dessous, Negligées und Korsette sowie eine aparte Home-Collection mit eigens entworfenen verführerischen Motiven an. Eine Designerin, die sinnliche Lingerie mit Haute Couture verbindet und dies auch in der Ausgestaltung ihres Shops als privates, aber auch öffentliches Lifestyle-Statement sieht.

Le « Magasin de la Séduction » propose lingerie, négligés, corsets ainsi qu'une collection séparée pour la maison portant ses propres motifs séducteurs. Un design combinant lingerie voluptueuse et haute couture et présentant ce savant mélange dans une boutique perçue comme l'évidence d'une vie à la fois privée et publique.

De 'winkel van de verleiding' biedt dessous, négligés en korsetten en een bijzondere huiscollectie met zelf ontworpen verleidelijke motieven. Een ontwerpster die zinnelijke lingerie met haute couture verbindt en dit ook in de vormgeving van haar winkel als intieme maar tevens publieke levensstijl formuleert.

Jewelry designer Mikimoto's second flagship store in the Ginza district elevates the art of sensuous surfaces to the highest level. This building, sprinkled with apertures apparently stamped into its facade, is the creation of master architect Toyo Ito and counts as one of the avenue's architectural highlights.

Beim zweiten Flagshipstore des Schmuckherstellers Mikimoto im Ginza-Quartier wird die Kunst der sinnlichen Oberfläche auf höchstem Niveau betrieben. Das mit unregelmäßigen, scheinbar in die Fassade gestanzten Öffnungen gesprenkelte Gebäude stammt vom japanischen Meisterarchitekten Toyo Ito und stellt eines der architektonischen Highlights an der Allee dar.

Le second magasin emblème du créateur joailler Mikimoto dans le quartier de Ginza, élève l'art des surfaces tactiles à son plus haut niveau. Ce bâtiment, ponctué d'ouvertures apparemment débitées dans la façade, est la création du maître architecte Toyo Ito et compte parmi les fleurons architecturaux de l'avenue.

Bij de tweede flagshipstore van het juweliershuis Mikimoto in de wijk Ginza wordt de kunst van het zintuiglijke oppervlak op het hoogste niveau bedreven. Het gebouw, dat is voorzien van onregelmatige openingen die in de gevels lijken te zijn ge-stanst, is van de hand van de Japanse meesterarchitect Toyo Ito en is een van de architectonische highlights van de laan.

romo

Air Flow

Aqua Sock

Duelist

87

Zoom Ultra

Air Mariah

88

Cooperstown

89

Air Trainer

This store also functions as an exhibition space. The history of speed is presented in a remarkably reduced version. Deliberately sparse installations, massive metal folds and sleek furnishings, all cast in a silver-gray, offer a retrospective of Nike's various running shoes, from its origins in the 1960s to the present day.

Das Geschäft dient ebenso als Ausstellungsplattform. Eindrucksvoll reduziert wird die Historie der Geschwindigkeit dargestellt. Bewusst sparsam eingesetzte Einbauten, massive Faltungen aus Metall, eine schlichte Möblierung und alles in einem silbrig-grauen Guss gibt einen Überblick über die einzelnen Laufgeräte von Nike, vom 21. Jahrhundert bis zurück zu den Ursprüngen in den 1960er Jahren.

Ce magasin est également un espace de présentation. L'histoire de la vitesse est retracée en une remarquable version condensée. Des présentoirs délibérément rares, des plis de métal massifs et un mobilier fuselé, tous d'un gris argenté, offrent une rétrospective des différentes chaussures de course de la marque, depuis ses débuts dans les années 60 jusqu'à aujourd'hui.

De winkel is tevens tentoonstellingsplatform. In deze winkel met massief geplooide metalen wanden en een sobere meubilering wordt de historie van de sportschoen indrukwekkend gereduceerd voorgesteld. Het geheel is gehuld in een zilvergrijze kleur en geeft een totaaloverzicht van alle afzonderlijke schoenen van Nike, van de eenentwintigste eeuw tot aan de beginperiode in de jaren zestig.

Zoom Maxcat

Mercurial Vapor

Air Zoom Katana

Mayfly

Air Presto

The extravagant presentation of Prada pieces stands in the foreground of this shop on famed Rodeo Drive. Walls which seem to be made of foam are used as display platforms into which clothing racks are anchored. They are designed to let light through without being completely transparent. The displays hanging from the racks turn shopping into a media experience.

Die extravagante Präsentation der Kleidungsstücke steht im Vordergrund des Showrooms auf dem berühmten Rodeo Drive. Wände, die aus Schaum entstanden zu sein scheinen, werden zu Ausstellungsflächen und fungieren als Verankerung für Kleiderstangen. Sie sind licht-, aber nicht blickdurchlässig. An den Stangen aufgehängte Displays lassen das Shopping-Erlebnis medial werden.

La présentation extravagante des articles Prada se trouve au premier plan de cette fameuse boutique de Rodeo Drive. Les murs, comme faits de mousse, servent de support de présentation et soutiennent les portants de vêtements. Ils ont été dessinés de manière à laisser pénétrer la lumière, sans pour autant être transparents. Grâce aux écrans suspendus aux portants, le shopping devient une expérience média.

De extravagante presentatie van kledingstukken van Prada treedt op de voorgrond in de showroom op de beroemde Rodeo Drive. Aan de muren, die van schuim lijken gemaakt, zijn kledingrekken vastgemaakt. Ze zijn zo ontworpen dat ze licht doorlaten zonder volledig transparant te zijn. De uitgestalde waren maken shoppen tot een echte media-ervaring.

The eye-catcher here is the gigantic wooden staircase undulating like a wave through this distinguished New York show-room. Take the time to try on some shoes or browse through the purses and accessories. Large metal cages hang from the ceiling construction and display various product lines. A translucent polycarbonate wall sheathes the existing brick wall, incorporating the original construction into the shop's design. You will find the changing rooms underneath the "wave".

Blickpunkt ist die überdimensionierte Holztreppe, die sich wie eine Welle durch den edlen New Yorker Showroom zieht. Hier können Schuhe anprobiert und Accessoires und Taschen begutachtet werden. Große Metall-Käfige hängen von der Deckenkonstruktion und präsentieren unterschiedliche Produktpaletten. Eine transluzente Wand aus Polycarbonat deckt eine existierende Backsteinmauer ab und bezieht damit die ursprüngliche Konstruktion mit ein. Unter der „Welle" befin-den sich die Umkleideräume.

Ici, c'est un escalier de bois surdimensionné ondulant tel une vague dans ce showroom distingué de New York, qui attire l'œil du visiteur. Prenez le temps d'essayer quelques paires de chaussures ou de flâner parmi les accessoires. De larges cages de métal tombant de l'armature du plafond présentent diverses lignes de produits. Un mur translucide en polycarbo-nate enveloppe le mur de brique pré-existant, assimilant cette construction originale au design de la boutique. Les cabines d'essayage sont situées sous la « vague ».

Blikvanger is de enorme houten trap die een golfbeweging door de hoogstaande New Yorkse showroom maakt. In deze win-kel kunnen schoenen gepast en accessoires en tassen worden bekeken. Aan de plafondconstructie hangen grote metalen kooien waarin verschillende artikelen worden uitgestald. Een doorschijnende wand van polycarbonaat verhult een bakstenen muur en neemt zo ook de oorspronkelijke constructie op in het interieur. Onder de 'golf' bevinden zich de paskamers.

The Prada Tower can be seen from a long way away. Swiss architects created this gigantic structure which comes across as a gigantic, glittering ice cube with slanted roof. On closer inspection, this turns out to be a composition of straight and arched glass rhombuses and diagonal braces, creating unusual views both inside and out. Inside, organically shaped hallways and other forms snake past the latest Prada creations.

Der Prada-Tower ist schon von weitem sichtbar. Die Schweizer Architekten schufen für Prada einen gigantischen Turm, der wie ein überdimensionaler gleißender Eiswürfel mit angesplitterter Dachschräge anmutet. Bei näherem Blick tut sich ein Geflecht aus geraden und gewölbten Glasromben und diagonalen Streben auf, die immer wieder ungewöhnliche Ein- und Ausblicke zulassen. Innen schlängeln sich organische Gänge und Formen an den aktuellen Prada-Entwürfen vorbei.

La Tour Prada est visible de très loin. Des architectes suisses ont créé cette gigantesque structure constituée de glaçons surdimensionnés, semblable à du verre soufflé, et possèdant un toit asymétrique. De plus près, celle-ci s'avère être une composition de losanges de verre plats ou bombés et d'armatures diagonales, créant des vues inhabituelles de l'extérieur comme de l'intérieur. A l'intérieur, des couloirs d'inspiration organique serpentent entre les dernières créations de la marque.

De toren van Prada is al vanuit de verte zichtbaar. De Zwitserse architecten ontwierpen voor Prada een gigantische toren die doet denken aan een reusachtig fonkelend ijsblok met schuin dak. Van dichtbij bekeken wordt een vlechtwerk van rechte en gewelfde glasoppervlakken en diagonale steunbalken zichtbaar die steeds weer ongebruikelijke doorkijkjes mogelijk maken. Binnen banen organische gangen en vormen al slingerend een weg langs de nieuwste creaties van Prada.

Wenge-wood floors, colorful walls, wallpaper, silver-coated alcoves, elegant mirrors, roomy changing rooms, comfortable chairs and poufs: this is the view that will greet you when you enter the designer's opulent Berlin department store.

Böden aus Wengeholz, farbige Wände, Teppiche, Einbauten mit Silberbelag, elegante Spiegel, großzügige Umkleide-kabinen, komfortable Sessel und Poufs: so stattete die Designerin das opulente Interieur des Departamentstores in Berlin aus.

Parquets de wengé, murs colorés, papier peint, étagères aux liserés argentés, miroirs élégants, cabines d'essayage spa-cieuses, fauteuils et poufs confortables : telle est la vision que vous offre l'opulent magasin multimarques de Berlin.

Vloeren van wengéhout, kleurige wanden, tapijten, zilverkleurige nissen, elegante spiegels, ruime kleedkamers, comforta-bele fauteuils en poefs: zo richtte de ontwerpster het weelderige interieur van de departmentstore in Berlijn in.

This Berlin concept store offers a unique mix of styles and products. Besides clothing you will also find select living accessories and 20th-century design classics. A subdued and understated interior has been developed to best present the wares on offer here. Slight curves draw the visitor inside. The classic parquet floor harmonizes with the white walls and furniture.

Der Berliner Concept Store bietet einen einmaligen Stil- und Produktmix. Neben Kleidung findet man hier auch ausgesuchte Wohnaccessoires und Designklassiker des 20. Jahrhunderts. Um das Angebot zu präsentieren, wurde ein zurückhaltendes, schlichtes Interieur entworfen. Leichte geschwungene Linien ziehen den Kunden ins Innere. Der klassische Parkettboden harmoniert mit den weiß gehaltenen Wänden und Möbeln.

Ce concept store berlinois offre un mélange unique de styles et de produits. En plus des vêtements, vous trouverez également une sélection d'accessoires ainsi que des classiques du design contemporain. La décoration discrète et élégante a pour but de mettre en valeur les articles présentés. Des courbes douces accompagnent le visiteur vers l'intérieur et le parquet s'accorde harmonieusement avec le mobilier et les murs blancs.

De Berlijnse concept store biedt een unieke stijl- en productenmix. Naast kleding vinden we hier ook prachtige woonaccessoires en designklassiekers uit de twintigste eeuw. Om de collectie onder de aandacht te brengen werd een ingetogen, sober interieur ontworpen. Lichte, gebogen lijnen trekken de klanten naar binnen. De klassieke parketvloer harmonieert met de witte wanden en meubels.

This shop for top of the range shoes and accessories in downtown Stuttgart is named after its proprietor. Sigrun has created a rich yet light and feminine locale. Brilliant white is contrasted by brightly colored graphic (cut-out) patterns on the walls and ceiling. This unusual combination underscores the fashion context while drawing attention to the smaller items, which are cunningly displayed against a neutral background.

Die Besitzerin gibt dem Shop für hochwertige Schuhe und Accessoires in der Stuttgarter Innenstadt seinen Namen. Entstanden ist ein prägnanter, aber leichter, femininer Ort. Helles Weiß wird von grafischen (Schnitt-)Mustern in kräftigen Farben an Wänden und Decke kontrastiert. Diese ungewöhnliche Kombination unterstützt den Modekontext und lenkt gleichzeitig die Aufmerksamkeit auf die kleinteilige Ware, die immer auf neutralem Grund präsentiert wird.

Cette boutique de chaussures et d'accessoires raffinés dans le centre de Stuttgart porte le nom de son propriétaire. Sigrun a créé un lieu riche et pourtant léger et féminin. Un blanc éclatant contraste avec des motifs graphiques (de découpage) très colorés sur les murs et le plafond. Cette association inhabituelle souligne le contexte « mode » tout en attirant l'attention sur de plus petits articles, astucieusement présentés sur des surfaces neutres.

De eigenaresse verleende de winkel voor eersteklas schoenen en accessoires in de binnenstad van Stuttgart zijn naam. De winkel is een markante, maar lichte en feminiene plek. Het heldere wit vormt een contrast met grafische (knip)patronen in krachtige kleuren aan de wanden en het plafond. Deze ongebruikelijke combinatie steunt de modecontext en vestigt tevens de aandacht op de producten die steeds op neutrale achtergrond worden gepresenteerd.

sigrun woehr

Stella McCartney's townhouse near Bruton Street is a true work of art. The retail areas house an exclusive perfumery, a tailor, a VIP room and an idyllic garden. And Matthew Williamson's shop in the same street offers a pleasing contrast with its light sandstone interior.

Das Stadthaus von Stella McCartney in der nahe gelegenen Bruton Street ist ein wahres Kunstwerk. Die Verkaufsräume beinhalten eine exklusive Parfümerie, ein Maßatelier, einen V.I.P.-Raum sowie einen idyllischen Garten. Und der Laden von Matthew Williamsons in derselben Straße bietet mit seiner Innengestaltung in hellem Sandstein ein gelungenes Kontrastprogramm.

La maison de ville de Stella McCartney près de Bruton Street est une réelle œuvre d'art. L'espace de vente accueille une parfumerie, un tailleur, un espace VIP et un jardin idyllique. De plus, la boutique de Matthew Williamson dans la même rue offre un contraste très plaisant, grâce à son intérieur de grès clair.

Het stadshuis van Stella McCartney in de Bruton Street is een waar kunstwerk. De verkoopruimten bevatten een exclusieve parfumerie, een maatatelier, een vipruimte en een idyllische tuin. En de winkel van Matthew Williamsons in dezelfde straat biedt met zijn interieur in licht zandsteen een geslaagd contrast.

Berlin is one concept store richer now, with a variety that is unique in this country. In Strange Fruit the most important internationally nominated New Young Designer labels for both sexes, incorporating accessories and lovingly selected lifestyle surprises, are spread over two floors and 4840 square feet (450 square meters).

Berlin ist um einen Concept Store reicher, der in seiner Art bisher einzigartig in Deutschland ist: Strange Fruit. Über zwei Etagen verteilen sich auf 450 Quadratmeter die international relevantesten Newcomer-Designerlabels für Frauen und Männer, Accessoires und liebevoll ausgewählte Lifestyle-Überraschungen.

Berlin possède un concept store de plus, sur un territoire déjà bien varié. Chez Strange Fruit, les marques les plus importantes de jeunes designers internationaux, comprenant des accessoires et un choix de fabuleuses surprises, s'étendent sur deux étages et 450 mètres carrés.

Berlijn is een concept store rijker en vooralsnog is deze enig in zijn soort in Duitsland: Strange Fruit. Op twee verdiepingen met in totaal 450 vierkante meter worden de internationaal meest gerenommeerde Newcomer Designerlabels voor vrouwen en mannen, liefdevol uitgezochte en verrassende lifestyleproducten en accessoires tentoongespreid.

Pure luxury. Even its clear, unblemished design is extravagant: handcrafted furniture, glass display windows set into ceiling-high walnut walls, the ceiling separated into little geometric islands of light. The effect both emphasizes the brand's elegance and comes across as über-stylish, akin to a computer-generated image.

Purer Luxus. Schon das klare und schnörkellose Design ist extravagant: handgefertigte Möblierung, Glasvitrinen eingelassen in raumhohe Walnusswände, die Decke unterteilt in Lichtinseln. Das wirkt zusammen einerseits der Marke angemessen elegant und anderseits extrem stylish, fast wie ein Wallpaper-Titel.

Le luxe à l'état pur. Même son design net et précis est extravagant : mobilier artisanal, vitrines de verre intégrées aux murs en bois de noyer, plafond séparé en petites îles géométriques de lumière. L'effet accentue à la fois l'élégance de la marque et un côté extra chic, qui relèverait de l'image de synthèse.

Pure luxe. Alleen al het heldere en sobere design is extravagant: handgemaakte meubels, glasvitrines in kamerhoge, walnoothouten wanden en een in lichteilandjes verdeeld plafond. Enerzijds maakt dit alles een, geheel in overeenstemming met het merk, elegante indruk en anderzijds doet het extreem stylish aan.

Revisionist room dimensions and flawless architecture offer a sleek backdrop to this store's delightful inventory. This new store's open display and the all-room display elements create a sense of transparency and clarity. Generously sized furniture partitions the area into different zones, enabling overall discretion, corner retreats and a multi-dimensional appearance. This fetish shop has opted for pure-form architecture as its sovereign corporate identity.

Bereinigte Raumverhältnisse und schnörkellose Architektur lassen das „reizvolle" Sortiment in den Vordergrund treten. Die neue offene Schaufensterfront und die raumübergreifenden Warenträger-Elemente schaffen Transparenz und Über-sichtlichkeit. Großzügige Möbel zonieren die Räumlichkeiten und schaffen damit Diskretion, Rückzugsmöglichkeit und Vielschichtigkeit. Klare Architektur als souveräne Corporate Identity eines Fetischshops.

Des dimensions spatiales revisitées et une architecture parfaite offrent une toile de fond bien léchée au délicieux inventaire de cette boutique. La vitrine de ce nouveau magasin et l'ensemble des éléments de présentation créent une impression de transparence et de clarté. Le mobilier de taille généreuse scinde l'espace en différentes zones, permettant une certaine discrétion, des angles où se retirer et une apparence pluridimensionnelle. Cette boutique fétichiste a adopté une architec-ture de formes pures, assimilable à l'identité de sa marque.

Verbeterde ruimteverhoudingen en sobere architectuur laten de aantrekkelijke collectie mooi uitkomen. De nieuwe open etalagegevel verschaft transparantie en overzicht. De grote meubels delen de ruimten in, zorgen voor discretie en bieden bezoekers de mogelijkheid om zich terug te trekken. Heldere architectuur als soevereine corporate identity van een fetisjshop.

Stephane Dou and Changlee Yugin's showroom in the historic Chungshan district emphasizes a sculptural vision of expressive shapes. Metal lamellae fold in front of the building's tall facade, metal air ducts wind their way through the interior like space-age furniture while metallic varnishes on the walls and floor catch your eye in this extravagant showroom.

Im historischen Chungshan-Viertel setzt der Showroom von Stephane Dou und Changlee Yugin auf die skulpturartige Wirkung seiner ausdrucksstarken Form. Die Metalllammellen falten sich vor der gebäudehohen Fassade, metallene Abluftrohre winden sich als Präsentationsmöbel durch die Innenräume und metallfarbene Wand- und Bodenanstriche sind die prägenden Elemente dieses extravaganten Showrooms.

Le showroom de Stephane Dou et Changlee Yugin, situé dans le quartier historique de Chungshan, s'appuie sur une vision sculpturale de formes expressives. Dans ce showroom extravagant, votre œil est accaparé par des panneaux métallisés qui se déploient devant la haute façade de l'immeuble, des colonnes d'aération métalliques qui envahissent l'intérieur telles un mobilier futuriste, tandis que les vernis métalliques recouvrent les murs et le sol.

De showroom van Stéphane Dou en Changlee Yugin in de historische wijk Chungshan zet in op het plastische effect van zijn expressieve vorm. De metalen lamellen plooien zich voor de hoge voorgevel, kronkelende metalen luchtpijpen presenteren zich als meubelstukken in de interieurs en de metaalkleurig geverfde wanden en vloeren drukken hun stempel op deze extravagante showroom.

WELLNESS AND SPA RESORTS

HEALTH & BEAUTY

The name of this luxurious spa is Sanskrit and means "garden of heaven". You will feel transported by this space. Warm colors and natural materials are accentuated with gold and silver highlights. The treatment rooms are bathed in soft light, ensuring a relaxed atmosphere. The spa combines traditional Thai elements with contemporary design.

Der Name dieses luxuriösen Spa kommt aus dem Sanskrit und bedeutet Himmelsgarten. Und in diesen soll sich der Besucher versetzt fühlen. Warme Farben und natürliche Materialien werden mit Highlights in Gold und Silber akzentuiert. Die Behandlungsräume sind in sanftes Licht getaucht und versprechen eine entspannte Atmosphäre. In diesem Spa wurden traditionelle thailändische Merkmale mit zeitgemäßem Design kombiniert.

En Sanskrit, le nom de ce spa luxueux signifie « jardin des cieux ». Vous vous sentirez transporté par cet espace. Les couleurs chaudes et les matériaux naturels sont rehaussés de pointes dorées et argentées. Les salles de soins baignent dans une lumière douce, assurant une atmosphère de relaxation. Le spa combine une décoration thaïe traditionnelle et un design contemporain.

De naam van deze luxueuze spa is afkomstig uit het Sanskriet en betekent hemeltuin – en hierin moet de bezoeker zich ook wanen. Warme kleuren en natuurlijke materialen worden met highlights in goud en zilver geaccentueerd. De behandelingsvertrekken zijn gedompeld in zacht licht en beloven een ontspannen sfeer. In deze spa worden traditionele Thaise kenmerken gecombineerd met eigentijds design.

This spa highlights the healing and purifying properties of water. This is achieved through pools kept at various temperatures, exotic baths and even a waterfall in a muted and elegant design. Gray slate walls and marble floors dominate the interior and harmonize with the various water basins.

Die heilende und reinigende Wirkung des Wassers steht in diesem Spa im Vordergrund. Erlebbar machen dies verschieden temperierte Pools, exotische Bäder und ein Wasserfall. Das Design ist schlicht und elegant. Graue Schieferwände und Marmorböden dominieren die Innenräume und harmonieren mit den verschiedenen Wasserbecken.

Ce spa insiste sur les propriétés guérisseuses et purificatrices de l'eau, par le biais de bassins à des températures variées, de bains exotiques et même d'une cascade, dans un cadre élégant et épuré. Des murs d'ardoises grises et des sols de marbre dominent l'intérieur et se marient harmonieusement aux différents bassins d'eau.

Het helende en reinigende effect van het water staat in deze spa centraal. Hiervan getuigen de zwembaden in verschillende temperaturen, exotische baden en een waterval. Het design is sober en elegant. Grijze leistenen wanden en marmeren vloeren overheersen de interieurs en harmoniëren met de verschillende waterbassins.

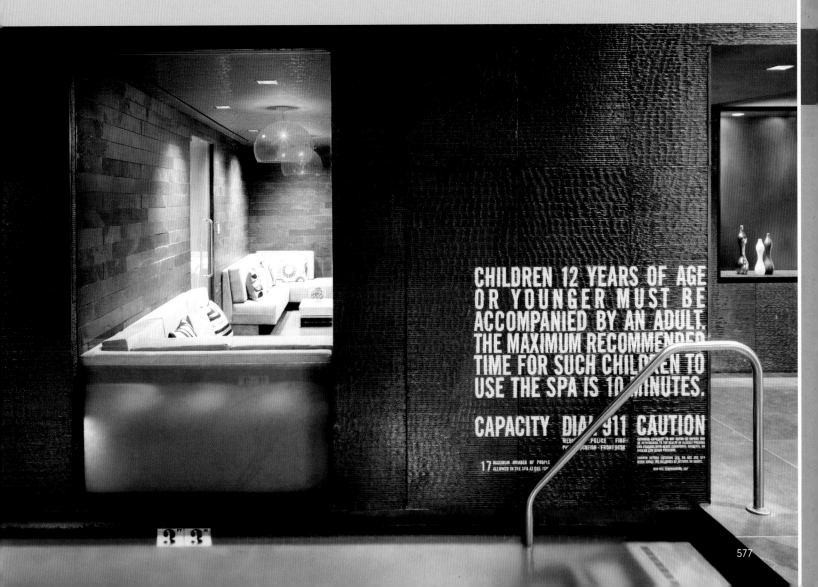

CHILDREN 12 YEARS OF AGE OR YOUNGER MUST BE ACCOMPANIED BY AN ADULT. THE MAXIMUM RECOMMENDED TIME FOR SUCH CHILDREN TO USE THE SPA IS 10 MINUTES.

CAPACITY DIAL 911 CAUTION

Located on the third floor of a highrise on 57th Street, this day spa offers an exceptional atmosphere. The interior is classically reserved, captured in subdued tones. Details like the glass walls enclosing small white feathers, walls of light gray velour leather and flattering lighting make this one of New York's most popular spas.

Im dritten Stock eines Hochhauses der 57. Straße gelegen, bietet das Day-Spa eine außergewöhnliche Atmosphäre. Das Interieur zeigt sich zurückhaltend und in gedeckten Farbtönen. Details wie Glaswände, mit Federn in den Zwischenräumen, Wandbespannungen aus hellgrauem Velourleder und eine schmeichelnde Beleuchtung machen diesen Spa zu einem der beliebtesten der New Yorker Society.

Situé au troisième étage d'un building de la 57ème rue, ce spa offre une atmosphère exceptionnelle. La décoration intérieure classique se pare de tons discrets. Des détails tels que les vitrines de verre renfermant des plumes blanches, les murs et les velours gris clair font de ce dernier l'un des spas les plus prisés de New York.

De day spa op de derde verdieping van een flatgebouw in 57th Street heeft een buitengewone ambiance. Het interieur is ingetogen en uitgevoerd in gedekte kleuren. Details als veren achter glazen wanden, met lichtgrijs suède bespannen wanden en een flatteuze verlichting maken deze spa tot een van de meest geliefde van de New Yorkse society.

The guest will find a very special spa on the roof of the Bayrischer Hof hotel. The space contains a pool and you can relax on the sunning terrace during nice weather thanks to the retractable glass roof. The interiors and furnishings are designed in subdued white and gray tones, contrasting with the bright blue of the pool. Austere shapes epitomize Andrée Putman's design concept.

Auf dem Dach des Hotels Bayrischer Hof erwartet den Gast ein besonderer Spa-Bereich. Hier befindet sich ein Pool und bei schönem Wetter kann mann auf der angrenzenden Sonnenterasse unter freiem Himmel entspannen. Das bewegliche Glasdach macht es möglich. Im Kontrast zum strahlenden Blau des Pools sind die Innenräume und die Möblierung in gedeckten Weiß- und Grautönen gehalten. Strenge Formen runden das Designkonzept von Andrée Putman ab.

Les hôtes découvriront un spa hors du commun sur le toit de l'Hôtel Bayrischer Hof. Cet espace comprend une piscine ainsi qu'une terrasse permettant de bronzer par beau temps grâce à un toit de verre escamotable. La décoration et le mobilier présentent des tonalités discrètes de blanc et de gris, contrastant avec le bleu de la piscine. Ces formes austères sont l'œuvre d'Andrée Putman.

Op het dak van het hotel Bayrischer Hof staat de gast een bijzondere spa te wachten. Er bevindt zich hier een zwembad en dankzij het verschuifbare dak is het bij mooi weer mogelijk om op het aangrenzende zonneterras te ontspannen onder de vrije hemel. Als tegenstelling tot het stralende blauw van het zwembad zijn de interieurs en de meubels in gedekte tinten wit en grijs uitgevoerd. Strenge vormen ronden het designconcept van Andrée Putman af.

Situated in the middle of the contemporary Falkenried property in Eppendorf, here you will find light-flooded yoga and pilates studios as well as separate massage and cosmetic rooms. Take the time before or after treatments to relax in the lounge area with its beautiful views of Hamburg. The spacious roof terrace is also for more than just relaxing: in the summertime it's used as a yoga space by small groups.

Inmitten des modern gestalteten Falkenriedgeländes in Eppendorf gibt es neben lichtdurchfluteten Yoga- und Pilates-Studios separate Massage- und Kosmetikräume. Im Lounge-Bereich bleibt Zeit, um vor und nach den Behandlungen und Kursen mit Blick über Hamburg zu entspannen. Die großzügige Dachterrasse lädt nicht nur zum Relaxen ein, sondern bietet im Sommer die Möglichkeit für Yoga in kleineren Gruppen unter freiem Himmel.

Situés au cœur de la propriété Falkenried à Eppendorf, vous trouverez ici des studios de yoga et de pilates inondés de lumière, tout comme des salles indépendantes de massage et de soins cosmétiques. Prenez le temps, avant ou après les soins, de vous relaxer dans le salon, jouissant d'une vue splendide sur Hambourg. Le spacieux toit-terrasse ne sert pas uniquement au repos : en été, de petits groupes de yoga profitent de sa situation.

Midden op het moderne Falkenriedgelände in Eppendorf zijn er naast lichte yoga- en pilatesstudio's ook separate massage- en schoonheidssalons. Het loungegedeelte biedt de mogelijkheid om voor en na de behandelingen of lessen te ontspannen met uitzicht op de stad Hamburg. Het ruime dakterras nodigt niet alleen uit om te relaxen maar biedt in de zomer ook de mogelijkheid voor yogalessen in kleine groepjes onder de vrije hemel.

Purity, seclusion and serenity – the visitor will find an island of peace and quiet here. The light swathes of fabric separating the treatment rooms add an open and airy atmosphere. With its well-chosen color scheme of bright whites, soft greens and warm eggplant hues, the spa still manages to come across as quite intimate.

Reinheit, Abgeschiedenheit und Ruhe – hier erwartet die Besucher eine Insel der Ruhe. Leichte Bahnen aus Stoff trennen die Behandlungsräume, sie wirken offen und luftig. Durch die geschickt ausgewählten Farbtöne, wie helles Weiß, sanftes Grün und warmes Aubergine wirkt dieser Spa im Ganzen jedoch sehr intim.

Pureté, solitude et sérénité : le visiteur trouvera ici une oasis de paix et de calme. Les légers rideaux de tissus séparant les pièces de soins contribuent à une atmosphère ouverte et aérée. Par ses tonalités chromatiques bien choisies de blancs lumineux, de verts tendres et de violines chauds, ce spa réussit toujours à diffuser une sensation d'intimité.

Reinheid, afgezonderdheid en rust – hier staat de bezoeker een oase van rust te wachten. Lichte stoffen gordijnen scheiden de behandelingsruimten af en deze lijken daardoor open en luchtig. Door de slim gekozen kleuren als helder wit, zacht groen en warm aubergine doet deze spa over het geheel echter zeer intiem aan.

The Abramson Teiger architects who designed this spa, which specializes in improving your skin's elasticity, designed grotto-like spaces for its treatment rooms. On sunny days you can open the front façade to let in the soft sea breezes. These "caves" are like their own little buildings.

Diesem Spa, der sich darauf spezialisiert, die Elastizität der Haut zu verbessern, gaben die Abramson Teiger Architects höhlenartige Schalen als Behandlungszimmer. An sonnigen Tagen kann man die vordere Gebäudefassade öffnen und die Meeresbrise hereinlassen. So werden diese Schalen zu eigenen kleinen Gebäuden.

Les architectes de chez Abramson Teiger ayant pensé ce spa, dont la spécialité est d'améliorer la tonicité cutanée, ont donné l'apparence de grottes aux salles de soins. Par beau temps, il est possible d'ouvrir la façade pour laisser entrer la douce brise du large.

De architecten van Abramson Teiger voorzagen deze spa, die erin is gespecialiseerd de elasticiteit van de huid te verbeteren, van grotachtige schalen als behandelingsruimten. Op zonnige dagen kan de voorgevel van het gebouw worden geopend om de zeebries binnen te laten. En zo worden deze schalen kleine gebouwtjes op zich.

The architect and designer Michael Young calls his work for Dr. James Plastic Cosmetic, a cosmetic surgery center in Taipei, "Dr. J". Together with his wife, who is responsible for the center's artwork, he has developed and combined new materials such as the electrically conducive and simultaneously imprinted and illuminated glass floors. The rooms contrast the absolute sterility of blank white with bright flowery colors.

Dr. J nennt der Architekt und Designer Michael Young seine Arbeit für Dr. James Plastic Cosmetic, einen Schönheitschirurgen in Taipei. Zusammen mit seiner Frau, die das Artwork verantwortet, entwickelte und kombinierte er neue Materialien wie stromleitende und gleichzeitig bedruckte und beleuchtete Glasböden. So wirken die Räume einerseits in absolut sterilem Weiß, anderseits wieder farbig und blütenhaft.

L'architecte et designer Michael Young appelle son travail pour le Dr. James Plastic Cosmetic, un centre de chirurgie cosmétique au centre de Taipei, le « Dr. J ». Avec sa femme, responsable de la partie artistique du centre, il a développé et intégré de nouveaux matériaux, comme les dalles de verre décorées et illuminées simultanément par conduction électrique. Les salles jouent sur les contrastes entre la stérilité absolue du blanc et les vifs motifs floraux.

Dr. J, zo noemt de architect en designer Michael Young zijn werk voor Dr. James Plastic Cosmetic, een schoonheidschirurg in Taipei. Samen met zijn vrouw, die verantwoordelijk is voor het artwork, ontwikkelde en combineerde hij nieuwe materialen zoals stroomgeleidende en tegelijkertijd bedrukte en verlichte glazen vloeren. Zo presenteren de vertrekken zich enerzijds in absoluut steriel wit en anderzijds ook kleurig en bloemrijk.

The husband and wife team of Dr. Barbara Polla and Dr. Luigi Polla run this cosmetic surgery institute. The fundamental concept is an abstract depiction of envelopment, as if the light itself is giving birth to the materials around you. The institute is characterized by an extravagant and stimulating atmosphere, an oasis of elegance and refinement.

Gemeinsam betreibt hier das Ehepaar Dr. Barbara Polla und Dr. Luigi Polla ein Institut für Schönheitschirurgie. Das grundlegende Konzept ist die Abstraktion der Umhüllung, so als ob das Licht die Materie gestaltet. In diesem Institut schuf man eine extravagante und anregende Atmosphäre, eine Oase deren Gestaltung sich durch Eleganz und Raffinesse auszeichnet.

Les époux Dr. Barbara Polla et Dr. Luigi Polla gèrent cet institut de chirurgie cosmétique. Le concept fondamental est une suggestion abstraite de l'enveloppement, comme si la lumière elle-même donnait naissance aux matériaux qui vous entourent. L'institut est caractérisé par une atmosphère extravagante et stimulante, c'est une oasis d'élégance et de raffinement.

Het echtpaar dr. Barbara Polla en dr. Luigi Polla leidt hier een instituut voor cosmetische chirurgie. Het basisconcept bestaat uit de abstrahering van het omhulsel, alsof het licht de materie vormt. In dit instituut creëerde men een extravagante en stimulerende atmosfeer met een kenmerkend elegante en verfijnde vormgeving.

Jean-Marie Massaud's spa has been conceived in a meditative Zen style, embodying the idea of all-round beauty. The Hi's architecture has been created as a place for fitness – not just of the body but of the senses as well. There are elliptical treatment tables, an egg-shaped bathtub, an unfinished bench and a botanical sofa. All the objects here have also been specially designed for this bathing area.

Das von Jean-Marie Massaud bewusst im meditativen Zen-Stil gehaltene Spa hat sich dem Konzept der ganzheitlichen Schönheit verschrieben. Die Architektur des Hi wurde als Stätte für die Fitness der Sinne konzipiert. Es gibt ellipsenförmige Behandlungstische, eine eiförmige Badewanne, eine unbehauene Bank und ein gegrüntes Sofa. Auch alle anderen Einrichtungsgegenstände wurden speziell für dieses Bad entworfen.

Le spa de Jean-Marie Massaud a été conçu dans un style Zen méditatif, personnifiant l'idée de beauté intemporelle. L'architecture du Hi a été conçue comme un endroit pour la forme, pas seulement du corps, mais aussi des sens. On y trouve des tables de soins elliptiques, une baignoire ovale, une baguette inachevée et un canapé végétal. Tous les objets ont également été créés spécialement pour cet espace de détente.

De door Jean-Marie Massaud bewust in meditatieve zenstijl uitgevoerde spa wijdt zich geheel aan de schoonheid. Er zijn ellipsvormige behandelingstafels, een eivormig bad, een onbehouwen en een met gras begroeide bank. Ook alle andere voorwerpen van de inrichting werden speciaal voor het Hi ontworpen.

The planners opted here for architectonic and space-forming materials in their interior design. This design concept incorporates a clever selection of glass, wood and raw stone, resulting in a stimulating interplay of shimmering glass surfaces and solid, primitive materials. A concept enhanced by austere geometric shapes. Specially crafted lighting is the final touch.

Bei der Innengestaltung waren die Planer darauf bedacht, mit architektonischen, raumbildenden Mitteln zu arbeiten. Zu diesem Gestaltungskonzept gehört auch die bewusste Auswahl der Materialien Glas, Holz und Naturstein, die zu einem spannenden Wechselspiel von glänzenden Glasflächen und solidem Urmaterial führt. Strenge, geometrische Formen unterstützen den Entwurfsgedanken. Den letzten Schliff erzielte man mit speziell ausgearbeiteten Lichtkonzepten.

Ici, les responsables ont opté pour des matériaux architectoniques et créant de l'espace. Ce concept créatif comprend une sélection savante de verre, bois et pierre brute, résultant en un échange stimulant entre les surfaces de verre brillantes et les matériaux solides et ancestraux. Un concept rehaussé par des formes géométriques dont la touche finale est donnée par un éclairage unique.

Voor de vormgeving van het interieur gebruikten de ontwerpers architectonische materialen als glas, hout en natuursteen. Dit leidt tot een spannend samenspel van glanzende glazen vlakken en solide oermateriaal. Strenge, geometrische vormen dragen bij aan het ontwerp. De finishing touch werd gerealiseerd door middel van speciaal ontwikkelde lichtconcepten.

You might be reminded of spaceships, dunes or perhaps oral hygiene: in any case, this practice's futuristic landscape will stimulate the visitor's imagination. Floor and ceiling are like a wave enclosing the entire space, letting you experience the practice as a three-dimensional creation. On top of this are amorphous pictures, acoustic backgrounds and an offbeat lighting concept. There are hardly any visible appliances and even the usual furnishings have disappeared, integrated into the sculptured space.

Assoziationen zu Raumschiff, Dünenlandschaft oder Mundhygieneraum: Die futuristische Praxis-Landschaft begeistert und weckt die Fantasie der Besucher. Boden und Decke formen sich zu einer Welle, die die ganze Praxis erfasst und sie als dreidimensionale Raumfigur erlebbar macht. Dazu gibt es amorphe Bilder, akustische Hintergründe und ein besonderes Lichtdesign. Es sind kaum Geräte präsent, das Mobiliar ist komplett verschwunden, indem es sich in einen skulpturartigen Raum integriert.

Vaisseaux spatiaux, dunes ou peut-être hygiène dentaire pourraient vous venir à l'esprit : quoi qu'il en soit, ce décor futuriste stimulera l'imagination du visiteur. Les sols et le plafond forment une vague comme englobant l'espace entier, vous laissant ressentir le lieu comme une création tridimensionnelle. Ajoutez à cela des motifs irréguliers, un fond sonore et un éclairage excentrique. Aucun appareil n'est visible et même le mobilier habituel a disparu, intégré à cet espace sculpté.

Associaties met een ruimteschip, duinlandschap of de behandelkamer van de mondhygiëniste: dit futuristische praktijklandschap inspireert en wekt de fantasie op van de bezoeker. De vloeren en het plafond vormen een golf die zich uitstrekt over de gehele praktijkruimte en tot een ruimtelijke, driedimensionale figuur wordt. Hierbij komen amorfe beelden, akoestische achtergronden en een bijzonder lichtdesign. Er zijn vrijwel geen apparaten aanwezig en het meubilair is volledig afwezig doordat het is geïntegreerd in de plastische ruimte.

The French designer's day spa is located on the fourth floor of the Kenzo House near the Seine. The interior is characterized by his typical mix of Asiatic and contemporary design elements. The walls and floor of the foyer radiate in pure, subdued white and soft floral décor. Massage rooms decorated in gold or hot pink are secluded behind equally white plush walls.

Im vierten Stock des Kenzo-Hauses, nahe der Seine, liegt der Day-Spa La Bulle des französischen Designers. Das Interieur nimmt die für ihn typische Mischung aus asiatischen Elementen mit zeitgenössischem Design auf. Wände und Böden des Eingangsbereichs erstrahlen zurückhaltend in Reinweiß mit sanftem Blumendekor. Hinter den ebenso weißen Plüschwänden verbergen sich jedoch Massageräume in Gold oder Knallpink.

Ce spa du designer français se trouve au quatrième étage de la Maison Kenzo près de la Seine. L'intérieur se caractérise par un mélange étonnant d'éléments asiatiques et contemporains. Les murs et le sol de l'entrée irradient d'un blanc pur et discret et de doux motifs floraux. Les salles de massage parées de doré ou de rose foncé sont isolées derrière des murs de peluche blanche.

Op de vierde verdieping van het Kenzogebouw, vlak bij de Seine, ligt de day spa La Bulle van de Franse designer. Het interieur pakt de voor hem kenmerkende combinatie van Aziatische elementen met eigentijds design op. De wanden en vloeren van de entree schitteren ingetogen in smetteloos wit met een zacht bloemenmotief. Achter de witte pluche wanden gaan echter massageruimten in goud en knalroze schuil.

The Lanserhof is characterized by soothing whites and blues, rounded corners and soft shapes and materials. The interior architect Regina Dahmen-Ingenhoven has developed clear spaces which offer the visitor both orientation and security. A special lighting concept is part of the overall design; the "healing light" aids the visitor's sense of wellness. This light never shines directly or too brightly but is cleverly subdued.

Beruhigendes Weiß und Blau, abgerundete Ecken, weiche Formen und Materialien sind die Gestaltungsmerkmale des Lanserhofs. Die Innenarchitektin Regina Dahmen-Ingenhoven entwickelte klare Räume, die Orientierung und Sicherheit bieten. Um das Wohlbefinden zu steigern, wurde zudem ein besonderes Lichtkonzept entwickelt: das „Healing Light". Dabei leuchtet das Licht nie direkt oder grell, sondern nimmt sich zurück.

Le Lanserhof se caractérise par des blancs et des bleus apaisants, des angles arrondis ainsi que des formes et des matériaux doux. L'architecte d'intérieur Regina Dahmen-Ingenhoven a développé des espaces aérés offrant au visiteur à la fois orientation et sécurité. Un concept particulier d'éclairage est partie intégrante du design : la « lumière soin » contribue au sentiment de bien-être du visiteur. Cette lumière ne brille jamais directement ou trop ardemment, mais sait se faire savamment discrète.

Rustgevend wit en blauw, afgeronde hoeken, zachte vormen en materialen zijn de stijlkenmerken van het Lanserhof. De binnenhuisarchitect Regina Dahmen-Ingenhoven ontwierp duidelijke ruimten die oriëntatie en zekerheid bieden. Om het welbehagen nog te vergroten werd een bijzonder lichtconcept ontwikkeld: het 'healing light'. Er is geen directe of felle verlichting, maar het licht wordt altijd gedempt.

The primary goal of this clinic's design was to create an incomparable ambience with the help of a total design concept. Organic shapes taken from nature such as plants and flowers have been used as graphic elements on the walls and ceilings. The carefully selected warm materials emphasize this sensuous impression. An organically shaped middle island separates the room, defining the exercise and lounge areas: the entry foyer faces the reception, the lounge area faces the operating theater and seminar rooms, as well as both waiting areas, and the curved hall along the treatment rooms.

Übergeordnetes Ziel der Gestaltung war es, ein unverwechselbares Ambiente mit Hilfe eines ganzheitlichen Designkonzepts zu schaffen. Organische Formen aus der Natur wie Blüten und Pflanzen wurden dafür als grafische Elemente auf Wände und Decken gebracht. Die sorgfältig ausgewählten warmen Materialien ergänzen den sinnlichen Eindruck. Eine organisch geformte Mittelinsel gliedert den Raum und definiert Bewegungs- und Aufenthaltszonen: der Empfangsbereich vor der Rezeption, Aufenthaltsbereiche vor dem OP und den Seminarräumen sowie vor den beiden Wartebereichen, der gekrümmte Gang entlang den Behandlungsräumen.

Le but premier de cette Clinique était de créer une ambiance incomparable, par le biais d'un concept novateur. Des formes organiques inspirées de la nature, telles que des plantes et des fleurs, ont servi d'éléments graphiques pour les murs et plafonds. Les matériaux chauds précautionneusement choisis accentuent cette impression sensitive. Un îlot central de forme organique sépare la pièce, délimitant les espaces d'exercice et de repos : l'entrée face à la réception, le salon face au théâtre des opérations et aux salles de séminaires, tout comme les deux salles d'attente et le hall arrondi le long des salles de soins.

Hoger doel van de vormgeving was om een onmiskenbare sfeer te realiseren met behulp van het gehele designconcept. Hiervoor werden organische vormen uit de natuur zoals bloemen en planten als grafische elementen aangebracht op de wanden en plafonds. De zorgvuldig uitgezochte warme materialen vullen de zinnelijke indruk aan. Een organisch gevormd eiland in het midden van de ruimte deelt de ruimte in en definieert de bewegings- en verblijfsruimten: de entree voor de receptie, de verblijfsruimten voor de OK en de congreszalen evenals de gekromde gang langs de behandelingskamers.

This cosmetic institute is located in a building dating from the 1960s and is characterized by a "backyard" feel. The architects of the Concrete Architectural Associates were responsible for modernizing the rooms, bringing them up-to-date with opulent chandeliers to appeal to a younger clientele.

Dieses Kosmetikinstitut befindet sich in einem Gebäude aus den 1960er Jahren und hat eher Hinterhofcharakter. Die Räume wurden von den Concrete-Architectural-Associates-Architekten modernisiert und zeitgemäß mit opulenten Lüstern ausgestattet, um einer jüngeren Klientel gerecht zu werden.

Cet institut de soins se trouve dans un bâtiment des années 1960 et aurait comme un air de « jardin ». Les architectes de chez Concrete Architectural Associates ont eu la responsabilité de moderniser les pièces, en les remettant au goût du jour grâce à d'énormes lustres pour attirer une clientèle plus jeune.

Dit schoonheidsinstituut bevindt zich in een gebouw uit de jaren zestig en heeft meer de uitstraling van een achterplaats. De vertrekken werden door de architecten van Concrete Architectural Associates gemoderniseerd en van weelderige eigentijdse kroonkandelaars voorzien om tegemoet te komen aan een jonger clientèle.

This floating spa has been conceived as a place where you can either moor up or dive right in. The building's focus on elementary design is achieved through its simplified use of interior shapes and its bold axial alignment. Windows fronting both sides create a light-flooded atmosphere, incorporating the surrounding water as a connective element in its design. From here you can look out onto the city, the power plant and the sun deck.

Das schwimmende Spa beschreibt einen Ort, an dem man landen und eintauchen kann. Eine reduzierte Formensprache im Inneren als auch die klare, axiale Ausrichtung des Gebäudes veranschaulichen die Konzentration auf das Elementare. Fensterfronten an beiden Stirnseiten erzeugen eine lichtdurchflutete Stimmung, schaffen eine unmittelbare Verbindung zum umgebenden Element Wasser und geben den Ausblick auf Stadt, Kraftwerk und Sonnendeck frei.

Ce spa flottant a été conçu comme un lieu auquel vous pouvez vous amarrer ou dans lequel plonger. Insistant sur un design élémentaire, le bâtiment jouit d'une utilisation simplifiée des formes intérieures et de son alignement axial audacieux. La double exposition permet à un flot de lumière d'envahir les pièces, jouant sur la présence de l'eau environnante pour renforcer cet élément du design. D'ici vous pouvez voir la ville, la centrale énergétique et le ponton terrasse.

Deze drijvende spa is een oord waar men aan land kan gaan of kan onderduiken. Het duidelijke, axiaal georiënteerde gebouw en de gereduceerde vormtaal binnen geven de aandacht voor de essentie weer. De raampartijen aan de beide kopeinden zorgen voor veel licht, creëren een directe verbinding met het omringende element water en bieden tevens uitzicht op de stad, de krachtcentrale en het zonneterras.

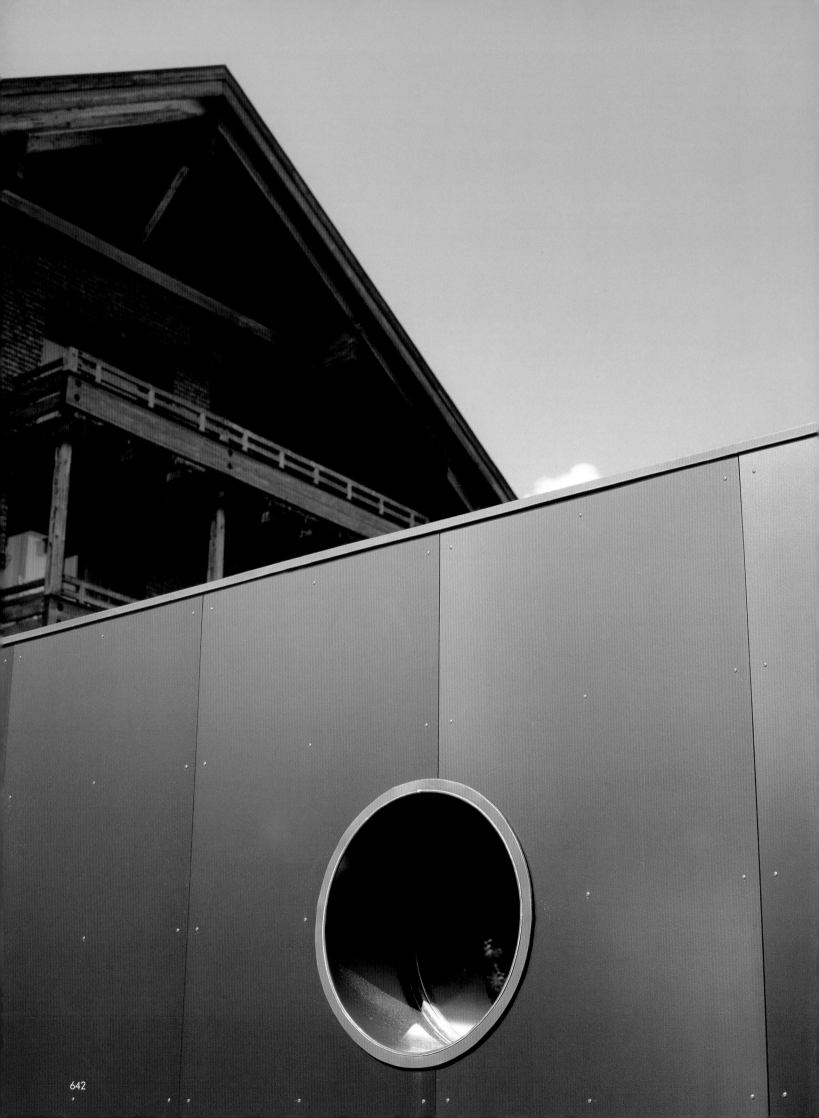

Susanne Kaufmann's spa area in the Hotel Post is subdued in its design, offering the guest a relaxing atmosphere in which to unwind. Everything is in pure white, from the walls, floors and furnishings to all the decorations. Raw materials taken from the Alpine flora of the surrounding Bregenzer Wood are used in the specially developed treatments.

Der Spa-Bereich von Susanne Kaufmann im Hotel Post nimmt sich in seiner Gestaltung zurück, um dem Gast eine entspannte Atmosphäre zu bieten. Von den Wänden, Böden und Möbeln bis hin zu sämtlichen Einrichtungsgegenständen und Handtüchern ist alles in Reinweiß gehalten. Die aus der alpinen Pflanzenwelt des umgebenden Bregenzer Waldes gewonnenen Wirkstoffe sind Bestandteil der speziell entwickelten Anwendungen.

Le design discret du spa Susanne Kaufmann situé dans l'Hôtel Post offre au visiteur une atmosphère relaxante dans laquelle se détendre. Tout est d'un blanc immaculé, des murs aux sols, en passant par le mobilier et la décoration. Les matériaux bruts issus de la flore alpine de la forêt de Bregenzer environnante composent les traitements, spécialement développés ici.

De spa van Susanne Kaufmann in het Hotel Post is sober vormgegeven om de gast een ontspannen sfeer te bieden. Van de wanden, vloeren en meubels tot aan de handdoeken is alles uitgevoerd in smetteloos wit. De uit de alpiene flora van het omringende Bregenzer Woud verkregen werkzame stoffen worden gebruikt voor de speciaal ontwikkelde behandelingen.

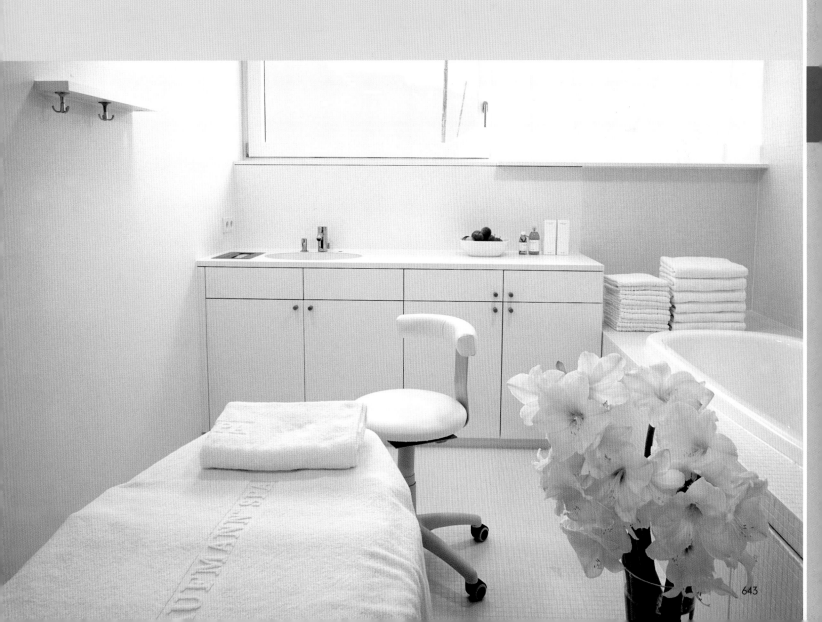

Therme Vals, constructed by architect Peter Zumthor, is an icon of international architecture. The building is made from local materials, including the 60,000 stone tiles of the exterior and interior facades. Inside you will experience water at different temperatures in various large basins and in different rooms. The natural materials and clear, stark architecture create a uniquely soothing atmosphere.

Die Therme Vals, erbaut vom Architekten Peter Zumthor, ist eine Ikone internationaler Architektur. Das Gebäude ist verwachsen mit den Materialien des Ortes, die 60.000 Steinplatten der Außen- und Innenfassade stammen von hier. Im Inneren erlebt man das Elementare des Wassers, der unterschiedlichen Temperaturen, der verschieden großen Becken und Räume. Natürliche Materialien und die strenge, klare Architektur schaffen eine einzigartig beruhigende Atmosphäre.

Les thermes de Vals, construits par l'architecte Peter Zumthor, sont une icône de l'architecture internationale. Le bâtiment est constitué de matériaux locaux, dont les 60 000 tonnes de plaques de pierre des façades extérieure et intérieure. Dans les thermes, vous jouirez d'une eau à différentes températures dans des bassins divers et des salles variées. Les matériaux naturels et l'architecture épurée créent une atmosphère apaisante unique.

De Therme Vals, gebouwd door de architect Peter Zumthor, is een icoon van de internationale architectuur. Het gebouw is vergroeid met de plaatselijke materialen, de 60.000 stenen platen van de buiten- en binnengevel stammen uit deze streek. Binnen worden de essentie van het water en de verschillende temperaturen gewaar. Ook de bassins en de ruimten zijn verschillend groot. Natuurlijke materialen en de strenge, heldere architectuur scheppen een unieke rustgevende sfeer.

It was important for the planners of Berlin's Yi Spa to design an Asiatic culture of relaxation in a modern ambience. Sleek elegance is skillfully combined with traditional motifs. Gray slate, white stone and dark wood contrast with bright floral-patterned glass panes. Exotic plants, exotic scents and subtile audio and light effects complete the design concept.

Den Planern des Yi Spa in Berlin war es wichtig, die asiatische Entspannungskultur in einem modernen Ambiente zu präsentieren. Dafür wurde schlichte Eleganz mit traditionellen Motiven geschickt kombiniert. Grauer Schiefer, weiße Steine und dunkles Holz stehen im Kontrast zu farbigem, floral bedrucktem Glas. Exotische Pflanzen und Düfte sowie intelligente Ton- und Lichteffekte vervollständigen die Entwurfsgedanken.

Il était primordial pour les responsables du Yi Spa de Berlin, de présenter la culture asiatique de la relaxation dans une ambiance moderne. L'élégance soignée est savamment combinée aux motifs traditionnels. Ardoise grise, pierre blanche et bois sombre contrastent avec les panneaux de verre aux vifs motifs floraux. Des plantes et des senteurs exotiques, ainsi que de savants effets audio et lumineux complètent ce concept.

De ontwerpers van de Yi Spa in Berlijn wilden de Aziatische ontspanningscultuur in een moderne ambiance presenteren. Hiervoor combineerden ze heel geschikt sobere elegantie met traditionele motieven. Grijs leisteen, witte stenen en donker hout vormen een contrast met het kleurrijke, met bloemmotieven bedrukte glas. Exotische planten en geuren en geraffineerde geluids- en lichteffecten vullen het ontwerp aan.

THE SMILE YOU GIVE WILL RETURN TO YOU

ART CENTERS AND CONCERT VENUES

CULTURE

Architect Santiago Calatrava developed these "Arts and Science" buildings, which contain five sights worth visiting: the Palau de les Arts Reina Sofia is an extravagant opera house. L'Oceanogràfic is home to the largest aquarium in Europe. The Museo de las Ciencas Príncipe Felipe displays a selection of natural laws. L'Hemisfèric, the 3-D movie theater, is a giant winking eye, opening and closing. L'Umbracle houses the botanical garden.

Die Gebäude der „Künste und der Wissenschaften" wurden vom Architekten Santiago Calatrava entworfen und umfassen fünf Sehenswürdigkeiten: beim Palau de les Arts Reina Sofia handelt es sich um eine extravagante Oper. L'Oceanogràfíc beherbergt das größte Aquarium Europas, das Museo de las Ciencas Príncipe Felipe zeigt eine Auswahl an Naturgesetzen, L'Hemisfèric, das 3-D-Kino, wurde als sich öffnendes und schließendes Auge konstruiert und L'Umbracle ist der botanische Garten.

L'architecte Santiago Calatrava a développé ces bâtiments d' « Arts et de Sciences », regroupant cinq sites à visiter : le Palau de les Arts Reina Sofia est un opéra extravagant ; l'Oceanogràfíc abrite le plus grand aquarium d'Europe ; Le Museo de las Ciencas Príncipe Felipe présente une sélection de phénomènes naturels ; L'Hemisfèric, un cinéma en 3-D, est un œil géant qui s'ouvre et se referme et enfin l'Umbracles accueille un jardin botanique.

De gebouwen voor de 'kunsten en wetenschappen' werden door de architect Santiago Calatrava ontworpen en omvatten vijf bezienswaardigheden: bij het Palau de les Arts Reina Sofia gaat het om een extravagant operagebouw. L'Oceanogràfic herbergt het grootste aquarium van Europa, het Museo de las Ciencias Príncipe Felipe is een natuurwetenschappelijk museum, L'Hemisfèric, de 3D-bioscoop, werd geconstrueerd als een oog dat zich opent en sluit en L'Umbracle is de botanische tuin.

659

This museum is characterized by its twisting tower and façade. The tower offers visitors fantastic views over San Francisco and the entire Bay Area from its lookout level. For the building's stately façade, thousands of copper plates were perforated and stamped with different designs. This was intended to integrate the construction's modern architecture into the natural landscape of the surrounding park, a solution which manages to lend the building and its distinctive personality a bit more liveliness.

Das Museum wird durch einen Turm und seine Fassade geprägt. Der Turm bietet eine für Besucher zugängliche Aussichts-etage und ermöglicht fantastische Ausblicke auf die gesamte Bay Area um San Francisco. Für die imposante Fassade wur-den tausende von Kupfertafeln mit individuellen Mustern geprägt und perforiert, um eine möglichst weitgehende Anpas-sung der modernen Architektur an die natürlichen Vorgaben der umgebenden Parklandschaft zu erreichen. Diese Lösung verleiht dem Bauwerk mit seiner so entschlossenen Persönlichkeit mehr Lebendigkeit.

Ce musée est caractérisé par une façade et une tour déformées par la torsion. Depuis l'étage d'observation, la tour offre aux visiteurs une vue fantastique sur San Francisco et sa baie. Pour l'imposante façade, des milliers de panneaux de cuivre ont été perforés et pressés de différents motifs, dans le but d'intégrer l'architecture moderne de la construction à l'environnement naturel du parc avoisinant : une solution ayant servi à rendre l'édifice et sa personnalité hors du commun davantage vivants.

De toren en de gevel van het museum kenmerken het gebouw. De toren beschikt over een voor bezoekers toegankelijke panoramaverdieping met fantastisch uitzicht op de gehele Bay Area van San Francisco. Voor de indrukwekkende gevel werden duizenden koperen plaatjes met verschillende patronen beslagen en geperforeerd om de moderne architectuur zo veel mogelijk af te stemmen op het omringende parklandschap. Hierdoor krijgt het bouwwerk met zijn bijzonder resolute karakter meer levendigheid.

Architekt Frank O. Gehry has managed to offer a striking contrast to the highrise glass rectangles now posing as office buildings and the monotonous white of "modern" art museums. Despite the irregular and asymmetrically shaped surfaces, Gehry has been able to achieve an aesthetic whole. A space for art which has itself become a work of art – a gigantic titanium sculpture.

Der Architekt Frank O. Gehry verstand es, einen Gegensatz zu den rechteckigen Glasquadern der Bürohochhäuser und den nüchternen weiß gehaltenen „modernen" Museumsbauten zu schaffen. Trotz der unruhigen und asymmetrischen Oberflächen und Linien gelang Gehry eine ästhetische Einheit. Ein Raum für Kunst, der gleichzeitig selbst zum Kunstwerk geworden ist – eine riesige Skulptur aus Titan.

L'architecte Frank O. Gehry a réussi à offrir un édifice contrastant efficacement avec les gratte-ciels rectangulaires de verre des centres d'affaires ou les habituels musées d'art « moderne » d'un blanc monotone. En dépit de surface irrégulières et asymétriques, l'œuvre de Gehry jouit d'une esthétique remarquable. Un espace dédié à l'art, devenu lui-même œuvre d'art : une gigantesque sculpture de titane.

De architect Frank O. Gehry slaagde erin een contrast tussen de hoge, rechthoekige glazen kantoorpanden en de sobere witte 'moderne' museumgebouwen te creëren. Ondanks de rusteloze, asymmetrische oppervlakken en lijnen realiseerde Gehry een esthetische eenheid. Een gebouw dat is ontworpen voor de kunst en tevens zelf een kunstwerk is – een reusachtige sculptuur van titanium.

Together with some of his artist friends, the painter, sculptor, art critic and philosopher Donald Judd has transformed a former Marfa military base (ammunition factory, hangar and garages) into a large, seemingly autarchic complex. His creation places art in a harmonious relation to nature and the existing structures in a new definition of space. This out-of-the-way location is visited each year by more than ten-thousand art lovers and architects from around the world.

Der Maler, Zeichner, Bildhauer, Architekt, Kunstkritiker und Philosoph Donald hat mit ausgewählten Künstlerfreunden in Marfa auf einem ehemaligen Militärgelände (Munitionsfabrik, Hangar, Werkstätten) eine große, autark wirkende Anlage geschaffen, die Kunst in der Natur mit vorhandenen Gebäuden in einem neuen Maßstab zu versöhnen weiß. Der abgelegene Ort wird jährlich von mehr als zehntausend internationalen Kunstkennern und Architekten besucht.

Accompagné de certains de ses amis artistes, le peintre, sculpteur, critique d'art et philosophe Donald Judd a transformé une ancienne base militaire (fabrique de munitions, hangars et garages) en un vaste complexe quasi autarcique. Sa création place l'art dans une relation harmonieuse à la nature et les nouvelles structures dans une nouvelle définition de l'espace. Ce lieu perdu au milieu de nulle part est visité chaque année par plus de dix mille amateurs d'art et d'architectes des quatre coins du globe.

De schilder, tekenaar, beeldhouwer, architect, kunstcriticus en filosoof Donald Judd heeft met selecte kunstenaarsvrienden in Marfa op een voormalig militair terrein (munitiefabriek, hangar, werkplaatsen) een groot autarkisch aandoend complex gerealiseerd dat op vernieuwende wijze kunst in de natuur met de bestaande gebouwen weet te verzoenen. De afgelegen locatie wordt jaarlijks door meer dan tienduizend internationale kunstkenners en architecten bezocht.

When the 250-year-old Edo-era temple became a little too cramped, a new and unique temple was constructed. Tadao Ando has created a building in which traditional Japanese elements are integrated into a contemporary context. A large space constructed of filigreed rectangular posts arranged at regular intervals is separated by glass partitions. Light from the outside world is cast within and viewers on the outside can watch the goings-on inside.

Da die Räumlichkeiten des 250 Jahre alten, auf die Edo-Epoche zurückgehenden Tempels nicht mehr ausreichten, entstand ein neuer einzigartiger Anbau. Tadao Ando schuf ein Gebäude, in dem traditionelle japanische Elemente in einen zeitgemäßen Kontext gesetzt wurden. So entstand ein großer Raum aus filigranen, rechteckigen Pfosten, die in regelmäßigen Abständen angeordnet und durch Glaseinsätze getrennt sind. So dringen Licht und Umgebung ins Innere, während man auch von außen wahrnehmen kann, was im Gebäudeinneren vorgeht.

Lorsque le temple de style Edo vieux de 250 ans fut un peu trop abîmé, on en fit construire un nouveau. Tadao Ando a créé un édifice dans lequel les éléments traditionnels japonais intègrent un contexte contemporain. C'est un large espace fait de poteaux rectangulaires de bois séparés par des panneaux de verre. La lumière du jour peut inonder la pièce et de l'extérieur, le visiteur peut observer ce qui s'y passe.

Aangezien de 250 jaar oude, uit de Edoperiode stammende tempel te klein werd, werd een unieke aanbouw gerealiseerd. Tadao Ando ontwierp een gebouw waarin traditionele Japanse elementen in een eigentijds kader werden geplaatst. Hij concipieerde een grote ruimte van rechthoekige palen die in regelmatige afstanden zijn opgesteld en worden gescheiden door glazen inzetstukken. Zo kan het licht en de omgeving naar binnen dringen en kan men tevens van buiten zien wat zich in het gebouw afspeelt.

The Graz art house seems to float like a bubble right in the historic center of town. A bluish, shimmering shell is suspended, unbuttressed, above the glassed-in ground floor, stretched over the two massive exhibition levels. So-called "nozzles" grow out of the surface of the acrylic glass „skin", prominent natural light openings which face the north to allow optimal viewing conditions. In the upper levels, bridges connect the new construction with the "Iron House", the cast iron under historic preservation status which was carefully renovated during construction of the art house.

Wie eine Luftblase schwebt die Kunsthalle im historischen Kern von Graz. Eine bläulich schimmernde Hülle über dem gläsernen Erdgeschoß umspielt stützenfrei die zwei grossflächigen Ausstellungsebenen. Aus der Oberfläche der „Skin", einer Haut aus Acrylglas, wachsen die „Nozzles", markante Tageslichtöffnungen, die nach Norden geneigt für eine optimale Beleuchtungssituation sorgen. In den Obergeschossen verbinden Brücken den Neubau mit dem so genannten Eisernen Haus, dessen denkmalgeschützte Gusseisenkonstruktion im Zuge der Errichtung des Kunsthauses Graz behutsam renoviert wurde.

L'espace artistique de Graz semble flotter tel une bulle en plein cœur du centre historique de la ville. Un chatoyant mollusque bleuté est suspendu, comme en lévitation, au-dessus du rez-de-chaussée de verre, étendu sur deux étages d'exposition. Des espèces de « canules » poussent à la surface de la « peau » de verre acrylique, des puits de lumière naturelle orientés plein Nord permettent des conditions de visite optimale. Aux étages, des passerelles relient la nouvelle construction à la « Maison d'Acier », une structure en acier, classée et protégée, soigneusement rénovée durant la construction de l'espace artistique.

Als een luchtbel zweeft het Kunsthaus in het historische centrum van Graz. De buitenzijde van het gebouw bestaat uit blauw getinte acrylplaten. Vanuit de 'skin' worden de 'nozzles' getild, markante op het noorden gerichte lichtschachten die voor daglicht zorgen. Op de bovenverdiepingen verbinden bruggen het nieuwe gebouw met het zogeheten Eisernes Haus. In het kader van de bouw van het Kunsthaus Graz werd de gietijzeren constructie van dit monument behoedzaam gerenoveerd.

Kunsthalle K21, the second location for the state of North-Rhine Westphalia's art collection, is spectacularly situated in an idyllic park not far from the state capital building. K21 Munich architects Kiessler + Partner transformed a former mansion, a showcase of 19th-century architecture, into a stunning museum topped with a stately glass dome.

Die Kunsthalle „K21", der zweite Standort der Kunstsammlung Nordrhein-Westfalen, liegt spektakulär in einem idyllischen Park ganz in der Nähe des nordrhein-westfälischen Landtags. Für K21 wurde das ehemalige Ständehaus, ein repräsentativer Bau des 19. Jahrhunderts, von den Münchner Architekten Kiessler + Partner in ein eindrucksvolles Museum mit imposanter Glaskuppel verwandelt.

Kunsthalle K21, le second lieu d'exposition des collections de l'état de Rhénanie du Nord – Westphalie est spectaculairement situé dans un parc idyllique. Les architectes munichois Kiessler + Partner du K21 ont transformé une ancienne demeure, fleuron de l'architecture du XIXe siècle, en une musée étonnant surmonté d'un imposant dôme de verre.

De Kunsthalle K21, de tweede locatie van de kunstverzameling van de deelstaat Noordrijn-Westfalen, is spectaculair gelegen in een idyllisch park vlakbij het parlementsgebouw van de deelstaat. Voor K21 werd het voormalige statengebouw, een representatief gebouw uit de negentiende eeuw, door de architecten Kiessler + Partner uit München getransformeerd tot een indrukwekkend museum met een imposante glazen koepel.

683

Situated in Austria's largest wine-growing region, Loisium is a center like no other. The visitors' center greets guests above ground while below a world of cellars opens up, housing installations meant to whisk visitors away into a world of the senses. With the construction of this building, Steven Holl has transformed the geometry of this network of cellars in an abstract, three-dimensional spatial language. The building's outer cladding is composed of brushed aluminum, while the inside surfaces are partially coated with pale corkwood.

In der größten Weinbaustadt Österreichs entstand mit dem Loisium ein Zentrum ganz besonderer Art. Oberirdisch empfängt die Gäste das Besucherzentrum. Unterirdisch öffnet sich eine Kellerwelt, deren Inszenierungen die Besucher in eine Welt der Sinne entführen sollen. Steven Holl wandelt mit seinem Gebäude die Geometrie des Kellernetzes in eine abstrakte, dreidimensionale räumliche Sprache um. Die Außenhaut des Gebäudes besteht aus gebürstetem Aluminium, innen wurden die Oberflächen zum Teil mit hellem Kork verkleidet.

Situé dans la plus grande région vinicole d'Autriche, le Loisium est un centre unique en son geure. Cet espace accueille les visiteurs dans un monde de caves, dotées d'installations propices à un feu d'artifice des sens. En construisant cet immeuble, Steven Holl a transformé la géométrie de ce réseau de caves en un langage abstrait, spatial et tridimensionnel. Le revêtement extérieur est composé d'aluminium brossé et les surfaces intérieures sont partiellement recouvertes de liège clair.

In de grootste wijnbouwstad van Oostenrijk ontstond met het Loisium een centrum van bijzondere aard. Bovengronds worden de gasten ontvangen in het bezoekerscentrum. Ondergronds gaat voor de bezoekers een onderwereld open die hun meeneemt op een reis door de belevingswereld. Steven Holl zette de geometrie van het keldernetwerk om in een abstracte, driedimensionale ruimtelijke taal. De buitenkant van het gebouw bestaat uit geborsteld aluminium en binnen werden de vlakken deels met licht kurk bekleed.

The basic shape of the new Mercedes-Benz Museum consists of three bands continually winding back in on themselves, reminiscent of a clover leaf. This design gives rise to paths which roll from one to the next like an architectonic Mobius strip, resulting in nine levels. An elevator transports visitors from the foyer to the top floor. The museum is viewed from top to bottom along a timeline which begins with the invention of the automobile and proceeds downward to the present. The building's exterior consists of spiraling bands of aluminum interspersed with the dark glass strips which are the windows.

Die Grundform des neuen Mercedes-Benz Museums besteht aus drei endlos in sich selbst zurückkehrenden Schlaufen, die an ein dreiblättriges Kleeblatt erinnern. Die so entstandenen Wege verschlingen sich ineinander und ergeben neun Ebenen. Der Besucher wird vom Foyer aus mit dem Aufzug auf die oberste Ebene gebracht. Von hier aus kann er sich bis ins Erdgeschoss entlang einer Zeitachse von der Erfindung des Automobils bis zur Gegenwart hinunterbegeben. Die Außenhaut besteht aus ineinander verschlungenen Aluminium- und dunkleren Fensterbändern.

La forme de base du nouveau Musée Mercedes-Benz consiste en un assemblage de trois bandes aux bordures découpées, rappelant une feuille de trèfle. Ce design a engendré un circuit d'exposition suivant une bande de Mobius architectonique, sur neuf niveaux. Un ascenseur conduit les visiteurs du hall d'entrée au dernier étage. On visite le musée du haut vers le bas en suivant une frise chronologique commençant avec l'invention de l'automobile, puis descendant jusqu'à aujourd'hui. L'extérieur du bâtiment est constitué de bandes d'aluminium circulaires, entrecoupées de bandes de verre sombre constituant les fenêtres.

De basisvorm van het nieuwe Mercedes-Benzmuseum bestaat uit drie eindeloos in zichzelf terugkerende lussen die doen denken aan een klavertje drie. De banen die op deze manier ontstaan, verstrengelen zich en vormen nieuwe etages. De bezoekers worden vanuit de foyer met de lift naar de bovenste verdieping gebracht. Van hieruit begeven ze zich langs een tijdlijn vanaf de uitvinding van het automobiel tot aan nu weer naar beneden. De buitenkant bestaat uit aluminium en donkere ramen.

689

Located between 53rd and 54th Street in New York, the buildings which make up MoMA were connected by a new annex in 2004. A glass cube was created, leading visitors into the museum proper. This light-flooded structure provides spectacular views of the Abby Aldrich Rockefeller sculpture garden and the Donald and Catherine Marron atrium. Besides the entry foyer at ground level, the interior houses variously themed galleries, each of which takes up an entire floor.

Das zwischen der 53. und der 54. Straße gelegene MoMA in New York bekam 2004 einen Anbau, der die bereits vorhandenen Gebäude miteinander verbinden sollte. So entstand ein gläserner Kubus, der die Besucher in das Museum führt. Der lichtdurchflutete Gebäudeteil lässt spektakuläre Blicke auf den Abby-Aldrich-Rockefeller-Skulpturengarten und das Donald-und-Catherine-Marron-Atrium zu. Im Inneren befinden sich neben dem Eingangsbereich im Erdgeschoss, verschiedene Galerien, die thematisch jeweils ein Stockwerk für sich beanspruchen.

Situés entre les 53ème et 54ème rues à New York, les bâtiments formant le MoMA ont été reliés par une annexe en 2004. Un cube de verre a été créé, conduisant les visiteurs jusque dans le musée. Cette structure baignée de lumière offre une vue spectaculaire sur le jardin Abby Aldrich Rockefeller et l'atrium Donald and Catherine Marron. En plus du hall d'entrée au rez-de-chaussée, l'intérieur accueille différentes galeries thématiques, chacune occupant un étage entier.

Het tussen 53rd en 54th Street gelegen MoMA in New York kreeg in 2004 een aanbouw die de reeds existerende gebouwen met elkaar moest verbinden. Zo ontstond een glazen kubus die de bezoekers het museum binnenleidt. Het lichte gebouw biedt spectaculaire gezichten op de Abby Aldrich Rockefeller Sculpture Garden en het Donald en Catherine Marron Atrium. Binnen bevinden zich naast de entree op de begane grond, verscheidene tentoonstellingsruimten met op elke verdieping een ander thema.

A conical 30-meter-high entry sculpture constructed at the foot of the Mori highrise aesthetically draws visitors into the building. The façade consists of a filigree steel frame and large glass panels surrounding a spiral staircase. The actual exhibit, however, is located on the 53rd and 54th floors. High-speed elevators whisk guests from the lobby up to the collections and offer breathtaking views of Tokyo.

Eine kegelförmige 30 Meter hohe Eingangsskulptur am Fuß des Mori-Hochhauses zieht den Besucher förmlich in das Gebäude hinein. Die Fassade besteht aus filigranen Stahlträgern und großflächigen Glaspaneelen und beherbergt eine spiralförmige Treppe. Die eigentliche Ausstellung jedoch befindet sich in der 53. und 54. Etage des Gebäudes, die durch extrem schnelle Aufzüge von der Lobby aus erreicht werden und atemberaubende Blicke über Tokio zulassen.

Une sculpture conique de 30 mètres de haut construite au pied du gratte-ciel Mori conduit majestueusement le visiteur à l'intérieur du bâtiment. La façade est constituée d'un cadre d'acier et de larges panneaux de verre surplombant un escalier en spirale. L'exposition permanente, cependant, se trouve aux 53ème et 54ème étages. Des ascenseurs à grande vitesse élèvent les visiteurs du vestibule aux collections et offrent une vue imprenable sur Tokyo.

Een kegelvormige, dertig meter hoge ingangssculptuur aan de voet van het Mori-flatgebouw trekt de bezoekers letterlijk naar binnen. De gevel bestaat uit filigreine stalen balken en grote glaspanelen en bevat een spiraalvormige trap. De eigenlijke expositie bevindt zich echter op de 53e en 54e verdieping van het gebouw. Deze kan vanuit de lobby worden bereikt met de uitzonderlijk snelle liften en bieden adembenemende gezichten op Tokyo.

The Quai Branly Museum captivates with the diversity of its architectural design. The visitor is led into the museum gallery by way of a series of small paths winding through a landscape of hills. The building is an irregular 729-foot-long (220-meter-long) block, most of which rests on pillars. Thirty eye-catching boxes protrude from the north façade, clad in bright-colored wooden panels. These form small chambers inside the gallery. The neighboring administrative building has been transformed into a vertical garden.

Das Museum am Quai Branly besticht durch seine Vielfältigkeit der Architektur. Der Besucher wird über kleine Pfade in einer Hügellandschaft zur Museumsgalerie geführt. Dieser ist ein geknickter 220 Meter langer Gebäuderiegel, der zum größten Teil auf Pfeilern steht. Markant stechen aus dieser Nordfassade dreißig Boxen heraus. Diese sind mit Holzpaneelen in kräftigen Farben verkleidet und formen im Innern der Galerie kleine Kammern. Das angrenzende Verwaltungsgebäude wurde in einen vertikalen Garten verwandelt.

Le musée du Quai Branly captive par la diversité de son design architectural. Le visiteur est conduit vers la galerie d'exposition par une série de petits chemins serpentant entre un paysage de petites collines. Le bâtiment est un bloc irrégulier de 220 mètres de long, dont une majeure partie repose sur des piliers. Trente boîtes immanquables se détachent de la façade Nord, recouvertes de panneaux de bois colorés. Celles-ci forment de petites chambres, à l'intérieur de la galerie. Le bâtiment administratif attenant a été transformé en jardin vertical.

Het museum aan de Quai Branly bekoort door zijn veelzijdige architectuur. De bezoeker wordt via kleine paadjes door een heuvellandschap naar het museum geleid. Het museum is een geknikt 220 meter lang gebouw dat voor een groot deel op pijlers rust. Uit de gevel aan de noordzijde steken dertig dozen. Deze zijn bekleed met houten panelen in krachtige kleuren en vormen binnen in het museum kleine kamertjes. Het aangrenzende administratiegebouw werd getransformeerd tot een verticale tuin.

701

For those of you with a sweet tooth, you will find the Ritter Museum right next to the chocolate factory. Smooth facades of light-colored limestone and spacious windows lend the architecture here a quiet, monolithic character. The building's 144 x 144 foot (44 x 44 meter) floor space is reminiscent of the chocolate maker's famous square package and is divided into two wings. The larger is devoted to the Marlies Hoppe-Ritter collection and changing exhibits. It also houses the museum shop and café. The smaller wing is where you will find the Ritter Sport visitors' center.

Direkt neben der Schokoladenfabrik befindet sich das Museum Ritter. Flächige Fassaden aus hellem, warm getöntem Kalkstein und große Fenster verleihen der Architektur einen ruhigen, monolithischen Charakter. Die Grundfläche des Baus von 44 x 44 Metern greift das für den Schokoladenhersteller kennzeichnende Quadrat auf und ist in zwei Flügel aufgeteilt: der größere ist der Sammlung Marlies Hoppe-Ritter und den Sonderausstellungen gewidmet und beherbergt Museums-Café und -Shop. Im kleineren Flügel ist das Besucherzentrum der Firma Ritter Sport untergebracht.

Ceux qui ont un faible pour le sucré trouveront le Ritter Museum juste à côté de la fabrique de chocolat. De douces façades de pierre calcaire claire et de spacieuses baies vitrées insufflent à cette architecture un caractère paisible et monolithique. Le sol de l'édifice, mesurant 44X44 mètres rappelle les emballages carrés du chocolat de la marque et se divise en deux ailes. La plus grande est consacrée à la collection Marlies Hoppe-Ritter et aux expositions temporaires. Elle accueille également la boutique et le café du musée. Vous trouverez dans l'aile la plus petite, le centre d'informations visiteurs de Ritter Sport.

Het museum Ritter bevindt zich direct naast de chocoladefabriek. Tweedimensionale gevels van licht, warm gekleurd kalksteen en grote ramen geven de architectuur een rustig monolithisch karakter. Het grondvlak van het gebouw van 44 x 44 meter verwijst naar het voor de chocoladefabrikant kenmerkende vierkant. Het gebouw bestaat uit twee vleugels: de grotere vleugel is gewijd aan de verzameling van Marlies Hoppe-Ritter en de speciale exposities en herbergt tevens het museumcafé en de museumwinkel. In de kleinere vleugel is het bezoekerscentrum van de firma Ritter Sport ondergebracht.

Copenhagen's new opera house is located in a place of great symbolic significance. Not only is it directly opposite from Amalienborg Castle, it also forms the end of an architectonic axis, stretching from the marble church and the octagonal rococo palace with its equestrian statue of Frederik V in the center through to the other side of the water. The opera house's acoustics are described as unique. A total of six stages offer artistic potential previously unknown in Copenhagen.

Das neue Kopenhagener Opernhaus steht an einem Ort mit großer symbolischer Bedeutung. Es liegt nicht nur direkt gegenüber Schloss Amalienborg, sondern bildet das Ende einer architektonischen Achse, die sich von der Marmorkirche durch die achteckige Rokoko-Palastanlage mit der Reiterstatue Frederiks V. im Zentrum hinüber auf die andere Seite des Wassers erstreckt. Die Akustik des Opernhauses wird als einzigartig bezeichnet und insgesamt sechs Bühnen bieten künstlerische Möglichkeiten, wie man sie in Kopenhagen bisher nicht kannte.

Le nouvel opéra de Copenhague se trouve dans un lieu très symbolique. Il ne fait pas seulement directement face au Château Amalienborg, mais forme également un axe architectonique, s'étendant de l'église de marbre et du palais octogonal d'influence rococo dont une statue équestre de Frederick V orne le centre, jusqu'à l'autre rive du fleuve. L'acoustique de cet opéra est qualifiée d'unique. Un total de six étages permet des possibilités artistiques encore jamais vues à Copenhague.

Het nieuwe operagebouw van Kopenhagen staat op een locatie van grote symbolische betekenis. Het ligt niet alleen recht tegenover slot Amalienborg maar vormt ook het uiteinde van een architectonische as die zich van de Marmerkerk via het achthoekige rococopaleis met het ruiterstandbeeld van Frederik V uitstrekt tot de overzijde van het water. De akoestiek van het operagebouw is uniek en het gebouw beschikt over in totaal zes podia.

Undulating like waves above the district, this hall rests on just two of the concrete supports traversing the entire market. Breaking through the façade, decorated with wooden panels on the building's south side, they support the 108 vertical, variously shaped laminated wooden arches which make up the roof's billowing shape. This steel construction, which is composed of 55,000 separate parts, is supported by a few steel braces and covered with a mosaic of 300,000 colored ceramic tiles.

In Wellen das Geviert überspannend, ruht die Halle auf lediglich zwei die ganze Markthalle durchziehenden Betonträgern. Auf der Südseite durchstoßen sie wuchtig die von Holzpaneelen geschmückte Fassade; vor allem aber tragen sie die 108 unterschiedlich geformten, vertikal laminierten Holzbogen, aus denen sich die Wogengestalt des Daches ergibt. Diese von wenigen Stahlstreben gestützte Holzkonstruktion aus 55.000 Einzelteilen wurde mit einem Mosaik aus 300.000 farbigen Keramikplatten gedeckt.

Ondulant comme la mer au-dessus du quartier, cette halle repose sur deux des poutres de béton traversant tout le marché. Ressortant par la façade, décorée de panneaux de bois sur le côté Sud du bâtiment, elles soutiennent les 108 arches de bois laminé verticales de formes variées constituant la forme ondoyante du toit. Cette construction en acier, composée de 55 000 pièces, est soutenue par quelques poutrelles d'acier et couverte d'une mosaïque constituée de 300 000 ardoises de céramique colorée.

De overdekte markt steunt slechts op twee betonbalken die door de hele markthal lopen. Aan de zuidzijde doorbreken ze krachtig de met houten panelen beklede gevel. Maar ze dragen vooral ook de 108 verschillend gevormde, verticaal gelamineerde houten bogen die verantwoordelijk zijn voor het golvende karakter van het dak. Deze door stalen balken ondersteunde houtconstructie van 55.000 afzonderlijke delen werd bekleed met een mozaïek van 300.000 kleurrijke keramische platen.

714

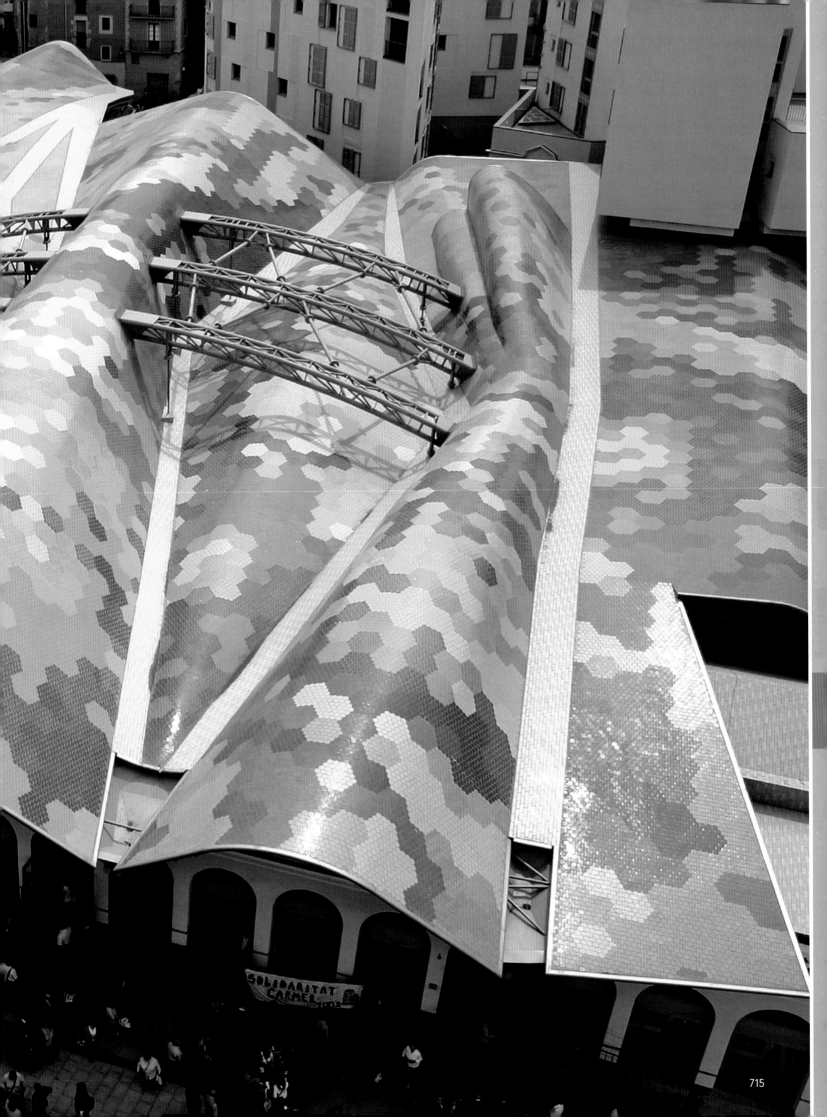

The Tate Modern was constructed in a former electrical plant on the shore of the Thames with an eye to providing more space for the ever-increasing number of modern artworks housed by the Tate Gallery. The building is constructed of two parallel blocks; the enormous turbine hall houses a dramatic entry area and space for the largest sculptures while the galleries are located in the boiler house, encompassing three levels. The Swiss architecture firm Herzog & de Meuron added a two-storey glass penthouse to the top of the building. This is lit up at night along with the old chimney, which is known as the Swiss Light.

Um der steigenden Anzahl moderner Kunstwerke der Tate Gallery neuen Raum zu geben, wurde in einem ehemaligen Elektrizitätswerk am Themse-Ufer die Tate Modern eröffnet. Das Gebäude besteht aus zwei parallel verlaufenden Riegeln. In der riesigen Turbinenhalle befindet sich der eindrucksvolle Eingangsbereich und Raum für große Skulpturen. Im Kesselhaus finden sich die Galerien, die sich über drei Etagen erstrecken. Herzog & deMeuron setzten dem Gebäude einen zweistöckigen gläsernen Riegel auf. Dieser sowie der erhaltene Schornstein werden bei Nacht beleuchtet und ergeben gemeinsam das so genannte Swiss Light.

La Tate Modern fut édifiée en lieu et place d'une ancienne usine électrique, sur les rives de la Tamise et dans l'esprit de réserver un peu d'espace pour le nombre croissant d'œuvres d'arts modernes appartenant à la Tate Gallery. Le bâtiment est constitué de deux blocs parallèles ; l'énorme salle des machines abrite un vestibule magistral, assez spacieux pour contenir les sculptures les plus imposantes, tandis que les galeries se situent dans le bâtiment des chaudières et occupent trois étages. Le bureau d'architecture Herzog & de Meuron a ajouté au sommet de l'immeuble, un penthouse de verre sur deux étages. Il est illuminé la nuit, tout comme l'ancienne cheminée, appelée aussi la Lumière suisse.

Om het groeiende aantal moderne kunstwerken van de Tate Gallery onder te kunnen brengen, verrees in een voormalige elektriciteitscentrale aan de oever van de Theems het Tate Modern. Aan het gebouw werden twee balkvormige verdiepingen toegevoegd. In de enorme turbinehal bevindt zich de indrukwekkende entree en ruimte voor grote sculpturen. De tentoonstellingsruimten zijn ondergebracht in het ketelhuis en bestrijken drie verdiepingen. Herzog & de Meuron plaatsten op het gebouw een glazen constructie van twee verdiepingen. Deze wordt 's avonds, evenals de behouden gebleven schoorsteen, verlicht en samen vormen ze het zogeheten Swiss light.

Peñafiel Castle stands on a hill high above the town of the same name in Spain's Valladolid wine-growing region. The wing which houses the exhibition halls, a wine shop and a restaurant was constructed right inside the castle's old defensive walls. The building's outstretched body, clad in filigree woodwork, is discreetly integrated into the existing castle structure. The choice of materials is also a reflection of the region's deep-rooted wine tradition, with wooden lamellae reminiscent of Barrique barrel staves.

Oberhalb des kleinen Ortes im Weinbaugebiet Valladolid liegt das Kastell Peñafiel. Inmitten der alten Mauern wurde ein Gebäuderiegel eingesetzt, der die Ausstellungsräume, einen Weinhandel und ein Restaurant beherbergt. Der lang gestreckte Baukörper wurde aus filigranen Holzelementen gefertigt und fügt sich zurückhaltend in die vorhandenen Gebäudestrukturen ein. Auch die Materialwahl ist eine Anspielung auf die Tradition der Weinherstellung: Die verwendeten Holzlamellen erinnern an Streifen der Barrique-Fässer.

Le Château Peñafiel domine une colline surplombant la ville espagnole du même nom, dans la région vinicole du Valladolid. L'aile abritant les halls d'exposition, la boutique de vins et le restaurant a été édifiée à l'intérieur même des anciens remparts du château. Le corps allongé de l'édifice, recouvert de planches de bois, est secrètement intégré à la structure pré-existante du château. Le choix des matériaux reflète également une tradition régionale vinicole bien ancrée, avec ses lattes de bois rappelant les tonneaux.

Boven het kleine plaatsje in het wijnbouwgebied Valladolid ligt het kasteel Peñafiel. Binnen de oude muren werd een bouwwerk opgetrokken dat de expositieruimten, een wijnzaak en een restaurant herbergt. Het langgerekte gebouw bestaat uit filigreine houtelementen en past zich terughoudend aan de structuren van de bestaande gebouwen aan. Ook de materiaalkeuze is een toespeling op de traditie van de wijnbouw: de gebruikte houten lamellen doen denken aan de duigen van barriques.

PUBLIC BUILDINGS AND PLACES OF INTEREST

LANDMARKS

The America's Cup Pavilion is an integral component in the refurbishment of the industrial harbor area and the heart of the America's Cup. Architect David Chipperfield's "veles e vents" (sail and wind) pavilion is an icon of the Cup, jutting out as it does into the harbor opposite the sailing teams' temporary constructions. The so-called Foredeck contains a four-storey pavilion with restaurants and bars, shopping, conference rooms and a viewing platform.

Der America's Cup Pavillon ist integrativer Bestandteil der Neuordnung des industriellen Hafengeländes und Kernstück des America's Cup. Stellvertretend dafür steht der Pavillon „Veles e vents (Segel und Winde)" vom Architekten David Chipperfield in exponierter Hafenlage den temporären Bauten der Segelteams gegenüber. Das so genannte Foredeck umfasst einen viergeschossigen Pavillon mit Restaurants und Bars, Einkaufsmöglichkeiten, Konferenzeinrichtungen sowie einer Aussichtsplattform.

Le pavillon de la Coupe de l'América est une composante indissociable de la réhabilitation de la zone du port de commerce, mais aussi le cœur de la Coupe de l'América. Le pavillon « veles e vents » (voiles et vent) de l'architecte David Chipperfield est une icône de la Coupe, se découpant dans le port, face aux constructions temporaires des équipes participantes. Le Pont avant, c'est son nom, est un pavillon de quatre étages, comprenant des restaurants, bars, boutiques, salles de conférence et une plate-forme d'observation.

Het America's Cup Pavillon vormt een integraal bestanddeel van de herordening van het industriële havengebied en kern van de America's Cup. Het paviljoen 'Veles e vents' (zeilen en winden) van de architect David Chipperfield bevindt zich tegenover de tijdelijke onderkomens van de zeilteams. Het zogeheten 'Foredeck' omvat een paviljoen van vier verdiepingen met restaurants en bars, winkels, conferentiezalen en een uitzichtplatform.

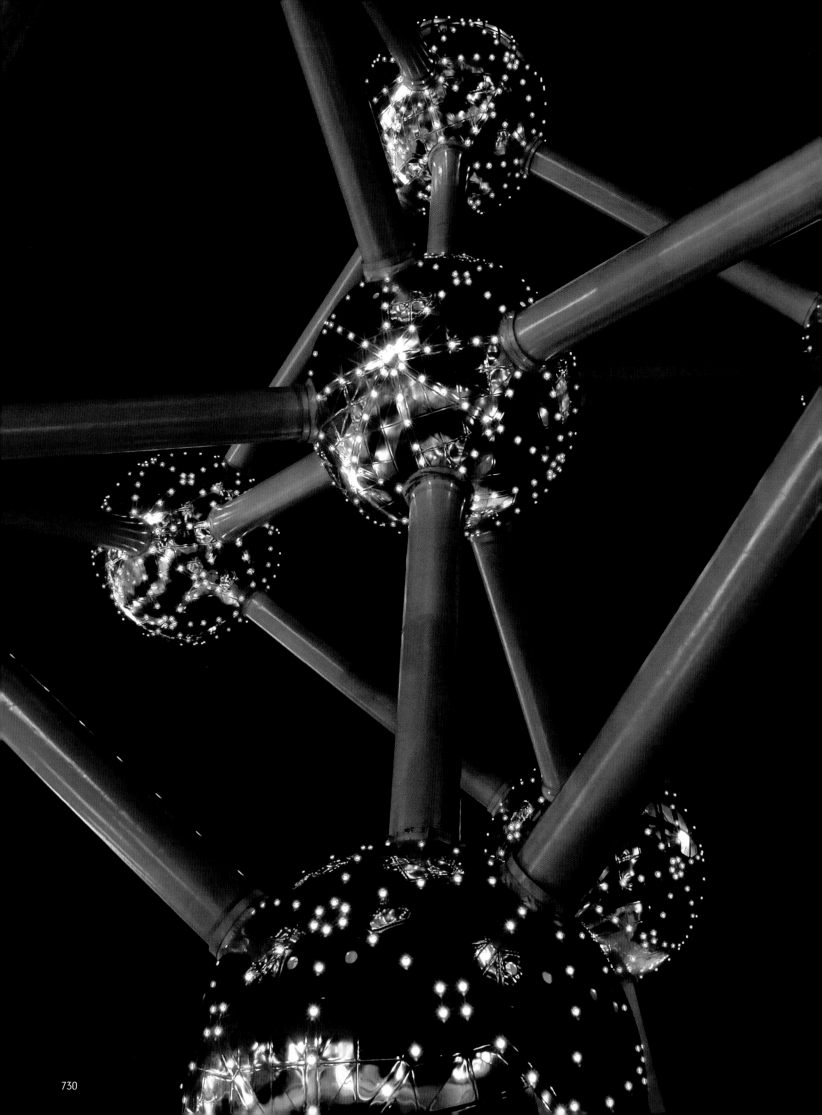

The Atomium in Brussels is considered one of the most innovative buildings in Europe, rivaling even the Eiffel Tower. It underwent extensive renovation in 2006. The lowest sphere, previously the entry area, is now devoted to the history of the Atomium's construction. Following the escalators, you first reach the special exhibits sphere, then the central sphere, where you can amaze yourself with interactive "Société de Pinxi" cartoons. The elevator will bring you to the topmost sphere, where a restaurant and panorama of the European capital greet you.

Das Atomium in Brüssel gehört neben dem Eiffelturm in Paris wohl zu den tollkühnsten Gebäuden in Europa und wurde 2006 generalsaniert. Die unterste Kugel, der ehemalige Eingangsbereich, ist der Entstehung des Atomiums gewidmet. Folgt man den Rolltreppen, erreicht man erst die Kugel der Sonderausstellungen, dann die zentrale Kugel, in der es interaktive Animationen von „Société de Pinxi" zu bestaunen gibt. Mit dem Aufzug gelangt man in die oberste Kugel mit einem Panoramablick und in das Restaurant darüber.

L'Atomium de Bruxelles est considéré comme l'une des structures les plus innovantes d'Europe, rivalisant avec la Tour Eiffel. Il a subi une rénovation complète en 2006. La sphère la plus proche du sol, servant auparavant d'entrée, est à présent dédiée à l'histoire de la construction de l'Atomium. En suivant les escalators, vous atteignez la sphère des expositions temporaires, puis la sphère centrale, où vous pourrez vous divertir avec les dessins animés de la société « De Pinxi ». Les ascenseurs vous emmènent ensuite vers la sphère du sommet, où un restaurant et une vue panoramique de la capitale vous attendent.

Het Atomium in Brussel behoort naast de Eiffeltoren in Parijs waarschijnlijk tot de vermetelste gebouwen in Europa en werd in 2006 volledig gerenoveerd. De onderste bol en de voormalige ingang is nu gewijd aan de ontstaansgeschiedenis van het Atomium. Als men de roltrappen volgt, bereikt men eerst de bol met tijdelijke exposities, vervolgens de centrale bol waarin interactieve animaties van de 'société de Pinxi' getoond worden. Met de lift bereikt men de bovenste bol met een panoramisch zicht en het erboven gelegen restaurant.

This colorful pedestrian bridge is the result of a collaboration between the Glass Museum and Dave Chihuly, the famed glass artist and Tacoma native. It represents a connection between the city's downtown and the shore of the Thea Foss Waterway. Visitors walk under a beautifully colored glass ceiling and past 20-meter-high glass sculptures to an enormous display case.

Die farbenfrohe Fußgängerbrücke entstand durch eine Zusammenarbeit zwischen dem ansässigen Glasmuseum und dem einheimischen Künstler Dave Chihuly. Sie stellt eine Verbindung zwischen der Innenstadt Tacomas und dem Ufer der Thea-Voss-Wasserstraße dar. Der Besucher läuft unter einer farbenprächtigen Glasdecke her, vorbei an 20 Meter hohen Glasskulpturen hin zu einer riesigen gläsernen Vitrine.

Cette passerelle colorée est le fruit de la collaboration entre le Glass Muséum et Dave Chihuly, fameux artiste verrier originaire de Tacoma. Il représente le lien entre le centre ville et les rives du port de Thea Floss. Les visiteurs déambulent sous un magnifique plafond de verre coloré et au côté de sculptures de verre atteignant 20 mètres de haut, jusqu'à une vitrine énorme.

De kleurrijke voetgangersbrug kwam tot stand door de samenwerking van het plaatselijke glasmuseum met de kunstenaar Dave Chihuly. De brug vormt een verbinding tussen het Washington State History Museum en het Museum of Glass. De bezoeker loopt onder een prachtig gekleurd glazen dak door, langs twintig meter hoge glassculpturen naar een grote vitrine.

The Craigieburn bypass is more than just a remarkable bridge; the copper cladding used in its construction was chosen for its changing appearance due to the oxidation process. As the copper oxidizes, gradual shades of reddish brown, gold and ultimately green will develop. After completion of this process, the typical green patina of oxidized copper will harmonize perfectly with the bridge's natural environment.

Der Craigieburn bypass besticht nicht „nur" als eine auffällige Brücke, die verwendete Kupferverkleidung wurde bewusst wegen der Veränderungen der Oberfläche im Verlauf des Oxidationsprozesses gewählt. Durch diesen Prozess werden sich allmählich Schattierungen von Rotbraun, Gold bis schließlich Grün entwickeln. Nach Abschluss dieser Oxidation wird die endgültige typische grüne Kupferpatina perfekt mit der natürlichen Umgebung harmonieren.

La bretelle de Craigieburn est bien plus qu'un simple pont; les panneaux de cuivre utilisés pour sa construction ont été choisis pour leur apparence versatile, en raison du processus d'oxydation. Lorsque le cuivre s'oxydera, des tonalités de brun-rouge, doré et enfin vert vont progressivement apparaître. Dès la fin du processus, la patine typique du cuivre oxydé sera en parfaite harmonie avec l'environnement naturel du pont.

De Craigieburn Bypass bekoort niet alleen als markante brug maar ook vanwege het gebruikte materiaal. De brug werd bewust bekleed met koper, aangezien dit in de loop van de tijd oxideert. Door dit proces ontstaat geleidelijk een roestbruine, gouden en tot slot groene oxidatielaag. Zodra het oxidatieproces is afgerond, zal het uiteindelijk kenmerkende groene koperpatina uitstekend harmoniëren met de natuurlijke omgeving.

This construction is intended to be viewed as a public operation: an installation of three "air trees" which function as a modern monument. They are viewed as a temporary densification of the tree population, a traffic pattern and encroachment upon existing urban space. They have been constructed as a temporary installation, to be used until the current deadlock is rectified and the local climate has been improved by the growth of new trees.

Der realisierte Vorschlag soll als eine Operation am öffentlichen Platz verstanden werden: eine Installation von drei „Luft-Bäumen", die als Mahnmal funktionieren. Es wird als temporäre Verdichtung des Baumbestandes gesehen, einer Anordnung der Verkehrswege und der Eingriff auf vorhandene städtische Oberflächen. Als temporale Bauten werden sie nur solange benutzt, bis der bisherige Stillstand korrigiert und die klimatischen Verhältnisse, durch nachgewachsene Bäume, verbessert wurden.

Cette construction vise à être comprise comme une opération publique: une installation de trois « arbres aériens » à valeur de monument moderne. Ils sont vus comme une densification temporaire de la population arboricole, un schéma de circulation et d'empiètement sur l'espace urbain existant. Cette installation est une construction temporaire, qui ne disparaîtra que lorsque l'impasse actuelle aura été rectifiée et le climat local amélioré par la plantation de nouveaux arbres.

Het gerealiseerde voorstel moet als een operatie op openbaar terrein worden opgevat: een installatie van drie 'luchtbomen' die als waarschuwingsteken dienen. Het wordt gezien als tijdelijke verdichting van het bomenbestand, vermindering en ordening van de verkeersroutes en aanpassing van het bestaande stedelijk oppervlak. Als tijdelijke bouwwerken worden ze zo lang gebruikt tot de tot nu toe geldende stilstand is gecorrigeerd en de klimatologische omstandigheden door nieuwe bomen zijn verbeterd.

Grande Arche, in the Paris La Défense area, is a modern interpretation of a triumphal arch. It forms a line with the Arc de Triomphe and the Arc de Triomphe du Carrousel, known as the axe historique, or historic axis. This almost cubical construction of glass and marble is not, however, positioned in an exact line of sight with the others: it is 6.5 degrees out of alignment with the axis. With its slight tilt, an optical depth is created when viewed from the distance, something that wouldn't be possible with a frontal view.

Grand Arche ist eine moderne Interpretation eines Triumphbogens im Pariser Vorort La Défense und bildet mit dem Arc de Triomphe und dem Arc de Triomphe du Carrousel eine Gerade, die so genannte axe historique. Das fast würfelförmige Bauwerk aus Glas und Marmor ist jedoch nicht exakt zur Sichtachse ausgerichtet, sondern um 6,5 Grad aus der Achse gedreht. Durch die leicht schräge Ansicht ergibt sich aus der Ferne eine räumliche Tiefenwirkung, die bei einer frontalen Ansicht nicht sichtbar wäre.

La Grande Arche, dans le quartier parisien de La Défense, est une interprétation moderne de l'Arc de Triomphe. Elle est alignée avec celui-ci et l'Arc de triomphe du Carrousel, connu sous le nom d'axe historique. Cette construction presque cubique de verre et de marbre n'est pourtant pas positionnée strictement dans l'alignement des autres : elle a 6,5 degrés de différence. Sa légère inclinaison crée une profondeur optique observable à distance, qui serait inexistante sans ce léger décalage.

De Grande Arche is een moderne interpretatie van een triomfboog in de Parijse buitenwijk La Défense en vormt met de Arc de Triomphe en de Arc de Triomphe du Carrousel een lijn, de zogeheten axe historique. Het haast kubusvormige bouwwerk van glas en marmer is echter niet exact op de zichtas georiënteerd maar is om 6,5 graden verschoven. Door het ietwat scheve aanzicht ontstaat vanuit de verte een ruimtelijke dieptewerking die bij een frontaal aanzicht niet zichtbaar zou zijn.

The Lantern Square with its diverse light installations and illuminated objects enjoys great popularity. Once used for marching drills, the square now offers amusement rides, numerous restaurants and even open air concerts. The square is free from the blare of advertising boards, a good thing because the park's lights create a unique atmosphere on their own. There are many thousands of these lights, reflected throughout the night in the surrounding pools, which illuminate the Chinese Tower and the numerous surrounding installations.

Größter Beliebtheit erfreut sich der Laternenplatz mit seinen vielfältigen Lichtinstallationen und Leuchtobjekten. Auf einem ehemaligen Exerzierplatz kann man sich in den Fahrgeschäften vergnügen, in den zahlreichen Restaurants schlemmen oder einem Open-Air-Konzert lauschen. Hier sind grelle Leuchtreklamen auf dem Gelände verpönt, und das ist gut so, denn Lampen vermitteln in dem Park eine Atmosphäre, die einzigartig ist. Viele Tausend Lampen spiegeln sich allabendlich in Wasserbecken, beleuchten den chinesischen Turm oder die vielen Installationen in der Anlage.

Le square aux lanternes, aux installations et objets lumineux, jouit d'une grande popularité. Autrefois théâtre de manœuvres militaires, ce square offre aujourd'hui des terrains de jeu, de nombreux restaurants et même des concerts en plein air. Aucun panneau publicitaire ne vient gâcher l'atmosphère unique créée par la lumière de ce parc. Ces lampes sont présentes par milliers, réfléchies dans la nuit par les bassins avoisinants, illuminant la Chinese Tower et les nombreuses structures qui l'entourent.

Het lantarenplein met de veelzijdige lichtinstallaties en lichtobjecten is bijzonder populair. Op een voormalig exercitieterrein kan de bezoeker een hapje eten bij een van de talrijke restaurants of genieten van een openluchtconcert. Felle lichtreclames zijn verboden op het terrein en dat is maar goed ook, want de lampen geven het park een unieke sfeer. Duizenden lampen weerkaatsen 's avonds in de bassins, verlichten de Chinese toren of de vele installaties in het park.

At 443 feet (135 meters), the London Eye is the tallest Ferris wheel in Europe. Visitors can let their vision wander as they travel high above the city. The ultramodern, closed glass capsules allow you to see up to 25 miles away on a clear day. Since its inauguration, the London Eye has been visited by more than 25 million people and has received 75 awards, including those for its design and construction. The London Eye has become a symbol of 21st-century Britain in practically no time at all, achieving a cult status around the world.

Mit seinen 135 Metern ist das London Eye das höchste Riesenrad Europas. Auf der anmutigen Fahrt können die Besucher die Blicke schweifen lassen – aus den hochmodernen, geschlossenen Glaskapseln lässt sich bis zu 40 Kilometer weit sehen. Seit der Eröffnung ist das London Eye von mehr als 25 Millionen Personen besucht worden, es ist 75-mal ausgezeichnet worden – unter anderem für Design und Konstruktion. In kürzester Zeit ist das London Eye zu einem Symbol für das moderne Großbritannien des 21. Jahrhunderts geworden und hat weltweiten Kultstatus erlangt.

Avec ses 135 mètres, le London Eye est la plus haute grande roue d'Europe. En voyageant au-dessus de la ville, les visiteurs peuvent laisser leur regard se perdre au loin. Les capsules de verre ultramodernes permettent de voir à une distance de 40 kilomètres par temps clair. Depuis son inauguration, le London Eye a été visité par plus de 25 millions de personnes et a reçu 75 récompenses, notamment pour son design et sa structure. Le London Eye est très rapidement devenu un symbole de la Grande-Bretagne du XXIe siècle, et devenu culte dans le monde entier.

Met zijn 135 meter is het London Eye het hoogste reuzenrad van Europa. Tijdens een ritje in het reuzenrad kunnen de bezoekers hun blikken laten gaan – vanuit de hoogmoderne, gesloten glazen capsules kan men tot veertig kilometer ver kijken. Sinds de opening is het London Eye door meer dan 25 miljoen mensen bezocht. Het is 75 keer onderscheiden – onder andere voor design en constructie. In de kortst mogelijke tijd is het London Eye tot een symbool voor het moderne Groot-Brittannië van de eenentwintigste eeuw geworden en heeft wereldwijd een cultstatus.

This prize-winning center for art, music, architecture and landscape design is located on the shore of Lake Michigan. Internationally renowned architects, designers and artists have had a hand in creating the park's landmarks. These include the Jay Pritzker Pavillion, an open-air concert space designed by Frank O. Gehry, the interactive Crown Fountain by Jaume Plensa, the modern Lurie Garden created by Kathryn Gustafson, Piet Oudolf and Robert Israel, and Anish Kapoor's "Cloud Gate" sculpture.

Das preisgekrönte Zentrum für Kunst, Musik, Architektur und Landschaftsdesign befindet sich am Ufer des Lake Michigan. Hier wurden besondere Anziehungspunkte von international renommierten Architekten, Designern und Künstlern geschaffen. Dazu gehören: der Jay Pritzker Pavillion, eine Freiluft-Konzertbühne von Frank O. Ghery, die interaktive Crown Fountain von Jaume Plensa, der moderne Lurie Garten, entworfen von Kathryn Gustafson, Piet Oudolf und Robert Israel, und die Skulptur „Cloud Gate" von Anish Kapoor.

Ce centre pour l'art, la musique, l'architecture et le design paysager, récompensé par de nombreux prix, est situé sur une rive du lac Michigan. Des architectes, designers et artistes célèbres ont contribué à créer les pièces maîtresses du parc : le pavillon Jay Pritzker, un espace de concerts en plein air pensé par Frank O. Gehry, l'interactive Crown Fountain de Jaume Plensa, le moderne Lurie Garden, créé par Kathryn Gustafson, Piet Oudolf et Robert Israel, ainsi que la « Porte du nuage » d'Anish Kapoor.

Het bekroonde centrum voor kunst, muziek, architectuur en landschapsdesign bevindt zich aan de oever van Lake Michigan. Hier werden bijzondere trekpleisters door internationaal gerenommeerde architecten, designers en kunstenaars gecreëerd. Daartoe behoren: het Jay Pritzker Pavillon, een concertpodium in de openlucht van Frank O. Gehry, de interactieve Crown Fountain van Jaume Plensa, de moderne Lurie Garden, ontworpen door Kathryn Gustafson, Piet Oudolf en Robert Israel, en de sculptuur 'Cloud Gate' van Anish Kapoor.

Originally built for the Olympic Games, this telecommunications tower is a prominent feature of Barcelona's modern city-scape. It rises from the Montjuic cliffs southeast of the city center. The architect Santiago Calatrava has created this graceful and elegant tower, which appears to be holding a single thin rod. An artificial pool lies at the foot of the structure.

Für die Olympischen Spiele gebaut, ist der Telekommunikationsturm ein weithin sichtbares Wahrzeichen Barcelonas geworden. Er erhebt sich auf dem südöstlich von der Stadt gelegenen Felsen Montjuic. Der Architekt Santiago Calatrava plante einen eleganten, filigran wirkenden Turm, der lediglich auf einer dünnen Spitze zu stehen scheint und an dessen Fuß ein künstlich angelegtes Wasserbecken liegt.

Construite à l'origine pour les Jeux Olympiques, cette tour de télécommunications est très représentative du paysage urbain et moderne barcelonais. Elle s'élève depuis les falaises de Montjuic, au Sud-est du centre ville. L'architecte Santiago Calatrava a créé cette tour élégante et gracieuse, tenant entre ses bras une fine tige. Un bassin artificiel s'étend au pied de la structure.

De telecommunicatietoren die voor de Olympische Spelen werd gebouwd, is een van ver zichtbaar symbolisch bouwwerk voor Barcelona. Hij verheft zich op de ten zuidoosten van de stad gelegen rots Montjuic. De architect Santiago Calatrava ontwierp een elegante toren die enkel op een smalle punt lijkt te balanceren. Aan de voet van de toren bevindt zich een aangelegd waterbekken.

Situated in the heart of the 15th Arrondissement in Paris, this park sits on the site of a former Citroën car factory. The park's postmodern style offers a stimulating contrast to the surrounding business and residential buildings. Besides two enormous glass houses, there are also smaller themed greenhouses which have been made to look like tree houses. The spacious center consists of ponds and meadows gradually sloping down to the Seine. You can stroll in a white, black, red or blue garden.

Die Parkanlage im Herzen des 15. Pariser Arrondissements entstand auf dem ehemaligen Gelände der Citroën-Automobilfabrik. Der postmoderne Stil bildet einen spannenden Gegensatz zu den umgebenden Wohn- und Geschäftshäusern. Neben zwei gigantischen Glashäusern sind kleinere Themengewächshäuser wie Baumhäuser konzipiert. Den großzügigen Mittelpunkt bilden Wasserflächen und Wiesen, die allmählich zur Seine hin abfallen. Bewundern kann man beispielsweise jeweils einen weißen, schwarzen, roten und blauen Garten.

Situé au cœur du 15ème arrondissement de Paris, ce parc remplace une ancienne usine de voitures Citroën. Le style postmoderne de ce parc offre un contraste stimulant avec les bâtiments professionnels et résidentiels avoisinants. En plus de deux gigantesques verrières, de petites structures semblables à des serres ponctuent la visite. Le vaste espace central est constitué de bassins et de prairies descendant graduellement jusqu' la Seine. Vous pourrez déambuler entre les jardins blanc, noir, rouge ou bleu.

Het plantsoen in het centrum van het 15e arrondissement van Parijs ontstond op het voormalige terrein van de Citroën-fabriek. De postmoderne stijl vormt een spannend contrast met de omringende woonhuizen en kantoorpanden. Naast twee enorme kassen van glas zijn er kleinere thematische kassen en boomhutten. Middelpunt vormen waterpartijen en weiden die zacht naar de Seine afhellen. Ook een witte, zwarte, rode en blauwe tuin zijn hier te bewonderen.

No contemporary architect has designed more religious structures than Mario Botta. The native Tessiner has created spaces of open spirituality where light and shadow interact in remarkable ways. His work with churches leads back to the fundamental values of architectural construction: gravity, light, shapes and materials – all structured in such a way that a dialog is created. All superfluities had to go. The 1:1-scale wooden model of the Borromini's San Carlino church on Lake Lugano, constructed with the help of architecture students, is also to be understood in this vein.

Kein zeitgenössischer Architekt hat mehr Gotteshäuser gebaut als Mario Botta. Im Spiel von Licht und Schatten schuf der Tessiner einprägsame Räume offener Spiritualität. Seine Arbeit an Kirchen führt zu den wesentlichen Werten der Baukunst zurück: Schwerkraft, Licht, Materialien und Formen – alle so strukturiert, dass sie einen Dialog schaffen. Alles Unwesentliche muss entfernt werden. So soll auch das zusammen mit Architekturstudenten entstandene 1:1 Holzmodell der Kirche San Carlino von Borromini auf dem Luganer See zu verstehen sein.

Aucun architecte contemporain n'a construit plus de structures religieuses que Mario Botta. Originaire de Tessin, il a créé des espaces de spiritualité ouverts, où l'ombre et la lumière interagissent de manière remarquable. Son travail sur les églises fait appel aux valeurs fondamentales de la construction architecturale : gravité, lumière, formes et matériaux (tous structurés afin de créer un dialogue). Le superflu n'a pas sa place. Le modèle en bois à l'échelle 1 :1 de l'église San Carlino de style Borromini sur le lac de Lugano, construite avec l'aide d'étudiants en architecture, doit aussi être envisagé dans cette perspective.

Geen andere architect van deze tijd heeft meer godshuizen ontworpen dan Mario Botta. In een spel van licht en schaduw creëerde de ontwerper uit Ticino sprekende ruimten van toegankelijke spiritualiteit. Zijn werk in kerken voert terug naar de wezenlijke waarden in de bouwkunst: zwaartekracht, licht, materialen en vormen – zo gestructureerd dat ze een dialoog teweegbrengen. Niet-essentiële elementen moeten worden verwijderd. Zo zou ook de, samen met architectuurstudenten, ontstane 1:1-maquette van de kerk San Carlino van Borromini in het Meer van Lugano moeten worden opgevat.

771

Multimedia artist Pipilotti Rist and architect Carlos Martinez have developed a public lounge area right on the street in the Raiffeisen district. Their goal was to lend the area a homogenous character and make it a more desirable place to just hang out. A bright red carpet covers the ground, benches, tables and even the fountains. This unique public art project occupies the space that was previously used by St. Gallen's textile industry for laying out fabrics for bleaching.

Um dem Quartier einen homogenen Charakter zu geben und die Aufenthaltsqualitäten zu stärken, entwarfen die Multimediakünstlerin Pipilotti Rist und der Architekt Carlos Martinez innerhalb der Straßenräume des Raiffeisen-Viertels eine öffentliche Lounge. Ein leuchtend roter Teppich bedeckt Boden, Bänke, Tische und Brunnen. Wo früher Stoffe der St. Galler Textilindustrie zum Bleichen ausgebreitet wurden, entstand ein einzigartiges Kunstprojekt im öffentlichen Raum.

L'artiste multimédia Pipilotti Rist et l'architecte Carlos Martinez ont développé un salon public en pleine rue, dans le quartier de Raiffeisen. Leur but était d'insuffler à cette zone un caractère plus homogène en y rendant la promenade plus désirable. Un tapis rouge vif recouvre le sol, les banquettes, les tables et même les fontaines. L'industrie textile St. Gallen entreposait autrefois ses tissus ici pour les blanchir.

Om de wijk een homogeen karakter te verlenen en de verblijfskwaliteiten te verbeteren, ontwierpen de multimediakunstenares Pipilotti Rist en de architect Carlos Martinez in de straten van de Raiffeisenwijk een openbare lounge. Een stralend rood tapijt bedekt de grond, banken, tafels en fonteinen. Waar vroeger de stoffen van de textielindustrie van St. Gallen werden gebleekt, ontstond een uniek kunstproject op openbare ruimte.

Located at 30 St. Mary Axe, the metal frame of "the Gherkin", as this unusually shaped office building is known to locals, is clearly visible from the outside and consists of an interlinked double helix. The façade of variously colored triangular and rhomboid glass components is flawlessly integrated into the structure's overall design. The interior office spaces are arranged in circles around the building's nucleus. These levels are interspersed with atria which are up to six storeys high and offer unique views of London.

Das nach außen sichtbare Tragwerk des Bürogebäudes in der 30 St Mary Axe besteht aus zwei ineinander verschlungenen Helixsträngen. Die Fassade aus verschiedenfarbigen, dreieckigen und rautenförmigen Glaselementen passt sich dieser Struktur gänzlich an. Die Büroflächen sind ringförmig um einen Versorgungskern angelegt. Unterbrochen werden diese Etagen immer wieder durch Atrien, die bis zu sechs Stockwerke hoch sind und einzigartige Ausblicke zulassen.

Situé au 30 St.Mary Axe, la structure de métal du « Cornichon », comme l'appellent les riverains de cet immeuble professionnel à la forme insolite, est facilement visible de l'extérieur et consiste en un motif de double hélice. La façade de triangles ou losanges de verre multicolores s'intègre parfaitement au design général de la structure. A l'intérieur, les espaces dédiés aux sociétés s'étendent en cercles autour d'une colonne vertébrale. Ces étages sont ponctués d'atriums pouvant atteindre six étages et offrant une vue unique sur Londres.

De aan de buitenkant zichtbare draagconstructie van het kantoorgebouw in de 30st Mary Axe bestaat uit twee verstrengelde helices. De buitenbekleding van verschillend gekleurde driehoekige en ruitvormige glaspanelen past zich aan deze structuur volledig aan. De kantoorruimten zijn ringvormig rond de kern opgezet. De verdiepingen worden geregeld doorbroken door atriums die tot zes etages hoog zijn en unieke uitzichten bieden.

Like an enormous jet of blue and red water, Barcelona waterworks' 32-storey highrise seems to shimmer in the air. The concrete construction is surrounded by an aluminum exterior whose surface boasts forty different colors. Another shell, consisting of glass lamellae, enhances the overall impression of an organic skin which changes colors throughout the day. Inside, however, cool hues dominate, accentuated only by a luminescent red.

Wie eine Wasserfontäne in Blau- und Rottönen schillert das 32-stöckige Hochhaus der Wasserwerke Barcelonas. Die Betonkonstruktion ist von einer Aluminiumhaut umgeben, deren Oberfläche in vierzig verschiedenen Farben lackiert wurde. Eine weitere Hülle aus Glaslamellen verstärkt den Eindruck einer organischen Haut, die je nach Tageszeit unterschiedliche Farbeffekte zeigt. Im Inneren dagegen dominieren kühle Farbtöne, akzentuiert lediglich durch leuchtendes Rot.

Telle un énorme jet d'eau bleue et rouge, la station hydraulique de Barcelone, haute de 32 étages, semblent luire dans les airs. La construction de béton est entourée d'une façade en aluminium dont la surface reflète quarante différentes couleurs. Une autre enveloppe, constituée de lamelles de verre, accentue l'impression générale d'une peau organique changeant de couleur au gré du jour. A l'intérieur, cependant, dominent de chaudes tonalités bleues, relevées seulement de touches d'un rouge lumineux.

De wolkenkrabber met tweeëndertig verdiepingen van het waterleidingbedrijf van Barcelona fonkelt als een waterfontein in blauwe en rode tinten. De betonconstructie is bekleed met aluminium en is gelakt in veertig verschillende kleuren. Een tweede huid van glaspanelen versterkt de indruk van een organische huid die afhankelijk van het tijdstip van de dag verschillende kleureffecten vertoont. Binnen daarentegen overheersen koele kleuren, enkel geaccentueerd door schitterend rood.

As in other Spanish cities, Alicante has had a new tram system installed with altered rail gauges. Alicante's planners seized the chance to integrate one of the new tram stops into a park plaza. Not only is the park now stunningly illuminated but the tram stop boasts curious roof constructions which, seemingly held up by nothing, appear to float like two oversized, perforated lampshades.

In Alicante wurde, wie in anderen spanischen Städten, eine neue Stadtbahn mit geänderten Spurbreiten eingeführt. Hierbei wurde die Chance genutzt, eine der neuen Haltestellen städtebaulich in ein neu angelegtes Parkrondell zu integrieren. Nun wird nicht nur der Park eindrucksvoll illuminiert, auch die ständerfrei wirkenden Überdachungen scheinen wie zwei überdimensionale perforierte Lampenschirme zu schweben.

Comme d'autres villes espagnoles, Alicante a vu apparaître un nouveau système de tram. Les responsables ont sauté sur l'occasion de pouvoir intégrer l'un des arrêts du tram à une grande place. Désormais, le parc est non seulement magnifiquement illuminé, mais l'arrêt du tram possède également une toiture fort curieuse : sans soutien apparent, les structures semblent flotter dans le vide comme deux abat-jours perforés.

In Alicante werd, evenals in andere Spaanse steden, een nieuwe tram met andere spoorbreedte ingevoerd. Men benutte de kans om een van de nieuwe haltes stedenbouwkundig in een nieuw aangelegd plantsoen te integreren. Niet alleen het plantsoen wordt prachtig verlicht, maar ook de overkappingen zweven 's avonds als twee enorme geperforeerde lampenkappen boven het plantsoen.

The highest and longest cable suspension bridge in the world spans the Tern Valley, leading from Clermont-Ferrand to Béziers near the French city of Millau. This over 1.5 mile (2.5 kilometer) long bridge reaches heights of 885 feet (270 meters) above the Tarn River. The roadway is supported by 328-foot-high (98-meter-high) steel pylons sitting atop the bridge's pillars. Thanks to the arrangement of its cables, the construction has an elegant and dynamic appearance despite its enormous dimensions.

Die höchste und längste Schrägseilbrücke der Welt überspannt das Tern-Tal und führt von Clermont-Ferrand nach Béziers in der Nähe der französischen Stadt Millau. Maximal 270 Meter über dem Tarn verläuft die zweieinhalb Kilometer lange Brücke. Auf den Brückenpfeilern stehen 98 Meter hohe Stahlpylone, an denen die Fahrbahn aufgehängt ist. Dank dieser Seilabhängungen wirkt die Konstruktion, trotz ihrer enormen Größe, filigran und dynamisch.

Le pont suspendu le plus haut et le plus long au monde enjambe la vallée du Tarn et mène de Clermont-Ferrand à Béziers, au niveau de la ville française de Millau. Ce pont long de plus de 2,5 kilomètres s'élève à une hauteur de 270 mètres au-dessus du Tarn. Le tablier est supporté par des pylônes d'acier, posé au sommet des piliers du viaduc. Grâce à la disposition de ses câbles, la construction garde une apparence dynamique et élégante, malgré une stature imposante.

De hoogste en langste tuibrug ter wereld vormt een verbinding over de vallei van de Tarn en gaat van Clermont-Ferrand naar Béziers, vlakbij de Franse stad Millau. De brug ligt op 270 meter boven de Tarn en is tweeënhalve kilometer lang. Op de brugpijlers staan achtennegentig meter hoge stalen pylonen waaraan het wegdek is opgehangen. Dankzij de tui-constructie doet de brug, ondanks de enorme afmeting, filigraan en dynamisch aan.

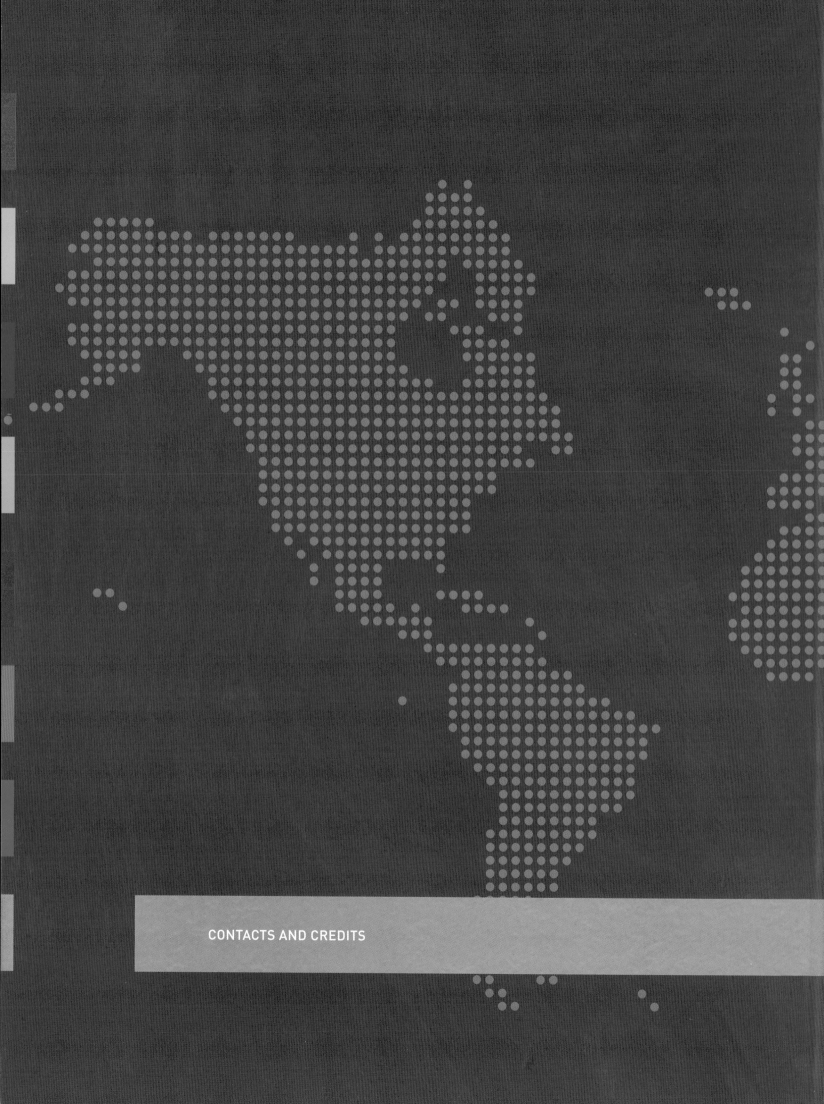

CONTACTS AND CREDITS

DIRECTORY